West Indian Pentecostals

Also available from Bloomsbury

Christianity as a World Religion, Sebastian Kim and Kirsteen Kim
Community and Worldview among Paraiyars of South India,
Anderson H. M. Jeremiah
Christianity in Africa and the African Diaspora, edited by Afe Adogame

West Indian Pentecostals

Living their faith
in New York and London

Janice A. McLean-Farrell

Bloomsbury Academic
An imprint of Bloomsbury Publishing Plc

B L O O M S B U R Y

LONDON · OXFORD · NEW YORK · NEW DELHI · SYDNEY

Bloomsbury Academic

An imprint of Bloomsbury Publishing Plc

50 Bedford Square	1385 Broadway
London	New York
WC1B 3DP	NY 10018
UK	USA

www.bloomsbury.com

BLOOMSBURY and the Diana logo are trademarks of Bloomsbury Publishing Plc

First published 2016

British Library Cataloguing-in-Publication Data
A catalogue record for this book is available from the British Library.

ISBN: HB: 978-1-4742-5579-0
ePDF: 978-1-4742-5581-3
ePub: 978-1-4742-5580-6

Library of Congress Cataloging-in-Publication Data
McLean-Farrell, Janice A.
West Indian pentecostals : living their faith in the cities of New York and London / Janice A. McLean-Farrell.
pages cm
Includes bibliographical references.
ISBN 978-1-4742-5579-0 (hb) – ISBN 978-1-4742-5580-6 (epub) –
ISBN 978-1-4742-5581-3 (epdf) 1. Pentecostals–New York (State)–New York.
2. Pentecostals–England–London. 3. West Indians–Migrations.
4. Emigration and immigration–Religious aspects–Pentecostal churches. I. Title.
BX8762.M35 2016
289.9'408968729–dc23
2015031590

Typeset by Deanta Global Publishing Services, Chennai, India
Printed and bound in Great Britain

In Memory of
Viola McLean, Sylvina White, and Ulalee Smith
My Ancestors in the Christian Faith

But we have this treasure in clay jars, so that it may be clear that
this extraordinary power belongs to God and does not come from us
(2 Corinthians 4:7 NRSV)

Contents

Acknowledgments

Many persons and institutions have contributed to this book, and to them I owe a debt of gratitude, in particular to the three churches and their members who invited me into their lives and shared their experience of being Pentecostal West Indian immigrants in New York and London. The New College at the University of Edinburgh's School of Divinity provided financial assistance that made the fieldwork possible. Colleagues at the Center for World Christianity at the University of Edinburgh and City Seminary of New York made valuable inputs into various chapters of earlier drafts and the post dissertation drafting of the manuscript: Afe Adogame, T. Jack Thompson, Brian Stanley, Mark Gornik, Maria Liu Wong, Carrie Myers, and Geomon George.

A number of relatives and friends provided me with food, shelter, and much encouragement at various stages of the research and writing: Lileen Ricketts and Yvette Nash in Brooklyn, Earlyn Edwards and family in London, Hillery Ingram-Smith, Margaret Acton, the members of the African Caribbean Christian Fellowship-Edinburgh and the Jamaican/Scottish group in Edinburgh, Nichelle Rosemond in Philadelphia, and Audley Richards in Atlanta. I am especially thankful for my parents, grandparents, mother-in-law, and sisters whose belief, encouragement, and sacrifice sustained me as I pursued this work. Finally, I acknowledge a great indebtedness to my husband Alan and son, Samuel, who provided me with the moral support and space without which I could not have completed this book.

Janice A. McLean-Farrell
New York

Introduction

Rooms echo my voice, I see
I was not a migrant bird.
I am a transplanted sapling, here, blossoming.

"Black Kid in a New Place" in James Berry, *When I Dance*
(London: Penguin Books, [1990] 1988), 42.

Growing up in a farming community in central Jamaica, I always knew that a day would come when I would migrate to America. For all those years, this foreknowledge produced excitement in me, as I looked forward to reuniting with my mother and living out my visions of the amazing life I would have in this land of opportunity. The eventual reality however was beyond all I could have imagined!

What I eventually came to understand is that the life of an immigrant is one of journeying toward the discovery of self. This is a journey that spans many years and is normally conducted without the assistance of therapists, counselors, or other professionals. Along the way, different aspects of the old home blend with one's experiences in the new home to create a unique evolving concept of self. For me, this journey began with feelings of displacement and disorientation as I sought to make sense of the strangeness and complexity of the new urban space I now inhabited. In probing, touching, embracing this strangeness—whether reflected in my awareness of being the other, or in the dissonance with the American culture that surrounded me—there emerged the knowledge that my world of yesterday had passed to never return in the same way. I was now like a migrant bird, originating from somewhere else and being marked by this new place in which I felt very little sense of belonging. In accepting this shift, I began to reorient myself toward the foundations and narratives that would help to brighten the seemingly "winter" experiences that overshadowed my life. By looking within, I began to draw on what were embedded there—religion, culture, history, community, dance, and music—and use them to fuel my interactions with the new world I was inhabiting. In the process, I discovered myself not as a migrant bird—the other who has no permanence of residence—but instead as a transplanted sapling that had found a place to flourish and blossom.

It is this journey toward the discovery of self—from the strangeness of the initial encounter with one's new home to finding a place of flourishing—that forms the focus of this book. This journey is not only that of those documented in this book, it is also mine, and that of my family. As immigrants, we are all on this pathway of discovering ourselves, both the individual and the collective self. In the process, we find a space that enables us as individuals and as a family to flourish and blossom in a new place.

In this book, I argue that the initial disorientation or culture shock, uncovers the immigrant's endeavor to regain equilibrium, that is, his or her efforts to integrate the new context and his or her experiences within it, into an existing frame of reference. This frame of reference is one that is carved out of the migrant's experiences in his or her homeland and therefore forms the primary interpretative lens through which the migrant will engage with the new context. For many West Indian migrants, the process of regaining equilibrium can become especially complicated (as it was for me) since they encounter an urban context, for which their predominantly rural frame of reference may prove inadequate. According to David A. Roozen, William McKinney, and Jackson W. Carroll, this inadequacy is primarily due to the complexity, dynamism, and fluidity of the urban context.[1] When religious plurality is added to these characteristics, the urban context becomes even more complex. Given this, the more communal nature of the rural context, along with its individualistic theology and competitive parish or county structure, is no longer adequate as a frame of reference.[2] This can result in a type of social instability and alienation or anomie. The immigrant's encounters with the host society and the adjustment processes he or she goes through not only address this anomie, but also create a unique space that facilitates the discovery of self and transforms the new context and the old frame of reference. It is within this space that immigrants—in the context of this book, West Indian immigrants—live, work, rear their children, live out their faith, navigate various transnational ties, and become inserted into the fabric of the diaspora.

In this book, the examination of this space will be conducted within the nexus existing between the home and the diaspora, which in this case are the urban centers of New York City and London, and investigate two specific issues: identity and Christian mission. These two issues are pivotal in underscoring the significance of the home and diaspora contexts in the life of immigrants, while also facilitating the expansion of the discussion about their interaction with the host society beyond an assimilation/ethnic binary to include the multiplicity of ways in which this interaction actually fosters the transformation of the immigrant, the host societies, and the home country. By focusing this study on two global cities we are able to consider how West Indian immigrants, who share a common culture and heritage, and who may be perceived as having similar experiences are in fact constructing divergent lives. This also allows for a unique cross-nation comparison into the complex and indirect ways that historical, social, political, urban, and economic realities in these urban centers contribute to the identification and missional process in which immigrants are involved.

Identity is an essential element in the lives of all human beings. Human beings are social beings; thus, they learn things about themselves and others through interacting with other humans. At the heart of this interaction, however, are their identities, which determine how they perceive themselves and others. In this regard, the notion of identity can be said to hinge "on the apparently paradoxical combination of sameness and difference."[3] We are the same in that we share a certain level of commonality—as humans and as women, men, etc. However, simultaneously, there are aspects of identity that highlight the ways in which an individual is unique and thus different from others. Given these dynamics, it is necessary to acknowledge some of the complexities accompanying identity and the process of identification. First, identity is not static. Instead it is fluid, undergoing dynamic changes as it interacts with various social, economic, political, and cultural factors in the surrounding environment. Second, it is not singular, that is, every individual will subconsciously or consciously identify in a multiplicity of ways, and these will in turn impact their other identities. Thus Steph Lawler argues, "It is not as though one could have a gendered identity, for example, and then, in addition to that, a raced identity. . . rather, race, gender and the rest interact, so that to be a white woman is not the same—in terms of meaning and experience—as to be a black woman."[4] It is needful to note that "the recognition of multiplicity . . . of identities does not mean that people are free to choose any identity they want or attach any meaning they want to a particular identity."[5] This is because the options and or labels available to people are normally determined by both the history and the current power relations of the particular context in which they find themselves.

Third, in the process of identifying with one thing, one also excludes something else. For example in choosing to identify as female, I automatically exclude those things that would accompany a masculine identification. Thus as Stuart Hall asserts, "identities are constructed through, not outside, difference."[6]

For it is only in relating to what is different, naming it in regard to what is excluded, that identity becomes a constructed reality.

Due to the above-mentioned dynamics, when identity is examined within an immigrant context, dynamics surrounding home, inclusion/exclusion, and similarity/difference attain seminal positions. For as immigrants settle in another nation-state and encounter a different socioeconomic, political, and religious context, their identities undergo a process of change, a way of becoming that is centered on renegotiation or construction.[7] The process of renegotiation and construction is very complex, involving a series of simultaneous and interrelated actions and the ongoing interchange between the country of origin and the diaspora. In this ongoing interchange, the history, culture, language, and conditions with the two contexts—home and diaspora—foster the consideration and articulation of what immigrants "might become, how [they] have been represented and how [this] bears on how [they] will represent [themselves]."[8]

In examining the process of renegotiation, I will focus on three aspects: transformation, maintenance, and adaptation. Transformation incorporates those aspects of the immigrants' identities that undergo marked changes as they interact with the new context. This would include a status change, for example, within the home as the female moves from being the secondary breadwinner to the primary one. Maintenance highlights the ethnic retention dynamic that accompanies the renegotiation of one's identity. Thus, an immigrant who did not participate in certain cultural activities while living in the West Indies, such as attending jam sessions, carnival, or church, when confronted with the realities of living in New York or London would see these cultural practices to be vitally important and as a means of distinguishing himself or herself from others. Adaptation is characterized by the multiple measures taken by the immigrant to integrate with the new context. The most common example of this is seen in relation to rearing the second and later generations. For instance, the common West Indian method of disciplining a child by spanking him or her is abandoned in favor of the host society's equivalent—time-out, or having a conversation with one's child. For many parents the impetus for this adaptation is twofold: one, what is seen as good parenting practice within the new context; two, the presence of the laws that govern child abuse.

The process of constructing one's identities is also marked by several actions as well as the dialectic relationship between the country of origin and the new home. At the two extremes are identities that either conform to or oppose the given norms of a society. For many West Indian youth in an urban context, this identity construction could follow one of two major paths, either by conforming to the norms of society associated with middle-class Anglo-Protestant culture or opposing this by becoming a part of an alternate/oppositional culture. However, in between these extremes lie a myriad of hybrid identities that are constructed from the integration of diverse aspects of country of origin and the new home in varying degrees.

As noted before, identification is about a process of becoming. As a result, within the diaspora context, immigrants may change identities over time, and in some cases may adhere to different identities at the same time depending on the circumstances they face. Thus, the dominant identities expressed by immigrants may be a product of their interaction with and reaction to: the socioeconomic, political, and cultural contexts within the host country; the heritage derived from their home country; and the identities ascribed to them by the wider society, other ethnic groups, and even their own ethnic group.

In addition to addressing the identification processes, this book will also examine how the concept of mission is being articulated and practiced by West Indian immigrants in New York City and London. Throughout the history of Christianity, the concept of mission has remained a dominant theme. Beginning with the mandates recorded in Matthew 28: 19-20 and Acts 1:8, mission has been presented as a cross-cultural exercise in which followers of Jesus are engaged. This has involved going into various contexts to be a witness of Jesus Christ and in the process seeing others become followers of Jesus. However, mission is not only something in which individual believers engage, it is also communal in nature and a fundamental feature of the church. According to David Bosch in *Transforming Mission*, "The identity of the church is missional by its very nature."[9] Thus it is the "space in the world, at which the reign of Jesus Christ over the whole world is evidenced and proclaimed. . . . The Church is the place where testimony and serious thought are given to God's reconciliation of the world with himself in Christ."[10] However, various questions have existed concerning how this process of reconciliation should be achieved. For much of the nineteenth and early twentieth century, this reconciliation was accomplished primarily through evangelism, social concern, or a mixture of both.[11] However, as colonialism and Western Christianity have undergone several critiques throughout the twentieth century, mission has come to also embody a commitment to the transformation of unjust societal structures, striving for the proper stewardship of the earth, and the recovery of the formative work of the Holy Spirit in all aspects of the Christian life.[12]

Taking three immigrant Pentecostal churches in both New York City and London as an additional place of inquiry, I argue that these intentional social organizations exist as a fundamental space where West Indian Pentecostals, individually and as a worshiping community, are engaged in both the process of identification and discerning what constitutes mission in their urban contexts of New York City and London. In terms of identification, within these immigrant religious communities another dimension is added—that of the Pentecostal religious identities. These religious identities also undergo a process of change within the new host context and are influenced by various social, religious, and cultural factors. Within immigrant Pentecostal churches, both the conception and practice of mission take on added dimensions as these religious communities strive to be a place where immigrants can renegotiate or construct their identities and navigate their new context while simultaneously functioning as a place where God is reconciling the world to himself. As a result, mission becomes an engagement in translation, one marked by dynamism and constant negotiation as the ideas and practices emanating from home and the urban host contexts are able to critique and affirm each other, while simultaneously providing the immigrants with a means of interacting with the wider community.

Role of churches in the lives of immigrants

For many immigrants, including West Indians, the religious communities in which they participate are a prominent feature of their lives. They enable them to creatively navigate and interact with the host context and live out their faith.[13] Religious communities accomplish this by providing a space where "members of an ethnic group can come together around cultural symbols and practices that resonate with them".[14] However, in the process of providing such a space for immigrants, many of these religious communities are commonly perceived by the various members of the host society to be functioning as a "virtual immigrant enclave"[15] or colony; an agency that impedes the migrant's social integration and which in turn produces further isolation and exclusion within the host society.[16] The end result of this isolation is that the immigrant continues to be perceived by the majority population as the other or an outsider, who ultimately is unable to assimilate into the host society and who by doing so prevents the society from functioning "properly." This perceived failure noted within the wider society is based on the assumption that assimilation is the norm. Consequently, the retention of one's ethnic, religious, and cultural distinctions may be perceived as a threat to the society and its structures. It is necessary to note that in both the American and British contexts, the values to which migrants are expected to conform are based upon those of the middle-class Anglo-Protestant culture. And in light of the events that occurred on September 11, 2001, and the role that second-generation Muslims played in the London suicide bombings in July 2005, these and other concerns have taken on added significance within the two societies.[17]

However, this perception of immigrant churches as places that primarily facilitate a colony mentality among immigrants is problematic because it ignores the ways in which they function as a source of cultural and social capital formation, an alternative family, and "a powerful forum for the [renegotiation and] construction of identities"[18] for their members. Simultaneously, such an assumption serves to exempt the host society from its responsibility in the development and perpetuation of certain social realities that make the presence of such organizations a pivotal resource for immigrants. As a survey of the residential patterns of West Indian immigrants in New York City and London reveals, a large percentage of these immigrants reside in enclaves within larger socioeconomically deprived urban areas. In the United States, these enclaves are located within predominantly black areas, while in London they are located within specific communities that include white British and other minorities. The location of and policies governing these enclaves, speak to the United States and Britain's perception and treatment of the other politically, economically, and socially. Thus, in both countries we see evidence of discrimination and prejudice toward different waves of immigrants and the ways in which they were seen as deviating from the dominant norms of organized society.[19]

For many immigrants, including those from the West Indies, both the formation of enclaves and their preservation have had a significant impact on immigrant life within the host society. First, when the initial group of immigrants arrived, these particular urban areas were the primary places available for them to reside. As others joined this group as a result of kin or community relationships, a more defined enclave was formed. Secondly, as the enclaves developed, they became sites where immigrants (both the newly arrived and the long-time residents) could find support, access to various kinds of social capital including jobs and knowledge on navigating the new context, and a place where aspects of their ethnic heritage, language, and culture were celebrated and preserved. Linked to this preservation role was the empowerment of the immigrant that was accomplished through several social organizations, especially those based on faith. For example, within the religious context, the order of service, hymns, and rituals were conducted in a manner that resonated with who the immigrants were, thus serving to affirm their ethnic and religious identities. Whereas these immigrants may face discrimination or be ostracized within the wider society, within the churches in which they participate their culture was celebrated and treated as normative. These religious organizations also functioned as places where many immigrants, who were normally relegated to a subservient position within society, could occupy various leadership positions. From a social perspective, these churches were also sites where members, who were often without biological family, could acquire a surrogate family and gain access to housing, social welfare, and employment opportunities while also creating "interlacing ties which reinforce parental authority and values vis-à-vis the second generation."[20]

Research questions

The research questions that this book will address are: What are the religious and ethnic identities being constructed and renegotiated among various generations of West Indian migrants? How are these identities expressed in the liturgy, sermons, documentation, auxiliary ministries, organizational structure, and life of church members? What are some of the specific factors within British and American contexts that facilitate this renegotiation and construction of identities? Does this process assist or inhibit the assimilation and/or integration of the immigrant into the host society, and what are the consequences of this?

This research will also seek to examine the conceptual understanding and practice of mission within West Indian Pentecostal churches. How is mission being conceived and practiced within West Indian Pentecostal churches in New York City and London? What effect does the renegotiation/construction of the religious and ethnic identities among its members have on the interaction between the religious communities and the wider social context? What is the impact of the coexistence of these identities on the transference of religious beliefs to the second and third generation?

Definitions of terms

West Indian

In this book the term West Indian will be used in a collective manner to designate the people who are from the Anglophone Caribbean islands. In making such a designation however, it is imperative to state that this term itself is a by-product of the existence of the diaspora and the migratory process in which many people from these islands are involved. For, within the Caribbean region national distinctions—histories, cultures, and identities—dominate and as a result this collective term is rarely used. One exception is found in the game of cricket, in which the islands come together to form the West Indian team.

It was only as the people from these former British colonies migrated to various global cities and began to interact with their new surroundings that several of their distinctive cultural features and identities became displaced by the emergence of more collective ones. This adaptation is especially the case in several social, cultural, and political spheres within the United States and Britain.

Although this segment of the population is currently designated as African Caribbean or Afro-Caribbean within the British context, there exists a long history of the usage of the term West Indian, both within the wider society and among the migrants themselves. Within the American context by contrast, it is the term West Indian that is more prominent. Given the comparative framework used by this book, it was necessary to use a common term that was applicable to the migrants in both contexts. In addition, this term had to be one that was used not only in the host countries, but also among the migrants. The term that best meets these criteria is West Indian. Having chosen to use this term, it is necessary to acknowledge that there are various ideological connotations, (imperialism, racial hierarchy, and black inferiority) associated with this term, especially within the British context.

Pentecostalism

Pentecostalism is defined in this book as a renewal movement within Christianity that places particular emphasis on a direct personal encounter with God, on the indispensable role of the Holy Spirit as power-for-mission, and on the importance of the miraculous and numinous within a mission strategy.[21] It is not a monolithic movement, but includes a range of theological beliefs and organizations. There are two major branches within the movement—the Oneness and the Trinitarian. Within the Oneness or Jesus Only branch of Pentecostalism, there is an adherence to the two-stage process of salvation, that is, conversion and the baptism of the Holy Spirit, evidenced by the speaking in tongues. However, among the Jesus Only Pentecostals, the classical Trinitarian doctrine is replaced with Unitarianism—Jesus is believed to be the name of God the Father, God the Son, and God the Holy Spirit. Drawing on the narratives

about the apostles' mode of baptism documented in the book of Acts, Oneness
Pentecostals teach that the correct baptismal formula is in the name of Jesus only.
Therefore to conduct baptism in any other formula is to commit a grave error.
Churches located within this branch include the United Pentecostal Church and
various Apostolic Churches.

The Trinitarian or classical Pentecostals uphold both the doctrine of the
Trinity and the Trinitarian baptismal formula—in the name of the Father, Son,
and Holy Spirit. However, this branch is subdivided into two groups—the two-
stage and the three stage Pentecostals. The two-stage Pentecostals believe that
there are two stages in the process of salvation—justification, which refers to
conversion and sanctification (which occur simultaneously and thus constitute
one stage), and the baptism of the Holy Spirit. The churches in this group
include Assemblies of God and Elim Pentecostal. Three-stage Pentecostals, in
contrast, recognize three stages—justification, sanctification, and the baptism
of the Holy Spirit. Churches located within this group are: The Church of God
(CoG)- Cleveland, CoG in Christ, CoG of Prophecy, and several independent
Pentecostal churches. It is within this Trinitarian stream and the three-stage
group that we locate the three churches that comprise this research.

Methodology

For this book, primary research data was obtained by conducting fieldwork in
Brooklyn, New York, and London. This took the form of a triangulation research
design, which incorporated an ethnographic and participant observation
methodology as well as case studies and comparative research designs.

In total, three churches were part of the study, two in Brooklyn and one in
London.[22] These churches were selected according to the following criteria.
First, the churches had to be located in areas having a large percentage of West
Indians. Both New York City and London are places that meet this criterion
since both historically have been the primary cities to which West Indians
migrate. Secondly, the churches had to be of the Pentecostal tradition. Thirdly,
the churches had to be founded by West Indian migrants and be predominantly
West Indian in membership.

During fieldwork, primary data was obtained from unstructured interviews
and participant observation. In both contexts, the sample population was
chosen to reflect the intergenerational dynamics of the immigrant family

as well as some of the demographics of the religious community being studied.[23] It is necessary to note, however, that the sample population was not selected to represent the gender distribution within the churches because, although the majority of the church members were female, the leadership was predominantly male. Since one of the main areas of study is the issue of identity within leadership as well as among the laity, it was important to have a number of informants for each gender where it was possible to do so. In New York, nineteen informants were interviewed. This consisted of five first-generation informants, two males and three females. Fourteen immigrant children were interviewed, two who were designated as 1.5 generation and twelve who were second generation.[24] Within this category, five were females and nine were males. Among the informants, ten were in leadership positions within the churches (five male and five females).

Within the London context, thirty-three informants were interviewed. This included twenty-three individual interviews and one group interview. Among the informants there were twelve first-generation immigrants, eight females, and four males. There were twenty-one immigrant children in the study, of which two were designated as 1.5 generation and eleven as second generation.[25] The remaining eight were third generation (three males and eight females). Of the informants, nine were in leadership positions. This included one first-generation female, three first-generation males, three second-generation females, and two second-generation males.

Primary data was also obtained through participant observation of various Sunday services, midweek services, and other auxiliary programs. The midweek services primarily consisted of Bible studies and prayer meetings, while auxiliary services included youth meetings, ladies meetings, Sunday school, church banquets, and some fundraising programs.

Outline of the book

The chapters in this book describe the different phases of the journey toward the discovery of self that the immigrant encounters in the process of migration and settlement. As such, each chapter builds on the previous ones and it is only when taken together that they present the full picture of what the journey is like. It is for this reason this book is structured like a beautiful tapestry, with each chapter contributing a portion to the finished product.

In the creation of tapestries, consideration about the specific pattern to be used is very important. This is particularly the case when the pattern is a reproduction, where both the pattern and technique employed in creating the tapestry are much-guarded familial or ethnic secrets passed on from one generation to another. In such contexts, great care is taken to preserve the complexity and overall confluence of the individual fibers used in the tapestry. In other contexts however, where a new pattern is being developed, greater flexibility may be the norm. For although the weaver may have a concept of what the finished creation should be, room is also given for experimentation, and for allowing the texture, contrast, and convergence of the fibers to determine how the tapestry is fashioned. For this book, it was the second mode of creation that dominated. For although Europeans, Amerindians, Africans, and others each contributed various fibers carrying specific embedded creative material, which within their own social contexts would follow a certain pattern, within the West Indies these predetermined patterns were no longer completely viable. Instead, each fiber combined with the others to create a unique combination of identities, ethnic and religious, that we now see in the people who self-identify as West Indians. As this group moved to London and New York City as immigrants, they encountered "new" contexts and conditions that resulted in entirely new fibers being added to the developing tapestry. Thus, the tapestry that came to symbolize their journey toward the discovery of self became even more extensive, diverse, and complex, characterized by sections of synergy and dissonance, and the incorporation of old predetermined patterns as well as new ones. In the creation of this tapestry, to try and separate the fibers that comprised it was an almost impossible task. In this monograph the finished creation will be examined from several perspectives, each of which form the main argument of the ensuing chapter, and gives specific attention to the major fibers that contributed to a particular portion.

Introduction

This chapter gives a brief overview of the book. The research questions and rationale for the research is presented as a brief description of the contextual and internal dynamics located within West Indian Pentecostal churches in New York and London. I argue that the encounter between the immigrant and the host society needs to be expanded beyond an assimilation/ethnic binary to include the multiple ways in which these interactions foster the transformation of the immigrant, the host society, and the home country. In focusing our study on West Indian Pentecostal churches that immigrants attend, we are given a unique lens that enables us to see the role that race, religion, and the immigrant experience play in the multiple transformative processes that accompany immigrant life in New York City and London.

Chapter 1. Formation: Ethnic and religious identities within the West Indian context

This chapter focuses on the construction and expression of ethnic and religious identities within the West Indian context. It examines the roles that the Spanish and British colonial systems, African slaves, Amerindians, and various missionaries played in the formulation of these identities. Building on this examination, the chapter further explores how these West Indian identities were and continue to be excavated from the history, geography, power apparatuses, personal realities, fantasies, memories, institutions, and religious revelations that existed within and outside of these island paradises. Continuing to use the metaphor of a tapestry, this chapter also outlines the parameters of the wider context in which the West Indian ethnic and religious identities were constructed as well as offers analyses of several of the more prominent fibers, that is, the role of Spain, Britain, Africa, European missionaries, and American Pentecostals in that formation.

Chapter 2. Island dreams and diaspora realities: Migration, transnationalism, and the formation of West Indian Pentecostal churches

This chapter examines the migration segment of the tapestry, giving particular attention to some of the fibers that contributed to the presence of West Indian immigrant and Pentecostal churches in New York and London. Beginning with the island paradises in which the migrants lived, this chapter investigates some of the regional and international features that facilitated the migration of West Indian migrants. Due to the complexity of the issues, I argue that a multidimensional approach is vital within this discourse. Therefore, this chapter will address the impact of regional and international socioeconomic and political issues, immigration laws and acts in the United States and Britain; and the perpetuation of particular "images" on migration within and outside of the West Indies. The second section of this chapter investigates the contextual realities within host societies that facilitated the formation of immigrant churches. Like all other social groups, these religious communities emerged within specific socioeconomic and political contexts and also at certain periods in the immigration histories of the receiving countries. It is within this context that the histories of the individual case studies will be considered and analyzed. This section also examines the manner in which both West Indians and the Pentecostal churches in which they participate are adapting to the host context. In this interrogation, particular attention is given to highlighting some of the salient transnational features that are found within the immigrants' lives and their religious communities.

Chapter 3. Finding space: Identification among first-generation West Indian immigrants

This chapter brings to the fore the settlement portion of the tapestry and focuses on the manner in which religious and ethnic identities are being renegotiated by first-generation West Indian migrants. I argue that for many first-generation immigrants, the processes of renegotiation whereby boundaries are legitimized and identities are articulated occur within a migration framework that connects their localities of origin and their new place of residence. As a result, this process in which they are actively engaged is a transnational one. This chapter investigates two primary areas of study. First, it examines the types of ethnic and religious identities being renegotiated by the first-generation migrant within this transnational context. Second, it will document the manner in which these identities and transnational features are being portrayed within the rituals and activities of West Indian Pentecostal churches.

Chapter 4. Creating space: Identity construction among West Indian immigrant youth

Chapter 4 continues to explore the settlement portion of the tapestry from the perspective of the immigrant youth. In this chapter the identity construction of West Indian immigrant youth is examined in the context of the creation of a place of belonging and freedom of expression. Within this chapter, this place is located within West Indian Pentecostal churches in which these immigrant youth are involved. Thus I argue that West Indian Pentecostal churches function as innovative places in which several ethno-religious and societal elements converge, thus facilitating the construction of particular ethnic and religious identities among immigrant youths. These elements are discussed in three sections within this chapter. The first section investigates how 1.5-, second-, and third-generation West Indian immigrant youth are interacting with their social contexts. In the second section, I argue that the identification process for immigrant youth is different from that engaged in by first-generation migrants. Therefore, this section will detail the various kinds of ethnic and religious identities that are being constructed by immigrant youth as well as document some of the reasons for this difference in identification. The third section illuminates features of the dialectic process in which immigrant youth and other members of the Pentecostal churches are engaged as they seek to negotiate the realities of living out their faith in the diaspora.

Chapter 5. Led by the Spirit: Mission within West Indian Pentecostal churches

This chapter explores the final section of the settlement portion of the tapestry, the conceptualization and practice of mission within West Indian Pentecostal churches. To accomplish this however, it will be necessary to present a brief overview of the understanding and practice of mission from a Pentecostal perspective—giving particular attention to two specific missional traditions—the North American and the West Indian. Following this investigation, the chapter highlights several of the ways in which the term mission is currently being conceptualized and practiced within three West Indian Pentecostal churches in New York and London. Specific attention is given to translation, where the ideas and practices emanating from the home and host contexts critique and affirm each other. In the process, some features of mission change, impacting the immigrants' daily activities and that of their co-patriots at home and throughout the diaspora.

Conclusion: Living their faith

This chapter summarizes the book, and highlights how each chapter contributes to the overall tapestry, that is, how West Indian immigrants are engaging in this journey of discovery. This chapter concludes by arguing that if we are to understand Christianity within contemporary contexts and know what its characteristics are in the twenty-first century, further attention needs to be focused on at least two areas: one, the religious lives of young people in general and immigrant youth in particular, and two, immigrant churches in the diaspora and global contexts. In regard to the religious lives of youth, in each society they constitute the frontline of cultural and social changes. As such, they have much to challenge and say to the church about discovering the way forward to a Christianity that is vibrant and addresses the needs of all its members. Second, as this book reveals, immigrant religious communities in the diaspora and global contexts are pivotal in the lives of immigrants. However as they continue to grow and proliferate they may also come to represent the forefront of a possible theological and power shift within world Christianity, especially as theologies and resources emerging from the Global South are brought to bear on the realities of life in the West.

Postscript: Engaging the field

This section discusses how I navigated the insider/outsider dichotomy in my research. I argue that while I may be considered an insider because I study co-ethnics, in reality my identification as an insider/outsider was not predetermined or static. It changed and fluctuated as a result of the specific particularities within the religious communities, the nature of the research, actions taken over the course of the fieldwork, and having to navigate certain familial relations and dynamics. Thus, in order to preserve the integrity of fieldwork and the overall research project, I had to continually engage in self-reflection and critical analysis of what I was observing and hearing in other words, I had to pay attention to what was spoken as well as what was unspoken, power structures, and other features governing the religious community, and where I was at any given time along the insider/outsider spectrum.

Formation: Ethnic and Religious Identities within the West Indian Context

In several conversations about West Indians and their interactions with people of other races I have been asked repeatedly, "Why discuss the issue of slavery?" In many ways this is a valid question to ask as I begin this chapter. Why should I give additional space to a subject about which Hugh Thomas, in 1997, while writing a history on the slave trade, says the following: "It may be said that that is now such well-ploughed ground that there is no room for any new cultivation."[1] This statement rings with resounding clarity especially as information generated from various conferences, discussions, articles, and books marking the bicentenary of the abolition of the slave trade in the British Empire are added to the volumes that already exist on the topic.

I begin with a discussion of slavery because it is a place of origin. It is here that the people now termed West Indian came into existence and where foundational aspects of their identities were formed, identities which were excavated from the history, geography, power apparatuses, personal realities, fantasies, memories, institutions, and religious revelations that existed within and outside of their island paradises. It was within these individuals, social groups, and societies that materials claimed from these areas were processed, given meaning, and embodied. Manuel Castells describes this embodiment as existing "according to social determinations and cultural projects that are rooted in their social structure, and in their space/time framework."[2] Having justified the necessity of beginning here with a discussion on slavery, I still take seriously Thomas' remarks provided above.

In approaching this section of the book, attention will be given to the manner in which the formation of West Indian ethno-religious identities, which highlights some salient aspects of the transatlantic trade, provides the primary element, that is, the people that will be discussed in the chapters that follow. As stated in the introduction, the subsequent chapters will be presented as a portion of a unique and complex tapestry, with each contributing to the overall finished product.

In discussing the West Indian ethno-religious identities portion of the overall tapestry, two additional preliminary statements are necessary. First, it needs to be reiterated that the pattern used in the overall creation of the tapestry and this particular portion was new. As Orlando Patterson states in his preface to *The Sociology of Slavery*,

> Jamaica, and the other West Indian islands, are unique in World history in that they present one of the rare cases of a human society being artificially created for the satisfaction of one clearly defined goal: that of making money through the production of sugar. . . . Both the British masters and their slaves, . . . were total strangers to the land upon which they were destined to build a completely new society.[3]

Thus, due to the artificial nature of the creation of West Indian society, a preexisting pattern incorporating all of the fibers—European, American, and African—was not available. Second, in examining the ethnic and religious identities formulated within the West Indian context, attention will be given to the value and beauty that lies primarily not in the characteristics of the individual threads but in the intricacies of the whole, that is, in the overall process of synergy and dissonance as the threads are woven together. We should note that the ethnicities and religious beliefs these threads represent are not singular; instead each is comprised of a multiplicity of other fibers. For with the successive arrival of each group of people to these exotic islands, coupled with the religious influences exerted by various European missionaries and American Pentecostals, another thread was introduced into the construction of what was to become the ethnic and religious identities that West Indian immigrants would take with them into the diaspora. Although the threads representing the Chinese, Indian, German, Portuguese, French, Syrian, and Jewish are important in the creation of the overall tapestry, they played a lesser role when compared to the contributions from the Spanish, British, African, European missionaries, and American Pentecostal fibers.[4]

The ethnic portion of the tapestry

The ethnic identities of West Indian people are a fusion of several external and internal fibers. These external fibers include the region's colonial heritage and interconnections with Europe and Africa. The internal fibers are dual, the indigenous peoples (the Tainos/Arawaks and the Caribs/Callinagoes) and the islands (their location, geography, climate, and topography).

In this chapter, the Spanish contribution to the formation of West Indian ethnic identity will focus on four specific strands. The first strand that Spain provided was the articulation of the ideologies that would subsequently be used to give biblical and social sanction to African slavery. The second and third strands are interrelated and will be discussed together. In its effort to "protect" the indigenous population that had seen a dramatic decrease resulting from Spain's arrival in the Americas, Africans were brought in as an alternative workforce. In the process, a link was established between Africans and slavery. This, both the workforce (Africans) and the work system (slavery), became Spain's second strand. Spain's third contribution to the West Indian ethnic tapestry was the introduction of a crop that necessitated the demand of a large workforce—namely sugarcane. In their attempt to maintain ownership of the islands in the Caribbean Sea, Spain recruited many slaves to fight with them by promising them their freedom. In the subsequent loss of several islands to other European countries, especially Britain, many of these slaves became a part of the free slave communities or Maroon towns. These towns, which had their inception in the collaboration between some of the indigenous population and the runaway slaves, constitute Spain's fourth strand, for by their presence, liberty, and acts of resistance they became a constant threat to the colonial system, and a catalyst for slaves in their fight for freedom.

By incorporating the four fibers contributed by Spain, the British introduced a measure of continuity and complexity into the West Indian ethnic portion of the tapestry. This emerged in the interlacing of four British prominent fibers, each adding a different form of embedded creative material to the tapestry. These four fibers were: one, the institutionalization of the plantation system; two, the absenteeism of the plantation owners; three, the creation of conditions that resulted in an increase in Maroon bands and other forms of slave resistance; and four, the development of a social classification that was systematically linked with color. We should note however that these fibers are not independent of each other; instead each facilitated the emergence and expression of the other. However, the individual fibers also received additional support in this process of facilitation from two structures, namely slavery and the transatlantic trade. As such, in discussing the characteristics, nature, and expression of these four fibers, space will also be given to highlight the role these structures played in the overall creation of the West Indian ethnic portion of the tapestry.

The African contribution to the West Indian ethnic portion of the tapestry were the slaves who upon their arrival to these islands disembarked from the holds of the ships carrying some precious fibers representing their heritage, history, language, religion, and various ethnic identities. Although confronted with several pernicious forces aimed at severing all ties to their past, they found a way of amalgamating many of these diverse fibers. This amalgamation took several forms and was expressed in various modes that may seem contradictory. There was the development of hybrid personalities (the trickster and Quashee), the inversion and acceptance of the prescribed British social and cultural mores, and the creation of new expressions of language, music, and dance. Due to the nature of the interrelation between the African and British threads, they will be examined together. Each impacted how the others were incorporated and expressed within the ultimate creation of this portion of the tapestry.

The Spanish contribution

Although European contact with the islands that were to become the West Indies did not occur until 1493 onward, the formation of the ethnic identity of the West Indian people commenced on the morning of October 12, 1492. As the resounding cry "Tierra! Tierra!" pierced the silence of the morning, the weaving of the West Indian ethnic tapestry commenced with Spain's first fiber. This cry, which signaled to Christopher Columbus and the other sailors the end of their ten long weeks at sea and the averting of a mutiny, inaugurated the colonization of the islands and lands later labeled as the "New World," and the "Christianization" and "civilizing" of the indigenous peoples who lived there. For hundreds of years this "discovery" marking "the very birth of the modern society as we know it" has been commemorated in the Americas and Europe.[5] However, for the indigenous peoples, this "discovery" and the subsequent interaction with the Spaniards resulted in the formulation and implementation of an ideology of exploitation and savagery that resulted in the loss of land, slavery, and the near extinction of entire people groups.

For Spain, the morning of October 12, 1492, came to signify a new beginning, one in which she was thrust into a privileged position that made her the envy of every European nation. She had "discovered" a "new world," a place later found to be abounding in riches—precious minerals, flora, people, and animals that seemed to defy medieval Europe's imagination. As "discoverer," Spain gained the right and responsibility of colonizing, civilizing, and Christianizing the people and the islands they inhabited. Legitimacy for committing these acts came in the form of Pope Alexander VI's perpetual appropriation to the Spanish monarch of the "dominions, cities, camps, places, and villages, and all rights, jurisdictions, and appurtenances all islands and mainlands found and to be found, discovered and to be discovered toward the West and South."[6]

What were the indigenous people that they encountered like? On the island of San Salvador, named as such by Columbus after "our Lord and Saviour," and which "was known to the natives as Guanahaní,"[7] Columbus found the Taino or Arawak nation to be

> a gentle and peaceful people and of great simplicity. . . . They go quite naked as their mother bore them; . . . They bear no arms, nor know thereof; for I showed them swords and they grasped them by the blade and cut themselves through ignorance; they have no iron. They ought to be good servants and of good skill, for I see that they repeat very quickly all that is said to them; and I believe that they would easily be made Christians, because it seemed to me that they belonged to no religion.[8]

Later in his explorations Columbus also encountered the Caribs or Callinagoes, whom he described as "a people who are regarded in all the islands as very ferocious and who eat human flesh."[9] According to Peter Martyr, the Caribs were

> cannibals [who] captured children, whom they castrated, just as we do chicken and pigs we wish to fatten for the table, and when they were grown and become fat they ate them. Older persons, who fell into their power, were killed and cut into pieces for food; they also ate the intestines and the extremities, which they salted, just as we do hams.[10]

Negative descriptions were also applied to the more "civilized" indigenous groups like the Incas, Aztecs, and Mayans, who were seen to engage in "uncivilized" and "bestial" behavior—specifically human sacrifice.

When engaging with the descriptions of the indigenous peoples given above, there is a need to interrogate the underlying ideological foundations. First, these descriptions were composed from the perspective of those whose agenda was to conquer a particular people. Labeling the Caribs as cannibals or the Aztecs as "uncivilized" helped to justify the Europeans conquering them. Second, they highlight the type of interactions that were experienced. The Caribs' active resistance to the threat to their sovereignty resulted in their characterization as a warlike "bestial" group. In contrast, the Taino were described as peaceful, primarily because they were accommodating and submissive to the Europeans and therefore more easily subjugated by them.[11]

The question that the Spanish had to answer as they embarked on the process of colonization, civilization, and Christianization was how would they relate to those whose culture and nature seemed to be so "bestial" and "uncivilized" when compared with their own. Was there any philosophy that would provide them with a framework on which to build a "right" perspective of these "new people?" The Spaniards found an answer in the Aristotelian ideology of natural slavery, which states "that one part of mankind is set aside by nature to be slaves in the service of masters born for a life of virtue free of manual labor."[12] This ideology underwent a process of synthesis with various Christian ideas articulated by both Thomas Aquinas and Albertus Magnus, so that "the term barbarus which, since the sixth century, had been used rather loosely to describe anyone 'out there' was now brought under closer scrutiny in the light of its use by Aristotle to classify a certain type of man."[13] And thus it came to be applied broadly to all non-Christian peoples, irrespective of race or religious beliefs, who behaved in what was perceived to be a savage or "uncivil" manner, that is, one unlike their own.

As can be seen from the description of the indigenous peoples documented above, there was no shortage of acts that lent themselves as evidence that such a label—barbarian—should be attached to the indigenous peoples of the "New World." The fundamental implication of such labeling throughout Europe was that "any creature so described, was somehow an imperfect human being."[14] Thus, for some Spanish thinkers, indigenous peoples, being imperfect human beings, were naturally meant to serve the Spanish invaders, who were civilized, enlightened, and possessed the intellectual ability and acumen to govern and, be their natural masters. For others like the scholar Vitoria, the high-culture Indians from central Mexico and the Andes possessed the characteristics of civilization and reason. However, in continuing to perpetuate such practices like cannibalism and human sacrifice, "they were like children, having the potential for use of true reason but not there yet."[15] Moreover, neither their maturation processes nor their environment or customs supplied what was needed to make this potential a reality. As a result, until they were grown, the Indians had to "remain in just tutelage under the king of Spain, [with their] status now slave-like, but not slavish."[16]

Having been allocated the majority of the lands and people of the "New World" by Pope Alexander VI, the Spanish monarchy believed that the papal bull also "conceded them the right not only to conquer but also to enslave the inhabitants of the Antilles."[17] This ideology, especially as it related to the conquering, Christianizing, and enslavement of the inhabitants of the Antilles, was readily adapted and firmly implemented by the conquistadores and the colonists and also formulized in the apportioning and forced labor of Indians through the encomienda system in 1503.[18] Although new laws were instituted in 1542 as a result of the debates within the Spanish courts cancelling the apportioning of Indians, the colonists in Peru "exploded in armed rebellion."[19] The Crown's reaction to the riot was to yield to the demands of the conquistadores and colonists and abolish the laws. Thus, the impact of the ongoing debates on life in the Americas was almost negligible because in the eyes of the conquistadores and colonists, the indigenous peoples were barbarians, imperfect human beings whose colonization was justified, even in the face of their visible demise.

Bartolomé de Las Casas in *A Short Account of the Destruction of the Indies* states, "When the Spanish first journeyed there, the indigenous population of the island [Hispaniola] . . . stood at some three million; today only two hundred survive."[20] In most cases, the indigenous peoples died as a result of exposure to diseases brought by the Spaniards for which they had no immunity. "[Thus] single epidemics reduced villages by half or more, and the people in many tribes were completely wiped out in a few decades. . . . The major killers included smallpox, measles, whooping cough, chicken pox, bubonic plague, typhus . . . and a variety of helminthic infections."[21] In *A Violent Evangelism* Luis Rivera gives several reasons that also contributed to the fatalities. He writes:

> The break down of agricultural production during war and mining exploitation was decisive. That created an arbitrary scarcity, accompanied by the physical weakening of the natives. Other factors were the lack of the care of the sick, the conditions not conducive to their recovery, and the overcrowding in homes and work situations that facilitated contagion.[22]

As a result of these causes and the harsh treatment by the Spaniards, the indigenous population of the Americas underwent a decline so dramatic that some have termed it a "process of genocide, an American Indian holocaust."[23]

Having discussed some of the ideologies that governed Spain's interaction with the Indians and their demise, we now turn our attention to the crop (sugarcane), the people (Africans), and the system (slavery) that constitute the second and third fibers of the tapestry under discussion. In 1493 on his second voyage to the Americas, Columbus brought a crop from the Canary Islands that would change the destiny of the islands and people of the West Indies forever—sugarcane.[24] This plant, which grows best in the tropics, is very labor intensive, requiring a large working population, and significant plots of land for ideal cultivation. According to J. W. Purseglove, "Sugar cane propagation is through stem cutting of immature canes 8–12 months old. These are called 'setts', 'seed', 'seed-cane' or 'seed pieces'. . . . It takes 12,500–20,000 setts to plant one hectare."[25] As a perennial crop, sugarcane "usually produces crops for about 3–6 years before replanting."[26] Given that various aspects of the cultivation of this plant, including planting and reaping, were done by hand, the dramatic decline in indigenous population created an urgent need for an alternative source of labor. For this the Spaniards turned to Africa, specifically West Africa. Although the Portuguese had founded a bustling slave trade upon their arrival in Western Africa, it was the coming of the Spanish that "multiplied it and catapulted it into a new means of production." This extensive need for slave labor resulted in "slavery, from that moment, [being] linked intimately with the Black race in a long history of oppression and resistance."[27] Built upon the ideological foundation laid by Spain in regard to the "others," the subjugation of the black race "took on a new ideological and paradoxical justification: the civilizing and evangelizing of the African."[28] Luis Rivera in *A Violent Evangelism* cites Carlos Dieve as stating:

> The attitude of the church toward slavery centered officially on its interest in having Black pagan idolaters received, through previous indoctrination and baptism, into the benefits and consolation of Catholicism. The Crown shared that view and also tried to see to it that Black slaves received religious instruction. Nevertheless, the interest . . . in having the slaves embrace Christian doctrine was not due only to apostolic zeal. . . . The Christianization of Africans also sought their easy subjection and was . . . a technique used to justify the market in Black slaves. . . . The body of the slave was chained so as to reward him with a soul that could be saved.[29]

Thus, slavery was viewed as beneficial for the slaves because it gave them the opportunity to give up their idolatrous and pagan practices to become Christians. This conversion, however, came at the cost of their lives and personhood.

One consequence of Spain being allocated the majority of the lands of the Americas was that she became the sole recipient of the wealth that was found there, namely gold and other precious metals. By holding such a position, however, she also became the target for other European nations who wanted a share of the wealth that was being generated. Initially, this took the form of various trade ventures and government-sponsored privateers. However, European nations later sought to acquire colonies within the region.[30] In 1655, after suffering a formidable defeat by the Spaniards in a battle over Hispaniola, the English turned their eyes to the poorly populated and "poorly defended island"[31] of Jamaica. In defending the island the Spaniards enlisted the help of their slaves, some of whom they freed in the process. Ultimately, the Spaniards were defeated and forced to withdraw from Jamaica and escape to Cuba. As they retreated, the Spaniards "left . . . their Negro slaves behind, who secreted themselves in the mountains."[32] These freed slaves, later called Maroons,[33] banded together to form thriving communities whose population was augmented by runaways, and became a force to be reckoned with during the British rule of Jamaica. The term Maroon was not limited to the freed African slaves and runaways in Jamaica, but also applied to bands of black Caribs in St. Vincent, the partly miscegenated Caribs (Caribs and runaway slaves) found in Dominica, and to runaways in general. Thus "true maroons were found at one time or another in virtually every plantation colony, however small."[34] The problem for most runaways, however, was the lack of ability to band together in a manner that would enable them to sustain themselves—militarily, agriculturally, socially, and politically.

Thus, with the formation of the Maroon communities, the final fiber contributed by Spain to the formation of the West Indian ethnic tapestry was added. This strand combined with the others—the Aristotelian ideology of natural slavery, which gave rise to the ideologies used to biblically and socially sanction slavery; the dramatic decrease of the indigenous population, which resulted in Africans being brought to the Indies for labor; and the introduction of a cash crop that had enormous earning potential—to pave the way for the next stage in the development of the West Indian ethnic tapestry: the British and African contribution.

The British and African contributions

By incorporating three specific Spanish fibers, Aristotle's ideology, the African link with slavery, and the presence of sugar, the British set into motion a complex structure that helped to transform the British Isles from a second rate nation to the world power by the eighteenth century and resulted in changing the face, language, and culture of the Americas.[35] At the base of this structure was the plantation system and its supporting components—the colonies in the West Indies, the institution of slavery, the transatlantic slave trade, and the auxiliary industries that were associated with them.

How were these fibers incorporated within the plantation system that the British implemented? On the one hand, the fibers justified, facilitated, and buttressed the plantation system, while on the other hand, the plantation system served to reinforce and further develop the role of these fibers within the ethnic tapestry. Thus, the ideologies that Spain had articulated and instituted in relation to the Amerindians and the African were further developed by the British to sanction this system. This sanction took the form of theological justification and the implementation of a racial discourse into all levels of society, both in Europe and the Americas, which resulted in an European belief in the superiority of whites and the innate inferiority of all other races, especially the Africans.

Theological justification was found in the curse of Ham theory, which was based on a particular exegesis of Genesis 9, where Noah curses Canaan and condemns him to a life of servitude. In the racist understanding, however, the curse was applied to Ham, Canaan's father, and his posterity. Thus, it was argued that since the black race was the descendant of Ham, it was their biblically ordained role, like that of their ancestor, to be subservient to the other races.[36] Within the social arena, justification came in the form of the racial discourses that were developed during the Enlightenment, and which essentially surmised that the black race failed "the Enlightenment test of humanity."[37] This racial discourse emerged from a multilayered analysis, one drawing on various philosophies, movements, authors, and scientific approaches. This resulted in the perpetuation of the belief among many Europeans that the black race was inferior, and deficient in every aspect of life—mentally, socially, biologically, psychologically etc.[38]

According to Samuel Yeboah, "The doctrine of inherent black inferiority" was the justification for not treating blacks the same way as whites. For him, this doctrine, which informed the ideology of racism, served several purposes. First, "It provided moral justification for the acts of bestiality," and prevented any possible indignation that may come from the home context. Second, "It soothed any vestige of conscience that the slave traders and colonists might have possessed, by enabling them to reconcile their cultural values with their brutal activities." Third, by undermining the self-esteem of the black man, this doctrine sought to prevent any resistance from the enslaved and the colonized, while simultaneously trying to convince him of the superiority of the white man and his right to rule.[39] We should note that within the colonization framework these racial discourses were also used to justify British expansion; since the blacks were believed to be lazy and deficient, they needed to be subjected to brutal force in order to achieve successful civilizing results.

In the early seventeenth century when the British began to make inroads in the Spanish monopoly over the West Indian islands, their attention was focused on the smaller islands. With Britain's arrival in Barbados in 1625, she entered a new phase in her history. In Barbados, Britain found its candidate for its first foray into an economic venture that would dramatically alter her existence and that of the West Indies—the sugar plantation. Up until the 1640s the majority of farmers in Barbados were involved in tobacco cultivation, a venture that was largely economically unsuccessful. Coinciding with these realities was the arrival of several Dutch farmers from Brazil who were knowledgeable in sugar cultivation and manufacture. "Within the space of a decade, this peasant stronghold was transformed into the advanced bastion of the plantation economy."[40] The immediate effect of the change to a plantation economy was the growing demand for more land and labor. Initially, the labor needs were satisfied by white indentured laborers who came primarily from Ireland, with a smaller number originating from the rest of Britain.[41] However, this solution was provisional due to the temporary nature of the contract; the lack of sufficient labor to replace those who had completed their contract; the servant's expectation of land upon completion of contract; and the difficulty in recovering a servant who had escaped, versus a slave, due to their color. For these reasons, plantation owners decided that slaves were the best alternative. They were cheaper, once bought they and their descendants belonged to the owners in perpetuity, and they were immune to tropical diseases.[42]

The sugar plantation system "dominated economic life in every sense. It occupied the best lands, the laws supported the slave system, and in general all commercial and other economic activity depended on the rhythm of activity of the plantation."[43] In both the West Indian colonies and Britain, the plantation, the slave system, and the transatlantic slave trade were intricately linked, and became something to protect and expand, sometimes at any cost. Primarily "because of the fabulous prosperity it brought to the English plantation owners directly, and indirectly to those cities, such as Liverpool and Bristol."[44]

The transatlantic slave trade was comprised of several parts. First, European ships would sail to Africa laden with bartering goods, arms, and liquor which they would trade for slaves. These slaves were transported on the same ships to the Caribbean to meet the continuous labor demands required in the production of sugar. From the Caribbean, these ships would convey Caribbean sugar, rum, and other by-products to the cities and palates of Europe. Evidence of the wealth generated from this trade and its interconnected systems—slavery and plantation—was visible in many of the geographical contexts governed by the trade. For several kings and chiefs in Bonny, Calabar, Dahomey, Lagos, and other areas of West Africa, the slave trade became a vital component in their societies' commerce.[45] The European products, especially weaponry, received in exchange for slaves, facilitated the expansion, strengthening, and consolidation of their rule over neighboring ethnic groups.[46]

In the West Indies, the transatlantic trade enabled several European farmers to change their economic status from being impoverished members of society to becoming wealthy plantation owners. Barbados, for example, an island which Thomas describes in 1645 as being inhabited by "more than 11,000 impoverished farmers of British stock, . . . owning about 6,000 slaves, and mostly growing third-rate tobacco,"[47] through the growth of the transatlantic slave trade, and the plantation and slavery systems became in 1667 at least in perception twenty times richer than it was prior to the introduction of sugar. What occurred in Barbados was to be repeated throughout the West Indies.

Who profited from this wealth? Unlike their counterparts in the American colonies, most of the beneficiaries of the wealth produced were not the merchants and common English citizens, but the gentry. For these members of society, their investment in plantations became a means of restoring their fortunes, and further cementing their place in the upper echelons of English society. According to Lord Brougham, the object of emigrants to the West Indies was "not to live, but to gain—not to enjoy, but to save—not to subsist in the colonies, but to prepare for shining in the mother country."[48] This mind-set among the plantation owners gave rise to absenteeism, which "drained the island of the very people it needed for leadership in all aspects of life."[49] It also undermined the growth of the infrastructure—schools, expanded public facilities, and good roads—necessary for the development of the colonies.[50]

As the pages of history reveal, absenteeism resulted in "a complete breakdown of religion and morality,"[51] which was most noticeable in the destruction of the institutions of family and marriage. In the case of Jamaica, this breakdown resulted in the "sexual exploitation of female slaves by white men."[52] The disintegration of family and sexual mores was also engendered among the slave population. We should note that these practices were not specific to the Jamaican context but were evident within slave communities throughout the Americas. This breakdown in some contexts, as Patterson asserts in regard to Jamaica, was due to the effects of absenteeism; however, it may have also resulted from several dynamics associated with the slave system, namely the lack of white women to marry, the encouraged cohabitation of slaves to increase the slave number, the harshness of the environment in terms of raising a family, etc.[53] The subsequent outcome was the notable acceptance of illegitimacy and the pervasiveness of cohabitation practices within West Indian society.

Absenteeism also created an environment that fostered the "gross mismanagement of the economic affairs of the island."[54] For some attorneys the planters' absence provided the opportunity to defraud them and live extravagantly at their expense.[55] Also, as they were responsible for a large number of plantations, the attorneys were incapable of properly managing them. By default, the running of the plantation was left to the overseers who also utilized the facilities for their own means,[56] and to obtain higher annual returns drove the slaves far beyond their physical strength. In *The Sociology of Slavery*, Orlando Patterson cites Henry Coor as making the following statement in his report to the Select Committee, "I have heard many of the overseers say, 'I have made my employer 20, 30 or 40 more hogheads per year than any of my predecessors ever did; and though I have killed 30 or 40 Negroes per year more, yet the produce had been more than adequate to the loss.'"[57] These work-practices resulted in a continuous demand for slave labor, which when combined with the plantations' potential as an income earner provided two major reasons for the necessity of the transatlantic trade.

Where did the slaves originate? The majority of the slaves that found themselves in the West Indies originated from West Africa, specifically the areas of the Gold Coast, Bight of Benin, Windward Coast, Angola, the Niger and Cross deltas, Cameroon, and Northern Gabon.[58] For many of them, once they became part of the transatlantic trade, their individual status as craftsman, prince, daughter, husband, or their ethnic group, was of no significance. Within the slavery system, they were the same—slaves—"all sailing away from the place that birthed them and toward a nightmare that had not yet taken shape."[59] According to Orlando Patterson in *The Sociology of Slavery*, "If we are to generalize about the extent to which masters abused their powers in the different periods we may say, first, that until about the middle of the second quarter of the eighteenth century brutality to the slaves was the norm."[60] To the planters, overseers, and others who benefited from the plantation system both in the West Indies and across the ocean in Europe and Africa, the slaves were a commodity, or chattel—something to be bought and sold at will. The main goal was to maintain the slave trade and continue to reap the profits that it produced. Thus, Eric Williams is correct when he asserts that "negro slavery was essential to the preservation of the sugar plantations. The considerations were purely economic. The slaves were denominated 'Black ivory'."[61] As such, they were of immense value to the overall economic system and its interlocked parts—manufacturing industries in Britain, the Atlantic trade in Africa and the West Indies, and the exports of tropical goods to Europe.

Driven by the plantations' need for slave labor, both its control and availability, while maximizing the system's agricultural earning potential, the slave system instituted within the West Indies and the United States was structured around keeping the slaves in perpetual bondage. This took the form of the erection of a society whose structures and systems sought to perpetuate the racial discourse discussed earlier. The intention was that eventually the slave would see himself/herself as what he/she was told he was—chattel. In her discussion of the United States context, Sidonie Smith describes the psychological effect of this assault on the slave in the following manner. "To survive . . . where he [she] was labeled a chattel and thereby stripped of his [her] humanity, condemned to inferiority, and denied uniqueness, the slave had to suppress all needs of legitimate self-assertion, all aspirations of self-fulfillment; in other words, the self had to be sacrificed or 'lost' in order for it to be 'saved'—physically."[62]

Smith's point about "losing" the self in order to "save" the physical does not, however, fully capture what was happening, especially in the context of the West Indies, as the slaves were trying hard to survive as well as subvert the plantation system by hitting "Massa [the plantation owner] where it hurt him most: in his pocketbook."[63] This was accomplished on two levels. First, by feigning sickness, breaking tools, working slowly, and interfering with plantation machinery, slaves were able to impede and greatly affect the operation of the plantation. For the women, another act of sabotage existed—fertility control, in order to ensure that their children did not become slaves, thus decreasing Massa's wealth.[64] The second level of subversion was the adoption of complex hybrid personalities; one set of behaviors were exhibited during the days while in Massa's presence and another was evident at nighttime and during the weekends spent in the villages. In Massa's presence it was the Quashee or mask personality that was portrayed. Through "manifestations of a persona of childlike inefficiency, frivolity, and ignorance,"[65] the slaves could mask their feelings, perpetuate the stereotypes that the Massa had of them, and give the whites, and the later chroniclers of slavery, the impression that they had indeed submitted to their place within the society. The reality was quite different as such a personality actually enabled them to preserve an inner freedom—what, according to the Jamaican proverb, is "playing the fool to catch wise."[66] According to Michael Craton, "There was no such creature as a genuinely docile slave."[67] Thus, adjustment on the part of the slaves in no form signified acceptance. The Quashee personality gave slaves the psychological satisfaction of duping and poking fun at the master and as Patterson points out, "If the slaves strongly resented an overseer or book-keeper and wanted to get rid of him, in the majority of cases they could achieve their objective by simply being the perfect quashee—stupid, bungling, exasperating and completely inefficient."[68]

For many of the slaves in Jamaica, the self-contempt that accompanied "playing the fool" before Massa, resulted in the deconstruction of the mythical

Anancy[69] stories they received from their Ashanti forefathers. This major character in Caribbean folklore is depicted as a spider with a human head who survives the odds stacked against him by using his quick wit, intelligence, and cunning tricks. In the Anancy stories, the slaves saw someone like themselves, that is, someone having to use cunning and scheming to survive and obtain an occasional victory in an unjust situation. Thus for slaves, the appeal of the Anancy stories lie not only in their drama and unpredictability but also in being able to perceive that these stories were not really about animals but about human beings.[70] In this manner, Anancy was able to provide the slaves with

> an object upon which [they could] displaced a great deal of their self-contempt and self-hate. First, by objectifying all the unpleasant features of Quashee, Anancy made it possible for the slave to reprimand and censor the undesirable part of himself [herself] without a sense of self-persecution. Second, having censored this part of himself [herself], the slave could then find it possible to laugh at it and even learn to live with and accept it.[71]

We should note, however, that in both the Quashee personality and the Anancy hero, the slaves subversion of the plantation system was conducted in a fashion which challenged the existing order through words and by masking their true feelings, while doing little to overthrow the system. For, as the Anancy stories reveal, "As soon as the prospect of resistance occurs, the trickster takes to his heels, changes disguise, and may even appear on the side of the order he used to flout,"[72] that is, on the side of Massa. Thus, through subverting the system and other acts of passive resistance, such as running away, committing suicide, feigning illness, injuring themselves, breaking machinery, etc., slaves were able to undermine the very system that depended upon their industriousness for productivity.

Throughout slavery, the act of running away was common.[73] As Michael Craton states in *Testing the Chains*, "Wherever there were slave plantations, there were runaways."[74] Though running away was often viewed as an "effective form of individual resistance to slavery" it did not produce any notable changes in either the overall structures within the slave system or society.[75] As such, running away functioned more as a short-term form of resistance, because once away from the plantations the slave then had to find a way to survive. In this case survival was dependent upon finding undeveloped land, preferably in the mountains, and other runaways with whom they could band together to form a Maroon village. Without these two necessities the slaves would find themselves in a vulnerable position, susceptible to being recaptured or starvation. In the case of Jamaica, the uninhabited mountainous parts of the central and eastern island provided the ideal location for the runaway slaves. Within the smaller islands, however, the lack of available land became a problem, and therefore other measures were adopted. These included migrating to another island or seeking employment in town, as was the case in the British Leeward islands.[76]

The most extreme form of passive resistance, however, was committing suicide. According to Patterson, this form of resistance "was largely restricted to the African group of slaves."[77] For many, their prior experience of freedom made them unable to accept the bondage of slavery, and thus suicide became "their intractable and stubborn refusal to accept their status as slaves."[78] For some slaves, the belief that they would return to Africa upon their death provided additional motivation to commit suicide, and ultimately refusing their slavery status.

Having highlighted some forms of passive resistance in which the slaves engaged, we will now discuss the different types of active resistance in which they participated. Active resistance took three forms; spontaneous rebellion, guerrilla warfare by the Maroons, and planned rebellion. The spontaneous rebellions were mainly restricted to a certain area or to a specific plantation. In this scenario, a particular outcome or decision by the slave master or overseer would stir the slaves to unite and rebel. There would be little strategic planning, and the events that were to take place (what was to be destroyed, who was to be killed, etc.) would be decided as the rebellion occurred. Although the reasons for rebellion varied, in most cases it was conducted "simply out of a desire to escape the terrors of slavery."[79]

From within their isolated communities the Maroons in Jamaica implemented a strategy governed by guerrilla warfare tactics against the plantation system and all the things to which it was linked. One strategy the Maroons employed were to stake out and attack remote plantations that could not offer resistance because they had very few people.

> By night they seized the favourable opportunity that darkness gave them of stealing into the settlements, where they set fire to cane-fields and out-houses, killed all the cattle they could find, and carried the slaves into captivity. By this dastardly method of conducting war, they did infinite mischief to the white without much exposing their own persons to danger.[80]

From the beginning of their occupation of Jamaica, the British have engaged in skirmishes with the Maroons. This culminated in 1725–40, with the British conducting an all-out war against the Maroons. At the end of that time period, the British armies had to concede defeat. The Maroon victory was due to several factors: their skill in guerilla warfare, their posting of scouts who provided adequate warning of the enemies' presence, and their location—the Windward Maroons were in the mountains of northeast Jamaica and the Leeward Maroons were in the cockpits, caves, and ravines of the northwest. These locations could easily be defended, even when their opponents had superior firearms. Patterson quotes the governor as describing the futility of the war in the following manner: "All former attempts against these slaves having being unsuccessful, or to very little purpose . . . the rebels openly appear in Arms and are daily increasing."[81] Although "the whites had spent £100,000 in attempting to suppress the rebellion"[82] between 1730 and 1734, it was all in vain. They could not gain the upper hand in regard to the Maroons. Eventually, the English were forced to seek peace with the Maroons and thus signed a treaty with them in 1739 granting them "ownership of lands . . . and the freedom to sell their provisions in markets in the neighboring towns as long as licences were obtained."[83] Although the signing of the treaty between the Maroons and the British essentially closed the door to freedom that running away presented to the plantation slaves in Jamaica, it also presented them with a visible example of blacks who had fought the system and succeeded. This example spurred many slaves after 1740 to revolt against the plantation system.[84]

Throughout the history of slavery, revolt remained a prominent feature. In the first years of slavery, the leaders of the revolts were primarily Africans. Against this threat whites responded with various measures geared toward keeping the slaves divided and suspicious of each other, and most of all under control.[85] The revolts during this period included the first great slave plot in 1675 in Barbados, the Greencastle revolt in Antigua in 1701, and Jamaica's Tacky revolt in 1760. In the years that followed, revolt remained a regular part of the slavery terrain but with one notable shift, the leaders were now predominantly Creole instead of African.

Following the highly successful Haitian rebellion that inaugurated Haiti's independence and the abolition of transatlantic slave trade in 1807, slave revolts within the West Indies experienced a dramatic increase. The slaves were convinced by conversations they overheard and by the rumors that had spread that the king had already granted them their freedom and that it was the Massa and overseers who were withholding their liberty.[86] Thus, the slaves, "moved by a passion for freedom and justice, . . . [and] relying on their own skills, their own courage, their own will, their own capacity for leadership and organization, waged war against the English . . . [to secure] recognition of their freedom and independence."[87] The rebellions during this period were larger than their predecessors in scope, and were meant to incorporate as many slaves as possible. One unexpected feature of some of the rebellions during this period was the prominent role played by Christianity. The shift from Christianity being used to support slavery to its role in rebellions and the empowerment of slaves will be discussed in the religious tapestry section of this chapter. Evidence of this shift was seen in the largest and most widespread rebellion in West Indian history, the Baptist war in Jamaica from 1831 to 1832. Sam Sharpe, the leader of this rebellion and a leader in the Native Baptist churches, declared prior to being hanged: "All I wished was to enjoy that liberty which I find in the Bible is the birthright of every man."[88] Lasting less than two weeks, the rebellion involved about "60,000 slaves in an area of 750 square miles and result[ed] in the death of 540 slaves (and 14 whites)."[89] According to Philip Sherlock and Hazel Bennett, "Although only fourteen white lives were lost the damage to property was very great—£1,132,440 12s.6d worth being destroyed and over £161,570 0s. 0d spent on suppressing the revolt."[90] It was this rebellion that combined with various abolition efforts to cast the final blow that toppled the slavery institution and brought about emancipation of the slaves in 1834.

With the emancipation of the slaves came the dismantling of the plantation system in its present form. However, it left intact the colonization enterprise that had also been implemented throughout the region. It was this that was to be Britain's most lasting contribution to the formulation of the West Indian ethnic portion of the tapestry. Built upon a similar foundation as the plantation system, colonization was able to reinvent itself and continue its dominance within the West Indian society following emancipation. During slavery, colonization was geared toward keeping the slaves in their position of subjugation. With their freedom, this framework had to be adjusted to, on the one hand, acknowledging the emancipation of the slaves while, on the other hand, maintaining a system that enabled the economy and the overall societal structures to continue. One of the major hallmarks of this structure was the racial discourses which articulated the superiority of whites over and against all other races. Within the colonial framework this belief was manifested in the orientation of the colonies toward Britain. Thus, Britain became the standard against which all were measured, and the repository of civilization, culture, education, history etc. In the West Indian context, these dynamics were mimicked in particular ways—specifically in regard to class and color. Since whites were perceived to be the standard, the more "white" you were, the more "civilized" you were, and the higher the class that you held within the society. The result was a stratified society in which the small white elite

was at the top, the colored in the middle, and the blacks at the bottom. For some of the emancipated slaves, this reality was worse than during slavery. For "the landed class, the ruling class, the social elite, the white minority were very much the same people."[91] Thus, it did not matter if the slaves continued to work on the plantations or lived in the free communities that they formed; the white minority was still in control. It was they who dictated the social, educational, economic, judicial, and religious framework in which all the lower classes lived. In such a system, however, all was not lost for the person whose genes had determined that they would have dark skin and thus relegated to the bottom of society. One could improve his or her lot and ascend to the middle class by internalizing the British colonial mind-set,[92] and expressing the "civilized" way of life in one's manner, speech, and conduct. Thus the colonial ideology was modified to assert that the more British and thus "white" you were in matters of conduct and beliefs, the more civilized you were deemed to be regardless of color.

The final strand contributed by the Africans to the ethnic portion of the tapestry was the Creole dialect and various forms of music and dance. From the beginning of Britain's control of the islands, English was designated as the official language; however, this "official" language was regularly displaced among the populace by the native Creole language. Creole is a dialect that combines various African and European syntax, lexicon, and words and in its creation and perpetuation reflects the amalgamation and vibrancy of the culture itself. The fusion process also occurred in the areas of music and dance—in the forms, rhythm, lyrics, and dances of the region (Calypso, Reggae, Soca, quadrille, mento, calinda, etc.)—where one can discern the African drumbeat and various European cultural influences.

The religious portion of the tapestry

In the previous section we have seen how various ideologies, sugar cultivation, and the association of African with slavery contributed by the Spanish, combined with the plantation system, and colonization under the British to produce a system of subjugation and development that forever changed the face of the islands. Central in this change was the Africans, who, in their enslavement, adjustment, and rebellion, also played a significant role in the formulation of the ethnic identities that the people of the islands would exhibit. Having discussed the ethnic portion of the tapestry we will now turn our attention to the religious portion of the tapestry.

The religious portion of the tapestry was a complex synthesis of fibers representing an African religious heritage and Protestant Christianity, as exemplified by the Church of England, the nonconformist denominations (Moravian, Methodist, and Baptist), and twentieth-century Pentecostal mission activities. Each of these belief systems, which are within themselves diverse, provided the messages, interpretations, and practices that became instrumental in the religious lives of West Indians. In their interaction, the fibers allowed the emergence of specific and sometimes contradictory realities—namely the reinforcement of the status quo, the growth of Afro-Caribbean and African religions, and engagement in sociopolitical activities.

From their introduction in the West Indies, many of the fibers contributed by the Church of England were focused on preserving the status quo. For much of the duration of slavery, the established church was dependent on the white elite and thus served their needs.[93] In the absence of residing bishops who could have provided spiritual leadership, the Church was greatly influenced by the plantocracy. While the governor of the colonies appointed the clergy, on the local level it was the vestry, comprised of plantation owners and merchants, who decided on ecclesiastical and civil matters. This governing body was also responsible by law to make provisions for the maintenance of the church—providing a church building, a salary, and accommodation for the minister.[94] Within such a context, the Church of England in general, and the clergy and masters in particular, made no attempt to Christianize the slaves and in the event that some efforts were made they were actively resisted.[95] Beginning in 1712 one such effort was conducted by the Society for the Propagation of the Gospel in Foreign Parts (SPG), a missionary organization of the Church of England, in Barbados on the Codrington estate, a sugar plantation owned and ran by the Society. On its plantation and within the organization itself, "the prevailing thought . . . for decades was that slavery, Christianity, and profits could co-exist." For many of its supporters and the society, this coexistence made Codrington the perfect estate to demonstrate this to other planters.[96]

Rationalization for overlooking the physical and spiritual welfare of the slaves, and barring them from baptism came from the idea that "the laws of England by which the colonies were governed forbade the enslavement of a Christian."[97] Thus to Christianize a slave was to grant the slave his or her freedom, and such action was in direct opposition to the plantation way of life. This notion was further supported by the argument that religion was essentially "an exercise of the intellect, [an activity,] which they regarded Black people to be incapable of exercising."[98] At the heart of these objections pertaining to the Christianization of the slaves, was the reality that to the churchmen, slave owners, and legislators, the slaves were essentially property, and the rights governing property needed to be safe guarded. To quell these apprehensions, Henry Compton, the bishop of London, issued a "memorandum concerning the church" in 1680, which reassured the planters that slaves, even Christian slaves, remained their property. Greater assurance came with the passing of several laws including the Jamaica Act for the Better Ordering of Slaves in 1696, which specified "that the status of slaves was unchanged by baptism."[99] The slave code which also stipulated that "all masters and mistresses who owned and employed slaves were to endeavor as much as possible to instruct their slaves in the principles of the Christian religion, to facilitate their conversion and to do their utmost to fit them for baptism," was met within the Jamaican Assembly with various administrative measures geared toward limiting its implementation.[100] Such measures were later formulized in the decision to set the fee required to baptize each slave, at an exorbitantly high price, which by the end of the eighteenth century, was over £3.[101] As a result of these prohibitive measures, the slaves were left on their own in regard to their religious beliefs and practices and to fill this gap they drew upon their African religious heritage.

With the advent of the Moravian's work within the British colonies in 1754, and that of the Methodist and Baptists in the ensuring years, other fibers were added to the religious tapestry.[102] Evangelical in their beliefs, missionaries within these denominations "saw the Christian life as a simple, practical expression of the biblical ideals of purity of life, personal saintliness, and deeds of mercy to the needy."[103] These fibers had specific expressions. One, their focus was the very people whom the established church had ignored. Two, within their interactions they sought to distinguish themselves from the local ruling class. Third, they took the time to learn "the distinctive rhythms and pronunciation of Jamaican creole and acquired a stock of idioms to convey their ideas."[104] Fourth, their presentation of the gospel was one aimed at "saving" the African soul without disrupting the social order.[105] They sought to achieve these expressions by teaching the slaves to be obedient, dutiful, and diligent in their service to their masters. Biblical justification for this teaching was taken from scriptures like 1 Corinthians 7:14, Colossians 4:22-24, and Philemon 1, which they interpreted as admonishing the slaves to remain in the "specified position" in which God had placed them. By behaving in such a manner the slave would eventually be rewarded by God in the afterlife for their diligent service.

The implementation of these fibers, especially the missionary's focus on the slaves and distinguishing themselves from the local ruling class, resulted in many slaves, and free colored and blacks becoming Christians. The most successful missionary group in terms of the number of conversions, however, was the Baptists. The origins of the Baptist denomination in Jamaica, the Bahamas, and later Trinidad lay in George Liele, an ordained minister and former slave from America who had been given his freedom because of his religious work. Beginning in 1784, he started a congregation in Kingston, where he preached to the poor and marginalized within the society, especially the slaves. In the years that followed, he "baptized four hundred people;" promoted a school which offered free education to children—free and slave; recruited Thomas Swigle, who served as a church deacon and the school's headmaster; purchased land and began the construction of a chapel; and enrolled "nigh three hundred and fifty members." As a result of the work of Liele and the other leaders, there developed within the Baptist denomination a "tradition of great freedom of evangelizing and of personal initiative by individual preachers, mostly uneducated, to collect their own flock." This tradition gained additional support from the denomination's principles of congregational independence.[106] In Liele and the other church leaders, the slaves encountered Africans in significant leadership roles. This development received further validation in the other nonconformist denominations, where, although slaves, free blacks, and colored people were not admitted into full membership, they "played a vital part in mission work; they were lay preachers, deacons, and advisers to the missionary."[107] As Shirley Gordon confirms, "In short the sustained work of the conversion of the mass of the population was affected by the efforts of free coloured and slave leaders."[108] The engagement of the free colored and slave leaders in the bulk of the "conversion" work among the slaves did not serve to marginalize the white missionaries, instead it pointed to the lack of sufficient leadership, a reality that remained pervasive throughout different spheres of the society.

As preachers, deacons, helpers, and members, black men and women, both slave and free, gained a level of authority and influence that undermined the structure of the plantation and the society.[109] In these roles the slaves gained a new status as God's instrument (one who declared his word), a model of a Christian for their fellow blacks, and through their membership tickets, co-ownership of mission churches and a place within a wider religious community. Within these denominations, however, the definition of a Christian had a strong emphasis on the outward manifestation of the effect of the conversion experience within the life of an individual, that is, the individual's behavior.[110] When this new status and authority was coupled with the slaves' functions as "free peasants," especially within the Jamaican context—the result was life changing.

The term "free peasant" refers to the provision-ground system where slaves were allocated a portion of land on which to cultivate their food (potatoes, plantains, yams, and other produce). According to Patterson, beginning in "the 1720's [a peasant] system had developed to the stage where the majority of slaves could provide for themselves and many of the more industrious had already began to sell their excess produce at the Sunday markets."[111] As a result of this commerce, some slaves were able to purchase and rear poultry, cattle, and small stock. As such, they became the sole producer of vegetables and cash crop for the free people by the middle of the eighteenth century. Thus the "slaves' functions as free peasants promoted the survival and development of precisely those intellectual capacities which the slave system was intended to destroy: curiosity about the world and determination to exert control over life."[112]

The full impact of the slaves' new status as a result of the mission churches and their function as free peasants combined to produce a unique development.

> To their established right to leave the plantation and trade at the Sunday market was added the opportunity to attend the mission churches; to their ability to earn money and buy goods was added the opportunity to contribute to their church and achieve status within it. The missionaries, moreover, addressed themselves to the slaves as people with souls to be saved, capable of intellectual and moral judgments, and the activities they encouraged were presented in a philosophical framework that posited the spiritual equality of all men. The slaves' rights as producers and traders encouraged them to develop a sense of their rights as laborers on the estates.[113]

For the slaves especially, the gospel "offered [them] a new, coherent worldview in which all men, whites as well as Blacks, were in the hands of a universally powerful God who called them, equally, to judgment."[114] Although the missionaries preached a salvation that addressed the slaves' spiritual bondage while encouraging them to submit to their physical bondage, the gospel that they heard was decoded, reinterpreted within the interpretive framework of their African religious heritage in such a manner that endued them with hope.[115] For many slaves, the decoding and reinterpretation of the gospel were accomplished through their fellow slaves who served as preachers, church leaders, and deacons. Thus, like their brothers and sisters in America, their encounter with slavery, racial discourses, and other forces that sought to keep them in perpetual bondage, was now mitigated by the presence of a God "who saw and listened to their sufferings, one who might reach out any minute to release them. This God had their interests at heart when it seemed no one else did."[116] Albert Raboteau confirms this in *A Fire in the Bones,* he states:

> In the conversion experience slaves realized—and realized it in the heart not just the head—that they were of infinite value as children of God, chosen from all eternity to be saved. Within a system bent on reducing them to a status of utter inferiority, the experience on conversion rooted deep within the slave convert's psyche a sense of personal value and individual importance that helped to ground their identity in the unimpeachable authority of almighty God.[117]

It is from this position of personal value, grounded in divine authority, that the slaves then engaged with the society in their efforts to gain their freedom. According to Michael Craton, "The phenomenally rapid Christianization of British West Indian slaves after 1783 clearly had a vital effect on the general slave consciousness and an important bearing on slave resistance."[118] We should note that in the years leading up to emancipation the majority of the rebellions were led by church leaders.[119] In this manner, Gordon is correct in her conclusion that "the Christian teaching of the worth of every human being had found its way into a culture of protest."[120] So while the missionaries intended the gospel to make the slaves more docile and accepting of their servitude the opposite was also the case, for the gospel initiated them into a culture of protest and the fight for their freedom.

Following emancipation both the nonconformist churches and the established church gained significant importance among the blacks and the planters. "They [the churches] were regarded as an important key to understanding the experiment in freedom. . . . The churches regarded it as their duty to create one society out of the various antagonistic social classes. The Anglican Church, which was favoured by the establishment, saw their task as a slow process of civilizing black people."[121] A major component of the slow process of "civilizing" the blacks was education. Administered in the form of the Negro Education Grant, which began in 1835 and ended in 1845, this grant was focused on providing compulsory primary education, some form of secondary education, and teacher training. In all three areas, however, the education provided was mediocre and geared toward preserving the status quo. The religious and vocational curriculum implemented in the primary education was oriented around teaching blacks to be hardworking, law-abiding, and God-fearing people who would be willing to work in the agriculture and carpentry sectors.

Coupled with this was a secondary school system structured around maintaining the current social system, in that only those with the financial resources could send their children to the secondary school. Blacks and colored people were in some cases able to secure admission, but it was normally in the intermediate secondary school, where they were trained to fill lower-level white-collar jobs—teacher, policeman, postmaster, catechist, etc. The grammar schools, where students were prepared to fill the high-level white-collar professional jobs within the society and gain admission into tertiary institutions in Britain, were still reserved exclusively for the children of the white population. Although some black and colored students were later admitted to the grammar schools by gaining scholarships to these institutions, the education they received still legitimized "the highly unequal social and economic structures within the society by convincing the masses to accept their subordinate role and thereby modifying their occupational and social aspirations."[122] In this manner, an ideology was implemented that led many among the masses to believe that their children could attain these high-level positions if they worked hard enough educationally, while simultaneously bolstering the overall system that perpetuated their subjugation.

Thus, we can conclude that underlying this "civilizing" process conducted by the churches was their deference to the status quo, in that they upheld the spiritual equality of black people to white people while maintaining the cultural superiority of the white race. For the ruling white elite, "the right kind of education would produce the right kind of society. Education [thus] became the guarantee that the society would not change, that Black people would remain at the bottom of the social ladder."[123] Upon realizing that the education that they were receiving was meant to produce a black person reconciled to the plantation system, some blacks refused to be involved in this venture. For them accepting such a position was to return the bondage from which they had just been freed.

Another area in which the churches, specifically the nonconformist denominations, sought to aid in the creation of a new society was through assisting the blacks to gain ownership of land and form free towns. This was accomplished by buying a large piece of land that were then subdivided into smaller plots and sold to denominational members. It should be noted, that even in this arena, the preservation of the social structure was also at work. For these villages were created in close proximity to the sugar plantations, with the expectation that the former slaves would continue to provide the labor required by the plantation owners.[124] Overall, this land ownership venture was a success and the blacks rewarded these denominations with their membership. However, as the church leaders in Jamaica came to realize, increasing numbers did not mean singular spiritual allegiance to Christianity.[125] According to Noel

Erskine in *Decolonizing Theology*, "Had [the church leaders] looked closely at what was happening in the Baptist churches in Jamaica, they would have noted that Black people had not relinquished Black religion, but were in fact allowing the practice of Christianity to coexist with African beliefs."[126] These African beliefs were expressed in various African-oriented religions, some of which were an amalgamation of African religions and Protestantism. These included Kumina and Revivalism in Jamaica; Winti in Surinam; Shango in Trinidad and Grenada, and Kele in St. Lucia. However, others re-created an African religious worldview—for example, Obeah—or became involved in an indigenous response to the issues within the society—for example, Rastafarianism.

Although the churches made great efforts to meet the spiritual and physical needs of blacks in terms of landownership, they failed to take the needs of the blacks for religious, cultural, and social equality seriously. As Frey and Wood confirms, "After 1838 the newly freed people of the British sugar islands found themselves free in name only; everywhere they were forced to contend with the enormous economic, political, legal, and social power retained by an unyielding plantocracy."[127] In this context, many blacks found the submissive and protective of the status quo characteristics within the Christian identities offered to them by the churches as not a viable option—it was too reminiscent of slavery. Frustrated, many turned to the African-oriented religious groups. Some of these groups took the Christian message presented by the missionaries and reinterpreted it within an African framework in a manner that addressed both realities, that is, their spiritual and physical (cultural/social) needs.[128]

The result was the emergence of an Afro-Christian perspective, the construction of identities derived from the black experience, and a recovery of a self-understanding among the black population. With these developments came the resurgence of some African-influenced cultural practices like drumming and dancing within religious worship; the rejection of Victorian views on marriage and sexual attitudes; and the reinterpretation of Christmas and Sabbath breaking. Throughout the rest of the nineteenth century, many white church leaders came to perceive these practices and Afro-Christianity itself, as further confirmation of the black people's moral and cultural inferiority. As a result, they renewed their efforts to fulfill the church's duty to "efface these flaws from the Black family character."[129] The end product was a divided society. On the one hand, the blacks and coloreds who had received substantial missionary instruction remained in the nonconformist and Anglican churches and embodied the ideals of Europe. For them, the concept of "blackness" was to be held in contempt. In contrast, for the other members of the black population, including the adherents of Afro-Christianity, their "blackness" was accepted and enthusiastically celebrated.[130]

It was into this divided society that the Pentecostal missionaries arrived in the first decade of the 1900s.[131] What fibers did they contribute to the religious tapestry? The Pentecostal contribution was its ability to provide an intermediate space for legitimate worship between Anglican and nonconformists churches on one hand and the Afro-Christian groups on the other. Thus, it presented the indigenous black population with another viable option of Christianity. Pentecostalism was able to "accommodate many of their customs—drumming, dancing, singing, possession (getting in the spirit), and glossolalia (speaking in tongues),"[132] while also stressing the outward manifestation of holiness as evidence that one had experienced Christian conversion—the "saint" identity, which the mission church expected of its members. The holiness that Pentecostalism presented was one of "careful self-examination, godly discipline, and methodical devotion and avoidance of worldly pleasures, [so that the believer] could live a life of victory over sin."[133] By incorporating these aspects, Pentecostalism gave the black population another articulation of black religious identity—one that linked blackness with acceptance, and empowerment as a vessel that God could use; separation from an evil world; and spiritual victory in the life to come.

In achieving this, however, Pentecostalism, like other forms of Christianity, did not seek to change the societal structures which governed the lives of its members. For underlying the message of empowerment and transformation that Pentecostalism provided for the marginalized and many lower-class women within the society was still the call to be law-abiding, hardworking, God-fearing workers.[134] Thus, although attention was given to converting many lower-class women from their sweetheart and common-law lifestyles and to assisting the poor and marginalized to live "holy" lives, very little attention was geared toward changing the structures within society that had created their marginalization. Finally, Pentecostalism, with its denominational affiliation with the United States, also represented a shift in the islands' orientation from Europe to America.

Conclusion

The West Indian ethnic and religious identities formulated as a result of the years of slavery, colonization, and Christianization were ones of cultural and religious dynamism, marked by survival and adaptation in the midst of adversity, as well as strength and empowerment. For these islands and their people, the complexities arising from the interaction of their various cultural and religious heritages are ones to be celebrated and embraced. For these are the strands that have produced the ethnic and religious portions of the tapestry that play such a pivotal role in their lives. As a result of the interaction between the Africans, Spanish, and British in particular, West Indians have come to identify themselves ethnically as a people who have a knack for surviving and overcoming. Through the Quashee and rebel identities, the slaves were able to survive and overcome the brutalities of slavery. However, by embodying an orientation toward Europe, the white elite was able to reaffirm their identities as members of what was perceived to be the superior race and thereby retain a place of prominence and privilege within the West Indian society.

In the religious arena the interaction between African religions and Christianity led to complex religious belief systems and identities. On the one hand were those belief systems that adhered to Christian "orthodoxy" and which advocated religious identities that simultaneously sought to maintain the status quo as well as to change the society; on the other were the African-oriented religions, which by their very presence served to undermine the societal structures within which their adherents were marginalized. Between these two systems were those individuals for whom religious belief was an amalgamation of both systems—thus enabling them to identify with and benefit from both. It is in this manner that the West Indian people continue to be—both in their ethnicity and religious beliefs—symbolically a portion of a tapestry, characterized by sections of synergy and dissonance, and the incorporation of old predetermined patterns and new ones.

Having being shaped in these particular ways—in their ethnic and religious identities—those who would later migrate to the United States and London, were armed with certain tools that enabled them to creative interact with the contexts they would encounter. In examining this interaction, it is necessary to begin our investigation with their actual movement, that is, migration. What was their experience of migration? What were the local, regional, and global factors associated with their movement across national borders? These questions along with the nature of their continued connection with their lands of origin form the basis of the next chapter.

Island Dreams and Disapora Realities: Migration, Transnationalism, and the Formation of Immigrant Pentecostal Churches

How calm and peaceful everything seems to be this morning. Everything seems to tell us it is the Lord's Day; . . . I watched the children in their nice clean clothes going to Sunday school and all smiling and happy. And I saw old Unc' Tom in his nice black frock-coat, and his clean white cravat, and his Bible under his arm, looking calm and pious.

Roscow Shedden, *Ups and Downs in a West Indian Diocese*
(London: A.R. Mowbray & Co. Ltd., 1927), 116–17.

Growing up I knew that I had separate clothes: you have your church clothes; you had your house clothes; you had your school clothes; and you wore the very best to come to church and I feel that, that is a pressure on people coming through the doors. If we were flexible in our appearance i.e. if a person wants to come in their jeans, and a t-shirt and trainers on a Sunday they can worship just as well as somebody who has got on a hat, that long frock and high heel shoes or even better sometimes.

Janice McLean, "Appropriating Faith within the City: An Examination of Urban Youth Ministry in Immigrant Churches," in *Reaching the City: Reflections on Urban Mission for the Twenty-first Century*,
eds. Gary Fujino, Timothy R. Sisk, and Tereso C. Casiño
(Pasadena: William Carey Library, 2012), 229.

In the two excerpts documented above, we locate similar descriptions of an aspect of West Indian religious life that according to Margaret Bailey represents "an important part of Jamaican life"[1]—the practice of going to church. In both descriptions we are told that engagement in this practice is linked to the wearing of one's "best" clothing. This aesthetic requirement marks this activity as significant, set apart from those engaged in during the rest of the week for which other clothes are worn.[2] Incorporated into this aesthetic requirement is an ethos of sanctification, that is, moral purity. This is reinforced in various behavior commitments geared toward the avoidance of any provocative types of clothing. The act of going to church may also demonstrate in a public manner that an individual is a Christian, and as such communicate on certain levels some of the beliefs this individual would adhere to.[3] In comparing the two excerpts, however, we also note two significant differences: that of location—the picturesque West Indian islands versus a metropolitan city; and the manner in which this activity may be undergoing changes in the diaspora context. This acknowledgment of difference, however, calls us to interrogate not only what is occurring during this particular practice but also what is being communicated through its perpetuation.

Thus this West Indian practice of going to church serves several purposes within this chapter. One, it links this chapter to the ones preceding and following it. The previous chapter highlights the formation of West Indian religious identities, within which this practice plays a pivotal role.[4] The chapters that follow provide a glimpse into some of the ideas and meanings that are being constructed and communicated through this practice. Two, the performance of this West Indian ritual within the diaspora calls us to further scrutinize several interrelated issues, specifically that of migration, transnationalism, and the formation of the religious communities within which this practice is being perpetuated. What were some of the reasons for migration becoming an attractive option for West Indians? What are some of the transnational ties that migrants are forming between their countries of origin and residence? What were some of the prominent factors within the new context which resulted in the formation of these religious communities? Examining the issues arising from these questions is essential because within much of the academic discourses on migration and the diaspora, the migrants have been presented as passive participants who were "forced" to migrate or to congregate within "safe" spaces. This unidimensionality is seen in the prominence of the push-pull theory of migration in explaining West Indian migration to both the United States and Britain. In regard to the formation of the religious communities, this passivity is expressed in the belief that racism was the primary reason for the growth of such churches in Britain, while in the United States, these communities are formed solely because the immigrants do not want to be identified with African Americans. Although these reasons are valid and do play a role in both migration and the formation of these religious communities they are not the only factors.[5] In contrast to the unidimensional approach, which emphasizes passivity or reactionism on the part of the migrant, I take into consideration the significant roles that history, global developments, racism, social contexts, and the migrants themselves play in migration, transnationalism, and the formation of religious communities, issues that this chapter will examine.

This chapter is divided into two sections and focuses on the migration section of the tapestry. The first section—Island Dreams—will examine some of the factors that have influenced West Indian migration in general, as well as the distinctive migration patterns to New York City and London. The second—Diaspora Realities—will investigate some of the complexities that the migrants encountered upon their arrival and during their settlement within these two metropolitan cities. In conducting this analysis, particular attention will be given to the ways in which the contexts facilitated the emergence and the continuation of the immigrant faith communities, as well as the creation of various transnational ties between the diaspora and home contexts.

Island dreams

To an overwhelming degree, the majority of studies conducted on Caribbean and West Indian migration have used an economic approach to explain why migration takes place.[6] These studies, which are normally conducted within the functionalist and historical-structural framework, perceive Caribbean international migration to be a classic example of the equilibrium theory, in which "human migration [is] conceptualized as an economic resource responding to the gradient of labor supply and demand within a macro-economic framework."[7] Thus, according to the functionalist interpretation, migration is a unidimensional process taking place according to the push-pull model. This model, which focuses on the socioeconomic conditions in both the sending and the receiving countries, pays considerable attention to the underdevelopment, overpopulation, and the social ills that plague the sending countries. This dismal picture is in turn contrasted with the abundance of opportunities to better oneself that are located within the receiving nation.[8] Thomas-Hope, in *Explanation in Caribbean Migration*, argues that within this interpretation, the individual's decision to migrate is perceived from the perspective of the "cost and benefits of moving from points of negative to positive attraction under forces articulated as 'pushes and pulls'."[9]

Within the historical-structural interpretation, a center-periphery model is applied to the global division of labor. Thus, the movement of the migrant is seen as part of an exchange and a transfer of value, in which labor, the migrant's only commodity, allows the global system to be equalized. This approach, like the functionalist approach, treats migration as a unidimensional process. This unidimensional focus is, however, problematic. First, the functionalist approach, which overemphasizes the push-pull model, does not give adequate consideration to the roles that various local and global developments play in cultivating and perpetuating these negative and positive factors in both the sending and receiving countries. This interpretation also does not give sufficient attention to the role that the perpetuation of a certain "image" plays in both the individual and familial decision to migrate. Image is used here to denote the process whereby a particular physical location become synonymous with certain physical, economic, and social qualities in the minds and perception of people. For in reality the immigrant is not a passive agent in this process—only reacting to outside forces; instead as the immigrant interacts with these external factors from the perspective of their individual or familial histories and contexts, he or she produces an image which may facilitate migration. This image, formulated from both a real and imagined world, is passed down from generation to generation. As a result, the real or perceived benefits and legacy of migration among West Indians are perpetuated and enforced. Second, the historical-structural intrepretation does not provide a viable explanation for the periods when migration exceeds the demands for labor, continues despite the lack of labor opportunities, or why similarly developed countries have different emigration rates.[10] This interpretation also does not address the other dynamics that play a part in the transfer or exchange of value that revolves around labor, for within the migratory process, there are some migrants who see the process as a means of not only selling labor but also acquiring capital.[11] This is most visible in the practice of sending remittances to those back home. For many seasonal workers the money earned provided the resources needed to build homes, start businesses, or assist family members—especially funding their children's education.

In this section I will argue that although the economic approach does explain some aspects of West Indian migration, its present focus is myopic in scope. For in reality, West Indian migration is not a one-sided process but involves an intricate confluence of several factors.[12] These include: the local or global factors that have created and continue to perpetuate the perceived "safety-valve" feature within West Indian islands; the manner in which immigration laws and acts within the United States and Britain continue to shape and influence migration from the West Indies; and the role that "image" plays in the decision of an individual and his or her family to migrate.

Local and international factors influencing West Indian migration

According to Anthony Payne and Paul Sutton, the Caribbean and, in particular, the islands of the West Indies are unique in that they are located within a matrix of relationships involving

> two of the great North-South systems of the twentieth century—the American hemispheric system with the US as metropolis and Latin America and the Caribbean as periphery, and the European imperial system with Britain, France and the Netherlands, and now the European Union (EU), as the metropolis and Africa, the Caribbean and the Pacific as the periphery.[13]

As a result, the islands are linked to the United States in terms of geography, language, and, in many respects, culture. Simultaneously, these islands also maintain an intricate historical and sentimental link to Europe.[14] The influence exerted by such linkages should not be underestimated in the migration discourse.[15] Therefore, in examining the historical, socioeconomic, and political factors that contribute to West Indian migration, attention will be given to the manner in which these two links influence the regional context. Although other nations or nation blocs, such as the Soviet Union, China, and even India, have had some impact upon these islands, their influence has been marginal compared to the United States and Europe, specifically, Britain.

For most of their history until the 1960s, many West Indian islands were British colonies. As such, the political and socioeconomic structures of the islands were shaped by the British model and implemented in a manner that would most benefit the Mother Country.[16] From the beginning, the economy operated within a closed system, one in which the islands along with the American colonies provided Britain with the tropical products that she required, and the necessary outlets for her export goods.[17] Thus, the capitalist system implemented was one that favored a mono-agricultural system. According to Selwyn Carrington, "Despite the general desire among West Indian planters to diversify their agricultural system, the British West Indian economy remained one based mainly on the production of sugar and rum. Given the demand for sugar in the American, British, and European markets, the planters were forced not only to continue but to increase production."[18]

Built within this system, however, was an unhealthy dependence upon beneficent and favorable external markets for both economic growth and progress. Evidence of this was seen in the islands' reliance upon the American colonies and Britain for their supply of food and lumber,[19] upon the British Empire markets, who were the exclusive buyers of their products, and upon the British policymakers, who determined the economic procedures that governed their economies.[20] In this vulnerable position, the islands and their economies were very susceptible to any changes that might occur in these relationships. Thus, during America's fight for independence in 1775, the islands were cut off from an economy with which theirs was intricately linked. This rupture produced widespread changes in the manner in which business was conducted in the islands. It inhibited their unrestricted access to cheap food items and lumber, and ended their usual practice of paying for those goods with tropical products. As a result, other suppliers within the Empire had to be found—albeit at a more costly price. The net result was the implementation of a system that eventually decreased the profitability of the plantation system and the overall economic well-being in the islands.[21]

In the years following the abolition of the slave trade in 1807 and slavery itself in 1834, this dependence on external markets left the islands at a disadvantage in their fight against those factors that undercut the profitability of sugar. These factors took the forms of reorientation within the consumer market, competitors, loss of "free" labor, and the eventual loss of the islands' monopoly on sugar. In the fight for the abolition of slavery, campaigns were mounted to encourage British consumers to consume sugar manufactured in East India.[22] This created a reorientation in the minds of customers toward other markets. Thus, when Cuba, Brazil, and the United States entered into the world sugar market, a potential market was already fostered among European customers. These competitors were a serious threat for three reasons: one, as slave owning nations, they had the necessary "free" labor needed to maintain profitability; two, there was greater investment into modernization techniques that increased their sugar production and made the process more efficient; and three, the land used for sugar production was not as overworked. With the end of the slave trade and slavery, the plantations no longer had a source of "free" labor. In the islands where the former slaves could choose not to work on the plantations, they became a surplus labor force. It was this group that eventually sought out other avenues of employment, first through regional and later through international migration.[23] Although indentured workers were brought in by the colonial government from India and China to work on the plantations, the damage was already done—the West Indian planters had begun to lose their monopoly on the world sugar production. For these planters, the decisive signal of their loss of monopoly came in the passage of the Sugar Duties Act by the British government in 1846. Essentially this act "provided for a reduction in the tariff on sugar until the tariff on sugar from all sources was equalized by 1854."[24]

Beginning in the 1880s the West Indian sugar industry experienced further setbacks fueled by the advent and the popularity of beet sugar within the global market. During this critical period the industry was dealt two additional blows by serious outbreaks of cane disease (the borer and blast stains) and several natural disasters—mainly hurricanes. The above factors, combined with the depression in world sugar prices, largely due to the increase and variability within the worldwide sugar production, profoundly impacted the West Indian economy. In the islands where sugar still maintained its economic dominance, the consequences were calamitous. First, it resulted in many sugar estates undergoing foreclosure due to nonpayment of the quitrent. Second, it produced economic hardships within the other industries that were associated with the sugar industry, such as peasant farming. Since the majority of their crops were sold to the plantation workers, the decline in sugar industry had an ensuing decrease in the peasant farmer's economic viability. Third, having emerged from slavery, some of the islands were experiencing increases in their population, namely due to falling death rates and rising birth rates. For years to come the region would be marked by population growth, high unemployment, underemployment, and limited resources for advancement. For blacks, life was a struggle to improve their condition, that is, to develop "a social conscience concerning their own affairs."[25] This took the form of offering alternative solutions, and conducting various protests and riots about prevailing conditions. In the 1930s the riots were so widespread that the British government could no longer deny the realities existing in the region.[26]

Having discussed the economic conditions associated with the sugar industry we will now examine some of the other regional and international factors that also encouraged West Indians to migrate. In 1834, as many emancipated slaves were leaving the plantations throughout the region, planters in Trinidad and Guyana were implementing programs to recruit these workers. The benefits being offered were: wages that were twice those of their home islands, and in the case of Trinidad—free passage and land for cultivation. These programs resulted in a large movement of seasonal workers mainly from the Eastern Caribbean. Workers from the northern Caribbean were numerically absent from this venture due to the travel distance that was involved. This regional movement highlights two significant developments: the plantocracies' need to preserve their labor; and the emancipated slaves exercising the benefits of their freedom by deciding what labor activities were most beneficial.[27]

Starting in the mid-1880s, the region underwent a dramatic shift in its orientation as the United States began to replace Europe as the dominant power in the area. The assertion of dominance by America was most visible when it intervened in Cuba—resulting in the Spanish-American War of 1898. America's victory resulted in the Treaty of Paris. Under its terms, America "secured" Cuba's independence and annexed Puerto Rico. Following Cuba's independence, US military governance was enforced, and this remained until the signing of the Platt Amendment in 1903—this dictated the relationship between America and Cuba thereafter. These two documents—Treaty of Paris and the Platt Amendment—were consistent with the new interpretation given to the Monroe Doctrine by Theodore Roosevelt that essentially allowed the presence of an international policing authority. From a regional perspective, the "Caribbean itself was to become America's closed sea, . . . [where] as assistant Secretary of State Loomis stated in 1904: 'no picture of the future is complete which does not contemplate and comprehend the United States as the dominant power in the Caribbean Sea'."[28] This dominance was further evidenced in the "huge foreign investment . . . in infrastructural projects such as the canal in Panama and railroads in Central America and Cuba. These investments accelerated the growth of export agriculture in those countries and, in the process, generated a considerable increase in the demand for unskilled workers from the British West Indies."[29]

For many West Indians, the beginning of the twentieth century marked a period of dramatic change in terms of migration. The completion of the Panama Canal in 1914 was followed by the crash in sugar prices in 1921, the implementation of restrictive immigration legislation, and the Great Depression in the United States. As such, several avenues that were previously open were now closed and many "West Indians were being repatriated from places like the United States and Cuba."[30] For many of these migrants who had become accustomed to higher wages and higher standards of living, the situation they encountered upon their return produced marked discontent.[31] While some fortunate West Indians were able to find work in the oil fields in Venezuela and refineries in Curaçao, these opportunities were limited and many workers had no choice but to remain at home. During the Second World War, as the United States experienced a labor shortage due to the deployment of servicemen, West Indian migrant workers were brought in to fill the gap. Simultaneously, many

West Indian men were called into the service of the Mother Country as she defended herself against the advance of Hitler's regime. In the years following the war, as the United States remained closed, many West Indians chose to migrate to Britain, where there were no barriers to entry. For these migrants, the decision to migrate was influenced by several factors, including responding to the appeal to come and help rebuild the Mother Country as well as seeking out opportunities to better themselves.

In the 1960s, as many West Indian islands gained their independence, they were faced with the task of how to advance the changes began after the Second World War, by shifting their economies from the traditional dependence on agriculture, especially the sugar monoculture, to a more diversified economy. Three industries that played a part in this were tourism, bauxite (Jamaica and Guyana), and oil (Trinidad and Tobago). The emergence of these industries formed the main thrust of the new development in the islands but were intially hindered by the lack of capital. Once again this was supplied by foreign corporations, primarily American, and this limited the contribution of these new industries to the overall economic growth of the region, for the profits were not reinvested in the West Indies but sent to the home to be invested there.[32] Also by providing the capital, these corporations dictated what was produced in the bauxite and oil industries, that is, primarily raw or intermediate material. As a result, the islands received minimal benefit for their ore or oil, since the real profitability was in the finished product—aluminum and refined oil. In regard to tourism, as a service-oriented industry it was susceptible to weather conditions as well as internal and external sociopolitical events (instability, travel restrictions, etc.). Despite these issues, these industries created substantial employment within the islands.[33]

The 1960s and 1970s saw the implementation of several programs aimed at developing the local economy—these programs allowed the active participation of the locals in the decisions that affected the economy as well as enabled the exercise of local majority ownership in the multinational companies operating within the islands.[34] In Jamaica some of these economic reforms were conducted under Michael Manley's leadership in the following manner:

> His government instituted price freezes and limited imports, especially on some luxury goods. He renegotiated his government's contracts with the six North American bauxite companies operating in the country, making it possible for Jamaica to receive increased taxes and acquire a majority interest in the country's important Bauxite mines.[35]

Through these reforms, the people of Jamaica were able to educate their children, acquire adequate housing, and receive sufficient compensation for their agricultural produce. During his tenure as prime minister, Manley "joined the campaign led by OPEC [Organization of Petroleum Exporting Countries] nations for a New International Economic Order, fought for an end to the isolation of Cuba, [and] campaigned . . . against South African apartheid."[36] Such actions, however, made Manley a "thorn in the side of Uncle Sam."[37] The consequences were immediate. According to Girvan, "retaliation by the Bauxite companies, a US-sponsored campaign of economic and political destabilization, and excessive public spending brought the economy to the brink of bankruptcy and into the jaws of the International Monetary Fund (IMF)."[38] Michael Manley described this as follows: "A country resorts to the IMF when it is experiencing a foreign exchange crisis. . . . Typically, the remedy begins with currency devaluation, strict control over spending in the government budget and a tight monetary policy aimed at restricting credit and increasing cost of money."[39]

These occurrences were not limited to the Jamaican context but were also experienced within other West Indian islands. The net result was an economic decline and an increase in political violence in several islands, specifically Jamaica, Guyana, and Grenada. Although the West Indian islands, except for Grenada, were never militarily invaded by the United States, American influence was still pervasive in that "their economies [were] restructured by US investment . . . [and the islands] continue to depend upon U.S aid, trade and tourism."[40] Thus the Caribbean, as a whole, became a region in which during the 1980s the "US [had successfully reshaped] the agenda of politics and political economy to the point where it was able to lay down the parameters of what could be done and even what could be articulated."[41] This reshaping was accomplished in two ways: through the implementation of the Caribbean Basin Initiative (CBI); and the adjustment measures imposed on several islands by the International Monetary Fund (IMF), the World Bank, and the US agency for International Development (USAID).[42] In all, these measures helped to create an environment within the Caribbean in which the islands' economic vitality and growth was dependent upon US investment, market opportunities, and tax/tariff regimes. As a result many countries placed their social and political stability in jeopardy as they strove, sometimes desperately, to grow economically within the international market place.

Immigration laws and acts

Due to the prominence of the economic factors in the discourse on West Indian migration, insufficient attention is given to the role that immigration laws and acts play in this process. Such oversight is problematic because it is the laws that determine the level of access that migrants have to diaspora nations. Thus, while economic factors may exist both in the sending and receiving countries that result in migrants having a desire to migrate, they will not be able to do so legally unless they are granted access via immigration laws. Since these policies also dictate which types of migrants have access, they are instrumental in determining the composition of the migrant population in any given country.[43]

The majority of West Indians went to Britain following the implementation of the Nationality Act in 1948. By changing their status from British subjects to British citizens, this act entitled them to the rights and privileges accorded to all citizens of the Commonwealth. Therefore, their entry into Britain was not based on the approval of a visa application but was secured by virtue of being born within the Commonwealth and occurred in the context of the United States imposing more restrictions on their entry.[44] The impact on West Indian migration was significant, a "colonization in reverse."[45]

Britain's openness was to change in 1962 with the approval and implementation of the Commonwealth Immigration Act, which limited the number of Commonwealth citizens entering Britain from Asia, Africa, and the West Indies. The 1962 act also increased the period of residence for Commonwealth citizens (plus British subjects and Irish citizens) applying for registration as citizens of the United Kingdom from one year to five years.[46] This act was followed by the Commonwealth Immigration Act of 1968, which highlighted the distinction made between the Commonwealth citizens who had close ties to the United Kingdom and who were allowed unrestricted entry into the country, and those citizens who had no such ties and were thus subject to immigration control. Further immigration restriction came with the Immigration Act of 1971, which introduced the right to abode concept, which essentially provided an individual with the right to enter the United Kingdom without government permission and to reside and to work in the country without restriction. However, under this act, Commonwealth citizens qualified for the right of abode only if they, their spouse, parents, or grandparents were closely associated with the United Kingdom, the Channel Islands, and the Isle of Man. So although this act allowed for family reunification, it restricted all other access to Britain.[47]

Within US immigration history, the majority of West Indian immigrants comprise a part of the "second wave" of immigration. This new wave of immigration began with the signing into law of the Hart-Cellar Immigration Reform Act in 1965 which removed the national quota system that was established in 1924. This law, which came into effect as Britain was becoming more restrictive, essentially produced a shift in the destination for West Indian migrants from Britain to the United States. Despite this shift, the influx of large numbers of West Indians to the United States did not occur until the beginning of the 1980s. Statistically, Jamaicans formed the majority of the West Indian migrants. According to Joseph Salvo and Ronald Ortiz, "In the 1980's alone, Jamaica sent 213,805 people to the United States—a full 9% of its total population of 2.5 million people."[48] These numbers are also mirrored for Guyana and to a smaller extent for Trinidad and Tobago, Barbados, and the other West Indian islands. According to Holger Henke, in this period "the immigrants from the English-speaking Caribbean consisted increasingly of single women or female-headed households."[49] This was due to two main reasons: one, "the liberation implied in the Hart-Cellar Act allowed women to take advantage of the family preference scheme,"[50] and two, "shifts in the United States labor market proved beneficial for a number of Caribbean women with or even without higher education," as many were able to find jobs as "general domestic helpers, or caregivers for children, the elderly and even pets."[51]

The access granted by the Hart-Cellar Act was supported by the Supreme Court decision in 1982, which ruled that "undocumented immigrant children had a right to go to school."[52] Thus West Indian children, who had entered the United States with their parents as illegal immigrants, were now entitled to an education and a means of advancing themselves. In its drive to tackle the illegal immigration, the United States implemented the Immigration Reform and Control Act (IRCA) in 1986. On the one hand it was argued that this bill would stem the wave of illegal immigrants who were "likely to displace Americans" in the workplace. The opposing view was that this act would result in the "undocumented being exploited until they are . . . deported."[53] The main features of this legislation were "establishing penalties against employers who hire illegal immigrants and legalizing those illegally in the country before 1982 [or 1986, in the case of agricultural workers]."[54] As a result one's legal status became the requirement for work eligibility. By the end of the 1980s America was again experiencing a drastic labor shortage especially in the health and educational fields. Consequently, legislation was introduced in 1988 "aimed at meeting the nation's purported labor needs."[55] For the next two years this legislation was argued within the House of Representatives and Congress and passed in 1990. The Immigration Act of 1990 served to revise "the quota preference system to provide substantially more immigration of skilled workers, more 'slots' to reduce delays for certain groups of immigration-eligible family members, and greater diversity in the countries of origin of the immigrants."[56] One effect was that many skilled laborers in the West Indies and other countries, like nurses and teachers, were recruited for jobs in America.

Perpetuating the image

Historically, the West Indies has maintained a strong migration culture. One extends from the migration pattern of the indigenous peoples, the voluntary migration of European sojourners, buccaneers, and adventurers, and the involuntary migration of thousands of Africans to the present. Within the history of migration, however, each movement occurred in a specific time period, and although related to the past ones, it was also distinct. Having stated this, one cannot dismiss the influence of the past on present migration. For the past migrations and, especially, the individual narratives they generated, served to link family members across generational and national boundaries, while also facilitating the process whereby each subsequent generation is "socialized in a way of life and livelihood conditioned by migration."[57] A crucial characteristic of this socialization is the construction and perpetuation of an image that is associated with a specific place.

This interaction with the past further highlights two factors that are vital within the migration process: the importance of the familial dynamic and the role of family in the creation of an image. The family not only approves of the migration and encourages members to leave, but also enables it. In many cases, they are the source of emotional, financial, childcare, and other types of assistance that make migration possible. As Mary Chamberlain rightly concludes, the decision to migrate is not solely an individual enterprise. It is a family endeavor, one focused on the welfare and the improvement of the family unit.[58] With regard to the formation of the image, it should be noted that the places involved—both the local and destination—gain meaning only in terms of how they are perceived by the individual. This perception is constructed from various fragments of information the individual receives and internalizes about a particular place. With respect to the local environment, the individual's personal experience also plays a crucial role in shaping his or her perception. For the distant place, the individual's perception is constructed from both the information (sometimes irrespective of the degree of accuracy) and the material goods that are received from that place. In many cases, the information, in the form of a narrative history, and the material goods, are supplied by various family members. Other sources of information come from the variety of American multimedia that is disseminated throughout the region as well as the numerous tourists who frequent the islands. For Britain, especially during the 1950s additional sources of information were found in the educational curriculum and various cultural and colonial practices perpetuated in the region.

Hence, the images constructed by individuals, and which influence the decisions that they make, are not formed in a vacuum but in the interaction with the external environment. This external world constitutes a place relative to their point of reference, be it a country, parish, or a district. Based on their evaluation of the local and external environments, coupled with the historical narratives received from others, an image is created which influences how individuals perceive and engage in migration. What are some of the images that are created about Britain and the United States that encourage families to migrate to these places? The two prominent images are the Mother Country and the Promised Land.

The Mother Country

Throughout the British colonies up until the late 1960s, Mother Country was the dominant image for Britain. It connoted the mother-like, nurturing, and caring relationship that Britain was perceived as having toward her colonies. From the imperial perspective, the islands of the West Indies owed their existence and history to Britain. She had "birthed" this region and orchestrated its liberty from slavery. In the West Indies, these beliefs found a place of acceptance, to the extent that "in more senses than one, Britain was the 'Mother Country' and commanded an intellectual, cultural and moral authority."[59] As an immigrant to Britain stated, "So much was taught down our throats about the Mother Country and so forth . . . from the time we were training school from Britannia, raise the flag on Jubilee day and drink your lemonade, you know, we think of England."[60]

Thus the information received from the educational institutions, from the culture exemplified by the white minority in their midst, and from the society at large, portrayed a magnificent mythical image of the Mother Country. It was a place of untold beauty, civilization, Christianity, morality, and culture. Like a loving mother, the Mother Country was perceived with open arms, ready to welcome her children. Thus, for many West Indians, "this imperial myth, [the 'Mother Country' image], had been translated into concepts of sanctuary and salvation, and had been memorised in the mnemotics of food and colour."[61] In both the dissemination of the information and the subsequent construction of the Mother Country image, space was not given to the white population inhabiting any class other than that of the elite. As a result, the reality the migrants encountered upon their arrival was a massive shock. For one respondent the fallacy of this image was revealed during a train ride from the continent to Britain. He says:

> While I was travelling on the train I looked out and I stood up, [and look] through the window and I said, "Oh my! I'm [not] where I thought I'm going, what I really thought England would be." You'd ask me, why do I say that? But you see coming to England, I saw a white man in the field and he's working . . . in the cabbage field. And I said, "I'm fooled!" You know, where I'm going is not what I thought because you see, [I] have never seen a white man [with a hoe] working in the field.[62]

Further confirmation of this fallacy was provided when he reached his destination and saw that "the English people, they sweep the floor."[63]

The Promised Land

For most of its history, the United States has been perceived as the Promised Land by countless groups of immigrants. For the Puritans and other Europeans in the seventeenth century it was a land of religious freedom—a place to practice their faith without religious persecution. Later, for the Irish, Italians, and Jews in the twentieth century, it was a land of opportunity—a place to rebuild their lives and thrive politically and economically. According to the American scholar Oscar Handlin, immigration is at the very heart of American history—"The immigrants [are] American history"[64]; they cannot be separated. For the West Indians, this image of the United States was not only alive and flourishing, but given the United States reach into the Caribbean it was one that was continuously being reinforced. Thus, for many of these migrants the United States was "abounding with economic opportunities for anyone willing to work hard and show some pluck and sense of adventure. [It was also a place where] a person could take charge of his [or her] own destiny."[65] One recurring theme among several second-generation respondents in Brooklyn was that prior to coming to America, their grandparents and parents did not have much. However, by coming to America they were able to provide a better life for their children and grandchildren. As a result, there was the expectation from the grandparents and parents that the children—and this was understood by the children themselves—would continue this legacy of hard work and take charge of their destiny. To surrender the available opportunities and become involved in criminal activities resulting in incarceration or deportation, was to dishonor the family and disgrace oneself.

This image of the Promised Land was not only synonymous with the United States but it was also attributed to one particular city—New York.[66] For many West Indians, New York was "the political and economic power base of [the current] capitalist system," one they saw as determining the vitality of the West Indian island economies. As a result, New York was a place abounding in opportunities to improve one's economic status and attain a level of modernity and civilization that their respective countries could not provide. New York was so prominent within the West Indian psyche that "no visit or residence in the United States [was] felt to be complete without at least one New York City experience."[67] Thus, migrating to New York came to signify for many immigrants the fulfillment of a dream, or the accomplishment of a great achievement. It was within this context that New York—and the United States by extension—became one of the principal places for West Indian migration.

Diaspora realities

This section will investigate two interrelated issues. First, it examines some of the social and historical reasons for the formation and perpetuation of West Indian religious communities in New York City and London. These reasons are not only multidimensional but also intricately related. Like all other social groups, these religious communities emerged within specific socioeconomic and political contexts and also at a certain period in the immigration histories of the receiving countries. It is within this context that the histories of the specific religious communities will be studied and analyzed. Second, it will highlight some of the transnational activities that West Indian immigrants and the immigrant Pentecostal churches are engaged in as they situate themselves within the social, cultural, and religious landscape of the diaspora contexts.

United States

Upon their arrival in the United States, many West Indians encountered a society that Mary Waters described as "fundamentally, a racist society."[68] For although the civil rights movement had resulted in certain rights and privileges for minorities, at its core American society was still racist. Instead of the blatant subjugation of African Americans, however, there was a "system based more on a subtle intersection of past economic discrimination, class and race interactions, and increasing separation of local political power from ultimate economic power."[69] Prior to their arrival, West Indians did not perceive American society through rose-tinted windows of racial equality and harmony, for they had some knowledge of the racial dynamics operating within the society.[70] However, as many later learned, this foreknowledge did not adequately prepare them for the stark reality of their present contexts. For within the poverty stricken, high crime, predominantly African American communities in which they lived, they encountered a system in which various levels of society were geared toward keeping African Americans at the bottom of the socioeconomic and political ladders.[71] Faced with this reality, many migrants realized how correct Derrick Bell was in his assertions that "the racism that made slavery feasible is far from dead [even] in the last decade of the twentieth-century America."[72] They also found sufficient evidence detailing how subtle discrimination was producing what Cornel West described as the shattering and demise of the African American community. This was a system driven by the "provision, expansion, and intensification of *pleasure*. . . . In the American way of life, [this] *pleasure* involve[d] [having] comfort, convenience, and sexual stimulation." The internalization of these ideas that endorsed "the predominance of the market-inspired way of life over all others" by some members of the African American population resulted in what West sees as "possible triumph of the nihilistic threat in Black America."[73] For many African Americans, the poor socioeconomic conditions within their residential areas not only inhibited their access to *pleasure* but also created an environment in which self-contempt and self-hatred became prominent features of their lives. This cycle of self-hate and nihilism was further buttressed by the daily barrage of television images stating "that theirs [was a] disgraceful form of living."[74]

Coupled with these factors were various political, socioeconomic, and education policies that were perceived as seeking to keep African Americans in their present state. Evidence of these policies is most visible in the comparison of poverty rates and median household income for African Americans to those of non-Hispanic whites and Asians. According to the US Census Bureau in 2013, African American median household income [$34,598] continues to be remarkably less than those of non-Hispanic whites [$58,270] and Asian [$67,065] households.[75] In regard to poverty, data revealed that the African American community still had the highest poverty rate of any racial group, 27.2 percent versus 9.6 percent for non-Hispanic whites and 10.5 percent for Asians.[76] These census findings are significant because they also indicate that poverty within the African American minority is predominantly located within metropolitan cities and the South.[77] Incidentally, these were some of the same cities in which the West Indian immigrants resided. As a consequence, many immigrants, like some of their African American counterparts, were continuously faced with the problems associated with nihilism, discrimination, drugs, crime, poverty, incarceration, and unemployment.

For many immigrants, the combination of these realities with the subtle insidious agendas that are focused on keeping members of the black population at the bottom of the socioeconomic and political ladders, have resulted in them seeking to distance themselves from African Americans. For many, failure to do so could result in them being perceived and treated as African Americans and given the predominance of the negative stereotypes attached to the African American population, this was not seen as a viable option. It is worth interrogating the "distancing" act in which many West Indian immigrants are engaged in, as by virtue of their phenotype the wider society *perceives* them as African American. Therefore the distinction they strive to perpetuate only becomes apparent when they speak or mention their country of origin. For the second-generation immigrant this distancing is particularly hard to maintain since they lack the distinct West Indian accent. As such they have to find other ways of intentionally articulating this distinction. "Distancing" is normally accomplished on three levels: residentially in enclaves, through social organizations and networks, and by embracing a strong work ethic.

One, by establishing distinctive residential enclaves, immigrants could intentionally preserve certain aspects of their ethnic heritage, language, and culture, thus enabling them to "maintain the distinction between themselves and American Blacks and to avoid relegation to poor Black neighborhoods or to American's most oppressed racial group."[78] Two, "by establishing networks, social clubs, organizations, festivals, and so on, Caribbean peoples who have migrated to North America have made it abundantly clear that they are not a somewhat casual gathering of rather disjoined individuals."[79] Instead the immigrants have "established themselves as a veritable and clearly identifiable community of people living in urban America."[80] Through these organizations, especially religious communities, the immigrants also found places of leadership, affirmation of their identities and culture, a surrogate family, access to social services information, and the reinforcement of parental values or authority in regard to their children. Among the immigrants were some who were affiliated with denominations that were already established within the American context and thus upon their arrival, they began to attend the neighborhood churches that were associated with these denominations.[81] However, many found the rituals and structures within these churches to be very different from what they were accustomed to in their home country. In order to recapture a worship style that was reminiscent of home, some immigrants began to meet for fellowship and prayer. It was from these prayer and fellowship meetings that many of the immigrant religious communities subsequently developed. This phenomenon is not limited to West Indian migrants but is also seen among African, Indians, Asians, and Indonesians as well.[82]

Three, by embracing a strong work ethic and by striving to attain economic mobility the West Indians migrants sought to separate themselves from their lower-class neighbors while aligning themselves with middle-class African Americans, a group which earned "between $34,000 and $54,400 (in 2003)" and was primarily comprised of university-educated individuals.[83] In this manner many West Indians fulfilled their goal of improving themselves while simultaneously avoiding becoming a part of a population that was perceived to be involved in social decline.

Brooklyn context

Having examined the wider US context, we will now give attention to the specific context in which our case studies were located. These two churches, Latter Rain Ministries and Beulah Church, were located in Brooklyn, the most populous borough in New York City. Within Brooklyn, Latter Rain Ministries was situated in the Brownsville neighborhood, while Beulah was found in the neighborhood know as Flatlands.

Brownsville[84]

Named for Charles S. Brown, the neighborhood started experiencing marked development in 1887. With the construction of several tenement buildings, garment workers from the Lower East Side moved into the area. Additional "settlement was spurred by the opening on the Fulton Street elevated railway in 1889" and the Williamsburg Bridge in 1903.[85] By 1910, Brownville was dominated by multifamily buildings and a predominantly Jewish immigrant population. Life in Brownsville was guided by the customs and practices of the Jewish residents.[86] Following the Second World War, many residents moved to the suburbs. With white-flight came a "cycle of decay, abandonment, vandalism, and arson."[87] Although various revitalization measures have been implemented over the years, "the neighborhood remained mostly low-income, with one of the highest densities of public housing projects in the city."[88] Today the population is predominantly African American with a small number of West Indians and Latinos.

Flatlands[89]

For most of its history Flatlands has been a primarily residential neighborhood. This was because it was not directly connected to the subway lines and bridges and thus developed after cars became affordable.[90] Today, the car remains the primary mode of transportation for residents; for those taking public transportation, Flatlands falls in a two-fare zone, that is, residents need to take a bus to get to the subway. Although Flatlands remains mostly Jewish, Italian, and Irish, since the 1980s it has become home to many West Indians.[91] According to a resident in the neighborhood, "These new immigrants have made the leap to the middle class and homeownership, supplanting older Jewish residents who have moved or died."[92] Today the Jewish population is undergoing an increase as orthodox Jewish families move into the area. Unlike Brownsville, Flatlands has mainly detached, semidetached, and attached houses. Despite its middle-class composition, Flatlands is not without its share of social issues, including failing schools, some gang activity, etc.[93]

A brief history of immigrant Pentecostal churches in New York City

Latter Rain Ministries[94]

Latter Rain Ministries was founded in 1971. It was the result of a meeting between Bishop Geoff Davids, the founding pastor, and eight people, during which he shared a vision to establish a church. Subsequently Bishop Davids and the eight people began to meet regularly for prayer meetings. Over time these prayer meetings became Sunday and midweek services and finally culminated in the establishment of a New York branch of a Jamaican denomination. The first official church service was held on Montvale Avenue, Brooklyn, with the overseer

of a Jamaican denomination as the guest preacher. Latter Rain Ministries was one of a series of church plants and pastorates launched by Bishop Davids.[95]

Beginning in 1982, the church embarked on several ventures that resulted in it becoming an independent entity and the headquarters of a "new" international ministry, of which Bishop Davids was the general overseer. First, there were a series of collaborations between Bishop Davids, church members, and other clergy to establish churches in Jamaica and the United States. Over the next twenty-five years, six Jamaican churches were added to the ministry—four churches via church planting and two through church affiliations. In the United States, two churches were instituted, the products of relocated church members who would meet together for fellowship and worship.

Second, in the late 1990s, there was a major renovation of the edifice. The new building provided the ministry with a larger sanctuary, with a seating capacity for about 600 people, multimedia capability, a sizable multipurpose room, several offices, and other meeting spaces. At the dedication in 2001, two significant events occurred. The first was the change in the name of the church to Latter Rain Ministries, which would be an independent organization separate from the Jamaican denomination. The second was the public announcement that the mortgage on the building was paid in full. The fulfillment of this financial obligation, positioned Latter Rain in a place where it could fully exercise the responsibilities that accompanied the church's status as the headquarters of the ministry, that is, it could pay leadership salaries and offer instruction and financial assistance to the other branches.

During my fieldwork Latter Rain had approximately 250–300 members.[96] Women constituted about 65 percent of the total church population, and were between the ages of twenty and eight-five. Teenagers and children comprised about 15 percent of the congregation, while approximately 20 percent were men, aged twenty and older. Within the leadership structure, the majority were men, with about 25 percent of the leaders females. According to the leadership, about 60 percent of the members lived in Brooklyn, with the other 40 percent residing in Queens and Long Island. However, it was observed that although many members lived in Brooklyn very few resided within the immediate neighborhood. During fieldwork it was observed that the majority of the members were employed in the healthcare and other professions (education, finance etc.). Among the young adults, the majority were graduates of universities, while most of the teenagers and children were regularly attending school. As a whole, the members of Latter Rain were upwardly mobile and in many respects could be considered to be a part of the middle-class African American community.

Beulah Church of God[97]

Beulah Church started as a Sunday school ministry out of the basement of Bishop Joshua Mitchell's home. The initial congregation included Bishop Mitchell, his wife, and their four children.[98] The original vision was to begin a Sunday school in their home and hand out flyers in the surrounding neighborhood to advertise the availability of this ministry. However, only two Sunday school sessions were held in their house because in December 1998, Rev. Vie Mitchell saw a building for rent in the Flatlands area of Brooklyn. This building, which was formerly a club, was eventually procured for their meetings. Having located a place for worship, Bishop Mitchell contacted the CoG denominational district overseer about officially establishing a ministry. In the two weeks that followed, Bishop Mitchell and his family worked to get the building ready for occupancy. On a Sunday in mid-December 1988, Beulah Church began, with a Sunday school session in the morning[99] and the official church opening that evening. The congregation remained at that location for eight years.

Prior to beginning this ministry in Brooklyn, Bishop Mitchell had been involved in ministry in various parts of England and it was during this time that he had received his ministerial license. In the 1980s the Mitchell family had been invited to relocate to New York by one of Bishop Mitchell's sisters, who saw the American context as a better one for improving oneself. Following the establishment of Beulah, Bishop Mitchell sat for and successfully passed his ordination exams. He was subsequently ordained as the minister of the congregation. In the mid-1990s, the church began the process of seeking a building to purchase. Several buildings were considered including their present location; however, they were all deemed inappropriate since they did not allow for any future expansion of the current building. Following these developments, Rev. Vie Mitchell contacted a real estate agent, who told her that the building they had previously considered was still available. As a result, a decision was made to acquire the building. According to Bishop Mitchell, "The Lord know what we should have, what was best for us."[100] After purchasing the building, it was discovered that the building was previously owned by the mafia. He further states: "From a human perspective this building would not have been good for our church. . . . Parts of the building were probably used for prostitution [and] where the choir sits used to be a stage which was used for dancing. [However] such a mindset would have stopped them from getting what God wants for you."[101] Along with the church sanctuary, offices, and church hall, the building also has several rentable apartments. These apartments, which are rented to members of the church and people in the community, have become a substantial source of income for the church.

Beulah had approximately 120 members, of which about 75 percent were women aged twenty-five and above.[102] The male members comprised about 10 percent of the total church population, and they ranged in age from twenty-three to seventy. The final 15 percent were made up of teenagers and children. In terms of leadership, about 90 percent were male and 10 percent were female. The majority of the members lived within Brooklyn, and several families including the senior minister resided in the immediate surroundings. The other families, who constituted the minority, lived in Long Island and Queens and commuted to church. The majority of the adult members retired or employed in the healthcare, technological, and other industries. Within Beulah, the majority of the young adults were university graduates. Although many members were economically upwardly mobile, there were some who are part of the low-income group. These members were typically retired with fixed incomes, and some were receiving financial assistance from their children.

Britain

The West Indian immigrants who arrived in Britain aboard the *Windrush*[103] in June 1948 and those who followed them entered Britain as citizens. For many, this journey marked a shift from the West Indian islands, which existed on the periphery, to the center, Britain. Upon arrival, however, many of the immigrants did not find the expected beneficent mother who would welcome her children with open arms. In her place they found an emotionally detached relation who treated them with disdain and marked coldness. This reaction, which on the surface seemed to convey a slight displeasure with the influx of West Indians, was in fact much more. According to Mike Phillips and Trevor Phillips, what the West Indian immigrants encountered was "an exclusive and impenetrable image of British society, backed up by the ideology of race and racial superiority, which had for so long been an essential pillar of imperial power."[104] It was an image that declared them not welcome! Their status as British citizens was inconsequential because to the British public, "culture and money in England do not, as in the West Indies, 'whiten'."[105] To be British was to be white. Consequently, the immigrants found themselves thrust into "a moral environment which steadfastly refused to acknowledge change, or the possibility of change, in the nation's self image."[106] Thus their arrival "in their light-weight suits and straw hats and felt sombreros, teeth chattering, shivering in the draughty, freezing, alien, impersonal, busy atmosphere of the railway stations," was perceived as an invasion that would "disrupt their stable pattern of life."[107] This romanticized notion of a stable pattern of English life thus became something to protect at all costs. It should be noted that this "protection" was not limited to one area, but was incorporated into several facets of daily life—specifically, employment, accommodation, and family life.

In these three areas, many West Indians were perceived to be the source for many of the social ills evident within society. In the employment arena, the denigrating stereotypes employers previously applied to the white working class, that is, lazy, irresponsible, uncultured, intellectually deficient, etc., were repurposed to describe blacks.[108] To their fellow employees and the trade unions' members, the West Indian immigrants were perceived to be a huge threat to their livelihood. Not only were they seen as "weakening their bargaining power" in the fight for higher wages, but their very presence was viewed as threatening the amount of overtime work that would be available, and diminishing the status of a job.[109]

For West Indian immigrants, their role as a scapegoat found its most prominent manifestation in the area of accommodation. As Ruth Glass argues in *Newcomers,* upon their arrival, the immigrants had very little choice in where to live. They were constrained by the location of their jobs, the inaccessibility of outlying areas, and the designation of central London regions for the white members of the working, middle, and upper classes. Their only option were "patches of inner London which [had] been neglected, and which [had] already been for some time in the process of decline and social downgrading."[110] In these deplorable conditions, they were subjected to further exploitation, harassment, and discrimination. Many of the migrants found themselves at the mercy of slum landlords and other extortionists who charged them exorbitant rents for small, deteriorating, and cheaply furnished living spaces.[111] Those who decided to seek alternative accommodation found themselves up against the color bar maintained by many white landlords.

In the area of family life, the migrants were declared deviant and dysfunctional, failing to conform to the professed "standard" of the British family. This standard, rooted in the Victorian period, espoused the image of a nuclear family into which children were born, as well as concepts of "control and self-discipline."[112] This Victorian "standard" also advocated that "the indiscriminate procreation of children has come to be regarded as improvident and uncontrolled; illegitimacy is a matter of shame and contempt; and the act of sex itself is usually invested with a puritan feeling of innate sinfulness."[113] Against this standard of propriety was placed the "deviant" West Indians' family lifestyle, noted for its high level of illegitimate birth and sexual promiscuity.[114] West Indian men were especially seen in a bad light—as men of sinister character who wanted to corrupt "proper" British society. For many within British society, the evidence spoke for itself, and the West Indians' lifestyle would eventually lead to moral disintegration in the society. Opposition to the perceived threat posed by the West Indian immigrants came in several forms. The most visible examples were the Nottingham and Notting Hill riots of 1958 and the subsequent implementation of the Commonwealth Immigration Act in 1962. Both mediums served to uncover the underlying feeling of rejection exhibited by the British masses toward the West Indian immigrants.

The West Indian immigrants' reaction to this treatment by the British masses was diverse and multifaceted. For many, their initial reaction was one of disillusionment. They had never expected that they would be unwelcome; after all they *were* British citizens, cultured in the history, language, and ways of the Empire. As a result, the immigrants came to realize that the claim that had been perpetuated in the West Indian islands that one's status could be based on merit—education, wealth, and manners, and not skin color—was a lie.[115] Within the British context, their skin color and national origin was of seminal importance and the dominant factor in their evaluation. As such, the country for which they had fought, pledged their loyalty, and given their strength, had no place for them. Another reaction was the creation of enclaves and social organizations. It is important to note that these enclaves and social organizations were formed due to both internal and external forces. The lack of housing options and the color bar that they experienced forced West Indians to live together in a manner that would form a buffer against outside society. Within the different enclaves and social organizations, many West Indian immigrants had their culture and personhood affirmed. They had found a space of belonging where they were no longer classified as outsiders. These enclaves also provided immigrants with a platform from which they could address the discrimination and racism that they faced within the society.

Upon their arrival, many of the immigrants were members of the established denominations—specifically Anglican, Methodist, and Baptist. However, the lack of welcome that they received in local congregations within these denominations coupled with the need for community resulted in them seeking alternative places to worship.[116] Thus, many became members of the emerging black-led Churches. These churches, mainly Pentecostal, were founded by West Indian migrants who were associated with various American denominations. After their arrival in Britain, many of these Pentecostals would conduct regular prayer meetings in their homes as a way to have fellowship and worship in a manner that was reminiscent of home. It was from these meetings that the many of the black-led churches developed.

London context

The above analysis has presented a brief overview of the British context that facilitated the emergence of the immigrant faith communities. However, it is also necessary to examine the specific context in which the case study is located. Kingsbridge Church is situated in one of the towns that comprise the borough of Brent, located in northwest London. Once a predominantly rural area, the locale underwent dramatic population growth beginning in the mid-1800s stimulated by the geographical expansion of the London metropolitan and the opening of a Metropolitan Railway station in 1879.[117] In the early part of the twentieth century as the town became a predominantly working-class area, a small Irish community was formed. This community experienced rapid growth during the Second World War. The community's population underwent further diversification with the coming of Jewish refugees following the Second World War and of migrants from the Caribbean and the Indian subcontinent in the 1960s. Beginning in the 1960s the area also began to experience an economic decline. Redevelopment was implemented within the area in the 1980s, when various business people operating along the High Road were allocated money to improve their businesses.[118] It is necessary to note, however, that although the area has undergone some redevelopment, it has more recently had several incidences of knife and gun crimes.[119]

A brief history of immigrant Pentecostal churches in London
Kingsbridge New Testament Church of God

The emergence of the New Testament Church of God (NTCG) denomination and the Kingsbridge Church was a direct result of the influx of West Indian migrants to Britain in the 1950s. Among the new arrivals from the Caribbean were several ministers and members of the NTCG, a West Indian Pentecostal denomination that was affiliated with the CoG denomination in Cleveland, TN, in the United States. Upon their arrival in England, many of these NTCG ministers and members were surprised at the lax attitude that the English exhibited toward religion and Sunday church attendance. As stated in the previous section, as many migrants sought to worship in the mainline churches of which they were members back in their homelands, some were faced with discrimination and rejection, while others were welcomed. For some of those who were welcomed within the established churches, the relationship proved to be a temporary one "as the newcomers seemed to be too noisy [to their British counterparts], [while for some of them] the worship was not as inspiring as they were used to 'back home'." Simultaneously, there was the growing awareness among some of the migrants of the rampant spiritual inertia and the lack of fellowship that was beginning to characterize the burgeoning West Indian community. In order to rectify what they perceived to be a significant problem they began establishing meetings in their homes to "preserve their spiritual life until they could return to the Caribbean."[120] It was one of these fellowships that gave rise to what is now Kingsbridge.

Pastor D. Love started Kingsbridge in the late 1950s. He along with six Christians met regularly for prayer meetings and house fellowships at his home. From this location, the group moved to a Scout hall located on the major street in the area. However, after a few weeks they had to relocate to another Scout hall in the neighboring town. The church remained in this location for several years and experienced tremendous numerical growth as believers from the Caribbean, especially Jamaica, were added to the congregation. While at this location, Pastor T. J. Bennet became the senior minister of the church. He was later replaced by Reverent K. T. Manners, who led the congregation in purchasing a redundant and dilapidated building in the 1960s. Following their relocation, the church's name was changed to Kingsbridge NTCG. The leadership and members of the congregation were committed to the building renovation and gave their time, skills, and money to the project.[121] In the years that followed, the church had several pastors, and in the mid-1980s, the current minister was transferred to Kingsbridge. During his pastorate the church has experienced several changes. The most notable has been the diversification of the church's leadership structure evident in the addition of two women and several second-generation members to the pastor's council[122] and the ordination of a woman as the youth minister.

In terms of demographics, the congregation was predominantly comprised of second-generation migrants. This was due to several of the first-generation members dying or relocating to the West Indies upon their retirement. However, despite these losses, the church continued to grow as several second-generation migrants and others became members of the church. As a result, Kingsbridge was a fairly large congregation having a membership of several hundred.[123] The female members represented 55 percent of the congregation, while the men and children/ youth were about 25 percent and 20 percent, respectively. The congregation was also very diverse in terms of economic status, with some of the members retired while others were employed in education, media, healthcare, and other industries. Like those at Latter Rain and Beulah, Kingsbridge's members were encouraged to gain various qualifications in order to improve their economic status. In terms of residence, the majority of the members lived within Brent and the surrounding counties of northwest London.

Transnationalism and the immigrants

Traditionally, scholars have viewed immigrants within a settler/sojourner categorization. As a result, the scholarship on immigrants has focused primarily on their acculturation, incorporation, and the ways they were "limited to the ethnic communities they created in the host society".[124] As per this categorization, the settler or immigrant underwent a process of permanent dissociation and relocation in which former life patterns were abandoned and new ones were forged[125]; sojourners or migrants, on the other hand, were conceived as transients whose residence in the host country was of a temporary nature since they would eventually return home or move to another location. This binary categorization has become increasingly less convincing as contemporary immigrants engage in "processes by which [they] forge and sustain multi-stranded social relations that link together their societies of origin and settlement"—including linkages between various diaspora contexts.[126] These include familial, religious, cultural, socioeconomic, and political relationships, which enable immigrants to simultaneously inhabit multiple worlds. The presence of transnational activities is not a novel phenomenon, however, as evidence of such activities abounds within earlier migrations. According to Portes et. al., "Precursors of present immigrant transnationalism have existed for centuries. . . . [But,] they lacked the elements of regularity, routine involvement, and critical mass characterizing contemporary examples of transnationalism."[127] For Portes and others, the growth of various technological revolutions in the telecommunication and travel industries has compressed space and time, which facilitates the proliferation and the continuation of the transnational networks with increasing efficiency and speed.[128] Although these globalizing features may have created an environment for the expansion of certain transnational networks, they are, not in themselves, the primary cause for the development of the networks. As documented earlier, one enduring aspect of West Indian life is a focus on regional and international migration. Pivotal within this framework is the establishment of various networks linking those who migrated and those who remained behind.[129]

The discourse on transnationalism covers a diversity of activities in which individuals engage, their social networks, their communities, and local and national governmental structures in three prominent sectors: economic, political, and sociocultural.[130] These activities include: various transnational economic initiatives (e.g. export/import, investments); the co-opting and mobilizing of the resources and loyalty of migrants by local and national governmental agencies in the home and host contexts; the proliferation of home-based religious and cultural organizations that institute branches in the host context as well as at home; and the maintenance of familial linkages across the national borders of the countries of settlement and origin. In regard to these activities, there is some debate concerning which ones should be considered transnational. For Portes, transnational activities are those that are regular, sustained, and primarily economic.[131] Although transnational economic enterprises have profound effects on various social processes including national development in the country of origin and the economic mobility of immigrants, such a focus overlooks the manner in which other everyday activities can be described as transnational. For as Itzigsohn et al argue, some transnational activities and the social networks that they facilitate are "constructed through the daily life and activity of immigrants."[132] Basch, Glick Schiller, and Szanton Blanc, in contrast, promote a more inclusive definition that includes everyday social practices—from economic ventures to the reconfiguration of social and cultural spaces.[133] However, this definition as Itzigsohn et al notes, "suffers from being too unspecified."[134]

Therefore, in determining what activities are transnational, one has to first: acknowledge the presence of both economic and everyday practices within the rubric of transnational activities. Second: realize that both the regular/ sustained transborder activities and the occasional ones play a significant role in "all aspects of [the immigrants'] life, from their economic opportunity, to their political behavior, to their individual and group identities".[135] Third: find a way to map transnational practices[136] and thus distinguish the different levels of engagement. All three of these issues can be addressed by implementing a typology of narrow and broad transnational activities. According to Itzigsohn et al, narrow transnational activities refer to the immigrants' participation in "economic, political, social, or cultural practices that involve a regular movement [across nation borders], a high level of institutionalization, or constant personal involvement."[137] In contrast, transnational activities in the broad sense refers to "a series of material and symbolic practices in which [immigrants] engage that involve only sporadic physical movement between the two countries, a low level of institutionalization, or just occasional personal involvement."[138] When applied economically, this typology will be as follows. Narrow activities would include having an importing business that requires the owner to regularly travel back and forth between the country of origin and the host to source and purchase products for sale. Board activities in contrast would include a long-time resident sending money to relatives in the country of origin at specific times, like during the Christmas holidays. It is this typology that will be implemented for the analysis of transnational activities by West Indian Pentecostal immigrants in New York City and London.

In regard to the discourse on contemporary migration it is not only immigrants who are challenging the traditional assumptions about their permanent dislocation from the homeland, but also the organizations in which they are involved—especially those of a religious nature. As Afe Adogame notes in regard to African diaspora churches, "These [religious] communities are connected through various ties in the realm of religion, economy, friendship, kinship, politics and increasingly so through the virtual space of telephone calls, new media such as the Internet which have become a central feature of development and maintenance of diasporic identity."[139] Another key feature of the transnationalizing of religion is that it "integrates migrants into a powerful, resource-rich international religious network they can access regardless of their political citizenship"[140] or their visa status. In this manner, diaspora churches also become subjects for interrogation and analysis.

In this section, transnational activities will be investigated from the perspectives of the West Indian immigrants and the Pentecostal churches and within the broad and narrow transnational typology. The transnational practices discussed will not be representative of all of the activities in which West Indian immigrants in New York City and London are engaged. It will focus on those observed during the ethnographic fieldwork that was conducted in both contexts. In so doing, we will be able to arrive at some specific conclusions about West Indian immigrants at a grassroots level within these urban locations.

Transnational activities of West Indian immigrants

Prior to discussing some of the transnational activities in which West Indian immigrants are engaged, it is necessary to state that the categories documented below do not exist as separate activities in the lives of the immigrants. They occurred simultaneously and in some situations each category facilitated the proliferation of the others. For example, running an import business required one to be aware of and possibly involved in various social (continuing to maintain certain tribal and network relationships) and political (the policies being implemented that may impact the exportation of products) undertakings in the country of origin.

Economic activities

The majority of the economic transnational activities in which the West Indian respondents were engaged in can be classified within the broad typology. For although the activities enabled the respondents to maintain contact with those in the home context, they were neither institutionalized nor did they involve constant transborder movements. One common transnational activity noted among West Indian migrants was the sending of remittances to relations in the country of origin. These remittances, which normally amounted to billions of US dollars, provided a means of extending the revenues of relations within the home context.[141] Among the respondents, the sending of remittances occurred within the contexts of supporting an aging parent, siblings, or a child living in the home country. According to one respondent, "My daughter spent her formative years in Jamaica. I was ill, and she had to go down and stay down there. I just couldn't manage to work and see to her. It was too much of a strain with my medical history and so she was down there for the first five years. You know intermittently I saw her but she started her schooling down there."[142]

It should be noted that although this quote did not expressly mention sending any remittances, within this particular context not to do so would be considered a grave offense and could have significant consequences for both the parent and the child. Within many West Indian families the sending of one's child to reside with a family member is normally coupled with an informal agreement that the parent will send money to help with the cost of rearing the child.[143] In some cases, the receipt of economic assistance can be directly related to the kind of treatment that the child left in the relative's care would receive.[144] Therefore if a parent broke this agreement they would not only lose status in the eyes of their relations and the community, but they could also place their child at risk of being ill-treated and perceived as the offspring of a "worthless" individual. The loss of status was not only borne by the parent but also by their relations. For in the context of the rising cost of living—evidenced in the price for food items, public utilities, transportation, and school tuition—remittances gave relations access to outside resources.

Coupled with the monetary remittances, West Indian immigrants also sent or carried food and consumer goods to relations and friends in the home country.

A common activity noted among some West Indians was the sending of barrels. This large cylindrical container, made of plastic or reinforced cardboard with a metal cover and bottom, was filled with various food, clothing, and other consumer goods and then shipped to relatives in the home country. This practice has resulted in the emergence of a phenomenon called "barrel kids" within the West Indian society. These "barrel kids" were children of individuals who had migrated and whose existence was intricately tied to the barrels that were shipped to the island.[145] Through these products, the immigrants were able to "provide the low-income sectors with access to consumer goods that these sectors could not buy with their local income."[146] As a result their relations were perceived by their neighbors to be "better off" and acquired status within the community. Thus, in a context where the remittances or consumer goods were not forthcoming, the relations would be demoted to the level of those in the community who were struggling to make economic ends meet.

An additional economic transnational activity noted among some of the respondents was the purchasing of properties and/or houses, or the building of houses in the country of origin. These economic transnational activities were conducted on a sporadic basis and were normally engaged in by those intending to relocate to their country of origin.[147] Notification about the availability of properties and buildings was acquired through various means. These included: advertisements in one of the diaspora newspapers or online national newspapers[148]; working with a real estate agent that specialized in return migration; and advertising within certain religious and/or social organizations. Within this process, the purchasing of properties and houses, as well as the construction of houses, were brokered through various agents, both in the country of settlement and their homeland. In some cases these agents were family members who would be asked to locate, inspect, and purchase property/house or oversee the construction process. David, the only respondent who had been involved in this process, described his experience as follows:

> I was buying Jamaica paper to look for land and house. . . . They can look at somebody's house, take the photograph and send it to you. So you have to be careful. So I said I want the land. . . . [During the service], the Lord spoke to [the visiting American Evangelist] and she said, "Who wants land come down"! Well I come down . . . because [I] want land. . . . Not long after that, I saw a land advertised in the Jamaican Gleaner [for] six acres of land. . . . So I phone the man, make contact and go and meet with him in Birmingham. . . . And I pay down something on it. When I go back down [to Jamaica], I go and see the land, [then] I phone to release the rest of the money for the land.[149]

The issue of return migration is particularly important within the transnationalism discourse because of the impact that it exerts on other transnational activities— for example, social and cultural. In order to return to their home country, the immigrant would need to maintain economic and/or social contacts with those in the home country. Simultaneously, the immigrant may also need to maintain various cultural/political distinctions that could continue to mark them as a foreigner within the diaspora context in order to prepare themselves for their eventual return.[150] Although many would not return to their home country, the hope of return continued to foster the maintenance of ties with home. For some immigrants this hope of return and the orientation toward home that it fostered was facilitated by the lack of belonging that they experience in the new social context.[151]

Social activities

The majority of the West Indian respondents were engaged in both narrow and broad social transnational activities. Of the narrow activities, the most common was communicating regularly with relations and friends in the homeland. For one respondent, this involved calling Jamaica several times every week. When asked about the frequency of her communication, she replied, "I have to do that, I love my family so I have to keep in touch with them."[152] For another respondent, the frequency of her contacts with her relations, especially her siblings, was due to her position within her family. She states, as the matriarch of the family, "I've had to really, you know, think not of myself. I have to think of them because . . . my mother passed [when] I was 32. So I just had to really take on that mantle."[153] This frequency of communication between London, New York City, and the West Indies was itself produced and perpetuated by the global expansion within the telecommunications sector. As a result of the internet and software like Skype and Windows Live Messenger, cost effective telecommunications, and low-cost phone cards, West Indian immigrants were able to maintain instantaneous and cost efficient communication with relations. Within the home context, this telecommunication process was further facilitated by the expansion of mobile communication services, resulting in individuals in remote rural areas now having greater communicative access to the wider world. One such organization is the Digicel group. Launched in Jamaica in 2001, it has since become one of the largest mobile operators in the Caribbean. Digicel is known for introducing the first GSM mobile service in Jamaica, enabling its customers to receive mobile coverage even in the most remote parts of the country. In addition, Digicel mobile plans are economically reasonable, making it possible for individuals from every stratum of the society to have a mobile phone. As a result, a common occurrence in many farming communities in Jamaica and the other islands was that of the farmer on his way to his farm talking on his mobile phone while riding a donkey.[154]

The broad transnational activities in which the respondents were engaged included: visiting their homelands and finding spouses. One common feature noted among many of the respondents was visits to their country of origin. The reasons for these visits were varied, and included vacation, weddings, funerals, finding a spouse, and family reunion. For many respondents, there was some level of overlap among their reasons for returning to their home country—thus a vacation could also include a family reunion, a wedding, or funeral. For two respondents, however, the primary reason for returning home was to find a spouse. For many West Indians, although there may be some pressure to marry "well" or within a certain ethnic group—as normally is the case among many East Indian families—the final decision is ultimately that of the two parties involved. Within the West Indian migration discourse, the practice of returning to the homeland to find a spouse has some precedence. However, in these instances the individuals involved normally had some prior relationship or friendship before one of them migrated. This did not seem to be the case for the two respondents.

One respondent, a 37-year resident in Britain, returned to his district or community in Jamaica to find a second wife after becoming a widower. From his interview and subsequent conversations with both him and his wife, it was determined that although they knew of each other, there was no evidence of them having any prior relationship or friendship prior to their marriage. In regard to the second respondent, she was the second wife of a widower who had spent some period of time living in New York. Here too there did not seem to be any prior relationship between them. When discussing her marriage this respondent noted: "He is from my district so he knew me. . . . He was married, his wife died, so he visited and after I came here he [got] married to me."[155] In examining the profiles of the wives, it was noted that both were single Christian women in their late forties to early fifties and both were committed members of the Pentecostal churches within their districts. The presence of this type of marital practice raises certain questions. Why was it important for the widowers to travel back to their respective districts in order to find wives? What were some of the characteristics found in these women that made them suitable as marriage partners? Some possible answers to these questions will be discussed in Chapter 3 of this book.

Cultural activities

For many West Indian immigrants, it was the cultural transnational activities that had the most prominent positions in their lives. These activities could also be categorized as narrow and broad. Narrow cultural transnational activities can be defined as those "practices and institutions [in which the immigrants are involved that facilitate] the formation of meanings, identities and values."[156] Through these practices and institutions, West Indians were able to define what it meant to be West Indian in the host nation context. Within the familial context, this definition took the form of parents ensuring that their children and grandchildren were not only familiar with their West Indian culture but also cognizant of their roots.

This cultural translation was accomplished in various ways. In regard to food, although American and British food may be eaten in the home, the principal place was given to food from the country of origin. Intricately associated with the familial diet was the West Indian ideology about the value of food—food should be received with gratitude and not wasted. A second-generation woman highlights this ideology in the following manner:

> My grandma . . . on a Sunday she gonna dish out your food and you better eat everything. [There] was a morning that my cousin didn't eat. He threw [the] food in the garbage and lied and said that, oh he ate it. He got beating. . . . When [grandma] was younger there used to be times when she could only have a cup of tea or something like that and they don't want it to be like that for us.[157]

Within the home, some children and grandchildren were reared in a similar manner to the way in which their parents and grandparents were brought up in their home countries. They are taught to be respectful to others, especially their elders, to be obedient, and to value education. As the quote above indicates, this may also include punishing the child or grandchild when they behaved in manner deemed to be reprehensible by the adults. For some of the respondents, however, the differences between the home and host context necessitated some modification in the way in which they parented their children. One respondent from London described her experience with her children in the following manner:

> We don't steal away their culture here from them, but . . . [at] the same time we let them know where their parents are coming from and what our culture is. And try to get them involved as much as we can in our culture as well [be] cause they like to [go] to Jamaica. . . . I think that's very important for kids,

very important [that you] don't take away the parents' culture, your culture from them but [get] them used to both cultures.[158]

Indelibly linked with the transference of West Indian cultural and behavioral practices was the need for children and grandchildren to know their roots and have a place of belonging. Given the racial dynamics in both the United States and the United Kingdom, and the manner in which they affected the lives of West Indian immigrants, including the respondents, having a place to which one could be linked was essential for the second and later generations of immigrants. During an interview, a respondent in New York narrated that one of her dreams had been to take her two grandsons to Jamaica so that they could see where she came from and where their great-grandparents had lived and worked. This dream was realized in 2006. According to the respondent, her primary reason for financing this trip was so that her grandsons would know their roots. This respondent's opinion about the importance of having and knowing roots was expressed as follows:

> I think part of the reason why we're having such a problem with our young Black youths is because of the fatherlessness in the home. I believe that young men needs to know their roots. I'm not saying it's not important for a woman but more so for a man because otherwise he's just out there. Where did I come from? Where am I going? You know, they don't have anything to anchor on to.[159]

For many West Indian Christians, religious training also played a pivotal role in the manner in which they reared their children. According to one respondent an important duty for her as a parent was "taking [her] children to church not just sending them, bringing them up in Sunday school, teaching them about God and things like that, and how to value human life, [and] things like that."[160]

Broad transnational activities covered a wide range of activities that would constitute a person as "being West Indian" though that individual may not have any direct link with the West Indian islands. Activities categorized in this framework would be those involving second- or third-generation immigrants who have had very limited contact with the islands and whose construction of a loosely affiliated West Indian identity was accomplished through periodically eating the food, listening to Reggae or Soca music, and trying to retain the language, that is, the dialects, pronunciation, and/or vocabulary of the islands. Included in the broad typologies were also the ways in which West Indian descendants have taken certain cultural markers and re-created them to form an entirely new entity within the new home context. One example of such re-creation found in both the United States and Britain was the adoption of dreadlocks, a visible marker that an individual was a Rastafari, as an expression of identity, pride, and fashion within the larger black community.

Transnational activities among Pentecostal churches

Having discussed various transnational activities in which the West Indian immigrants are engaged, it is also important to investigate the kinds of transnational activities in which the religious communities they attend are involved. One common transnational feature noted in all three congregations was the sending of money to the Caribbean. This activity took three particular forms: financial assistance to specific individuals, contributions to a church and community projects, and disaster relief. The first two forms were conducted on an ongoing basis, while the latter was engaged in only during an emergency. All three activities were brokered through former members of the churches who had relocated to the Caribbean or though the church's position as the headquarters of the ministry—as was the case for Latter Rain. By using their former members as brokers or ministry ties for these financial activities, the home church was able to receive ongoing updates while reducing the risk of being defrauded.

Another activity noted specifically within the New York context was the expansion of the diaspora church to other contexts, particularly back to the country of origin. Speaking of African diaspora churches Afe Adogame notes that this expansion "demonstrates a kind of 'spiritual remittance mechanism'."[161] This feature was evident in Latter Rain Ministries, which has eight branches in three countries—The United States, Canada, and Jamaica. As the headquarters, Latter Rain Ministries-Brooklyn functions as a key resource for financial and personnel assistance for the other branches. The transnational links between the headquarters and the branches were reinforced in several ways. First, through the weekly church's Sunday bulletin, which listed the names of the minister/pastors of all branches along with the names of members who needed prayer due to illness, or some other circumstance. Second, through the financial contributions and the founder's frequent visits to the church branches, as well as his continuous involvement in the ministry of these churches. Third, through the local and global dynamics that comprised the ministry of the church—in that programs organized on the local level also have global links to the other churches. This included the exchange of preachers, invitations, and letters of greeting between the branches. For example, while conducting fieldwork, the minister in charge of a branch in Jamaica died. In preparation for her funeral, a special offering was collected in the Brooklyn branch to aid with the financial requirements. Condolences and well-wishes were sent to the members of the branch through Bishop Davids who was going to Jamaica to officiate at the funeral.

Another area in which a local/global dynamic was demonstrated was in church membership, which can be conceptualized in terms of the local church as well as the international organization. This was the case when a member relocated from their local context to another one where a branch of the church already existed. In this situation, they would not have to deal with the series of requirements needed to acquire a new membership; instead their membership could be transferred from their former church to the new one.

For Beulah and Kingsbridge the expansion dynamic noted above did not exist and the transnational links with the West Indies were more tenuous. One reason for this was due to denominational connection. For both Beulah and Kingsbridge, their primary denominational connection was to the CoG headquarters in Tennessee. So although they were comprised of West Indian immigrants, their denominational orientation was toward the United States and specifically the southern state of Tennessee. One outcome of such an orientation was the lack of any formalized organizational connection/affiliation with churches in the West Indies. In the case of Beulah, what was noted, were the differences between the church's official name and what it was called by some of the members. Officially the church is Beulah Church of God; however, among some of the members it was called Beulah NTCG. It was in this designation that one found the link to the West Indies. When the CoG denomination sought to register in Jamaica following its organization in 1925, there was already a denomination bearing the name CoG.[162] Therefore, they took the name NTCG. When the members from these churches migrated and became a part of CoG churches like Beulah, they continued to call it, albeit in an "unofficial" capacity, by the name of the denomination they had left behind. The existence of this "unofficial" designation attests to the presence of a link that continues to be perpetuated both in the minds and lives of its members.

For Kingsbridge NTCG, the most prominent links with the West Indies or other contexts were brokered through the activities of their individual members. On a denominational level, it was noted that although the NTCG in Britain bears the same name as its counterpart in the West Indies it did not seem to have much contact with that denomination. As stated previously, the NTCG in Britain was affiliated with the CoG denomination in Cleveland, United States. The prominence of this link was seen in the presence of several NTCG national executive council members at a CoG conference in the United States and that of CoG leadership during the NTCG annual convention in Britain.

Conclusion

This chapter, which forms the migration portion of the tapestry, has argued that when examining immigrants and the immigrant faith communities in which they participate, one has to allow for a diversity of perspectives. For although these topics have at times been presented as simple, straightforward issues, the reality is that they comprise several converging elements. It is in this manner that many empirical studies that have been conducted on West Indian migration are problematic. With their overwhelming dependence upon the push-pull model, they have failed to take into consideration the other factors that have influenced and continue to influence the migratory process of many West Indians. In the area of economics, space needs to be given to scrutinizing the West Indian islands' economic past, because it is there that the foundations of the islands' present economies were laid and the contemporary "safety valve" features are explained. In conducting this investigation specific attention also needs to be given to the manner in which the proliferation of certain relationships[163] between the West Indian islands and the metropolis facilitated the migration process. Finally, a critical investigation of the individual, the family, and "image" is essential. For many migrants, it is the family that makes their migration a possibility—by providing the much-required money for traveling, the emotional support, and the care for children who may be left behind. The perpetuation of an image is also significant because it forms the basis by which people in the West Indies are socialized in relation to their ongoing migratory culture. Thus, it is only in examining internal and external socioeconomic and political factors, immigration laws, the role of family, and the perpetuation of certain images that one can give adequate attention to why immigrants choose to migrate.

When discussing how West Indian migrants interact with their new host countries, a multidimensional approach is also necessary. For the West Indians who came to Britain and the United States from 1948 and 1965 onwards, respectively, it was their racial encounter in their largely disadvantaged urban communities that would lay the foundation for their future interactions. Although West Indians had arrived in Britain as citizens, they found themselves as the object of a racial system whose goal was to relegate them to one of the most oppressed ethnic groups within the society. In the United States, West Indian migrants encountered a society plagued by racism and associated issues. Within these contexts, West Indians utilized their ethnic and religious resources to create spaces of belonging and empowerment and which also served as a means of acquiring social and cultural capital. One such space was the immigrant faith community. Within this community, these immigrants were able to find many of the resources that enabled them to navigate the terrains of the diaspora. Coinciding with this process was the forging of multiple ties between their home and the host contexts, which allowed the migrants to simultaneously inhabit multiple worlds. Within these worlds, they were able to use the culture, heritage, and ways of home as a template for adapting to the new context. As a result, many migrants discovered a voice that allowed them to articulate just what it meant for them to be West Indian in a foreign land. One primary part of this articulation is the construction and negotiation of identities. This will be discussed in the chapters that follow.

As immigrants settle down and begin to make meaning of their lives in the new context, they are still maintaining some connection to their country of origin. Using the board-narrow typologies in regard to transnationalism, this chapter highlighted some of the economic, social, and cultural activities that West Indians immigrants and the Pentecostal church in which they participate, engage in as they remain connected to their former island homes.

In functioning as a transition between previous chapter and those that follow, this chapter has documented the diaspora realities that will give rise to the identities that will be negotiated by the first generation and constructed by the immigrant children, and the ways in which the concept mission will be articulated and practiced within the Beulah, Latter Rain, and Kingsbridge churches. It is in this regard that this section of the tapestry can be seen as strands that connect these pieces within the larger whole.

Finding Space: Identification Among First-Generation Immigrants

In this chapter and the one that follows the theme of identity is given centrality of place. Here, we will see which strands from Chapter 2 remain and which ones change. We will also discover what factors facilitated the differences in both the appearance and pattern of these strands within the overall tapestry.

As stated previously, identity is an essential element in the lives of all people—one that is rooted in the history of an individual or a group. Although it is shaped by past experiences, it also enables a person to live in the present and move into the future. Thus, "identities are in transition, involved in a multiplicity of crossovers and mixes."[1] As Stuart Hall states, "Identities are never unified and, in late modern times, increasingly fragmented and fractured; never singular but multiply constructed across different, often intersecting and antagonistic, discourses, practices and positions."[2] Identity, therefore, is not static but fluid. It provides a source of significance, meaning, and experience for both the collective group and the individual. Identity also allows one to articulate how he or she sees himself or herself in relation to the other—both the real and the imagined— this in turn enables an individual to construct his or her concept of self and the other.[3] However, it is only in the process of internalization and the construction of meaning around this internalization that identity becomes identity.[4] From this construction and internalization results the legitimization of boundaries— which are then articulated through various cognitive and performative actions directed toward oneself and the other.

For first-generation immigrants, the construction and internalization processes whereby boundaries are legitimized and identities are articulated occur within a migration framework. Thus, the myriad connections linking their localities of origin with those of the diaspora forge a nexus from which emerges their "new" concept of the self and the other. For some migrants, the migration framework also consists of a religious dimension, one that simultaneously anchors them to their home country as they engage with the host country.

Given the prominence and the politics of migration within the current global landscape, an investigation into the renegotiation of identities among first-generation migrants within a religious arena is highly warranted.

In this chapter, the analysis of identities exhibited by first-generation West Indian immigrants will be conducted within the context of their involvement in Pentecostal immigrant churches. In this chapter, I will argue that because immigrant churches are themselves located within the migration framework, they provide us with a suitable environment for investigating how ethnic and religious identities are being renegotiated by first-generation West Indian Pentecostals in the diaspora. This chapter will examine the types of ethnic and religious identities being renegotiated as a result of certain transnational ties and their interactions with the host societies. It will also document some of the ways these identities are represented within the immigrant Pentecostal arena.

Renegotiating identities

Due to their engagement within the migration framework, West Indian Pentecostals are intricately connected to multiple contexts—home and various diaspora contexts where they live and/or have familial and social connections. These connections not only allow immigrants to engage in various sociopolitical, economic, and religious activities, but also function as a seminal element in their reconstruction of the self and the other. For it is in the interaction between these contexts that the transference and rearticulation of concepts occur, thus enabling the renegotiation of their identities. What identities are being renegotiated by these first-generation West Indian immigrants? Within our examination, specific attention will be given to the role that immigrant faith communities, which are themselves products and facilitators of these connective ties, play in the renegotiation of identities.

Ethnic identities

New York

Ethnically, the majority of those who I interviewed in New York described themselves within a black or West Indian-oriented rhetoric. There was one individual who ascribed to a nationalistic identity—she called herself Jamaican. For this individual who had immigrated to the United States in June 2001, Jamaica was still very much her home. Her primary reason for her being in the

United States was her husband—"he's the one who filed for me to live here." When asked if she would consider going back to Jamaica if the circumstances made such a move possible, she replied, "For right now I can't really give you a straightforward argument but I'm always considering Jamaica. I love Jamaica. I rather live in Jamaica than here but for right now, [laugh] I say I wouldn't definitely say. I want to go back you know. [The] experience is good and being here is a different experience from back home and I can always go back you know, we adjust."[5]

For those who expressed an identity constructed within the collective black/West Indian orientation, two purposes were at play. The first was to call attention to themselves, as a group that has historically suffered from double invisibility within the US national context—as blacks and as black foreigners.[6] The second was to highlight the diversity that exists within the commonly perceived homogenous black America—especially the distinction that some of them, as West Indian immigrants, believed existed between themselves and African Americans. Rooted in the rhetoric of distinction is the idea of West Indians as "good blacks" or "model migrants" who will achieve the much-lauded "American Dream" and their own individual dreams through hard work and sacrifice.[7] Interestingly, this stereotype was not only attributed to West Indians by the wider society[8] but was also willingly embraced and reinforced by the immigrants themselves. This idea of the "model immigrant" was expressed by a grandmother's assessment of her two grandsons in the following manner. The eldest, who she ascribes as being more West Indian, is "on the honor roll, well behaved and loves the Lord, all that good stuff. . . . [He got] saved at eight [years old] . . . and he's just that steadfast in the Lord." In contrast, her other grandson, who is "more" African American, is more of a challenge. Not only is he 10 ½ years old and not saved but "you could tell him 'if you don't have Jesus you going to hell!' It [doesn't] mean [any]thing to him." From her interview it seemed that this grandson was having some difficulty in school. Thus, she was planning on sending him to the Sylvan Learning Center[9] because she "can't afford for him to go down the drain. *I mean it's just not, not going to happen in the name of Jesus.*"[10] Thus, although she perceived her grandson as "African American" in several ways, for her, his success and subsequent upward mobility within society was nonnegotiable. This became a goal to which she gave her time and money.

What we see in this grandmother's assessment of her grandsons is a dilemma many West Indian immigrants encounter—what will be their children's identity? Will they adhere to a West Indian identity and embody the "model immigrant" stereotype that accompanies it, or will they embrace an African American identity, specifically a urban African American one, and become a part of the underclass? These are some of the questions that will be considered in Chapter 4. As we see from what this grandmother expressed, this "battle" is one that is waged on a daily basis and for her part, it is one she cannot afford to lose because it is not only her grandson's life but also the sacrifices that the family has made that are at stake.

Other characteristics associated with being a "model immigrant" are an emphasis on hard work, sacrifice, education, and being upstanding members of the society. One man articulated these ideals in the following manner:

> I say to the young folks . . . "do [the] right that [you] can do." "Try and get an education and it [will] turn into a good job." That's a very good thing in this country, not in this country alone but all over the world, education is a very good thing. When you have that, you can choose and you can refuse and get the right package. . . . You can make a lot of money, if you have the right education. And you can get a good job and you can take care of your family.[11]

Although this emphasis on hard work, sacrifice, and education is also seen on the lives and experiences of other immigrants, the direct link between getting an education and a good job, expressed in the above quote is rooted within the historical West Indian ideology, whereby education was used as a means of legitimizing "the highly unequal social and economic structures within the society by convincing the masses to accept their subordinate role and thereby modifying their occupational and social aspirations."[12] This mind-set was cast in the philosophy that if an individual worked hard enough and embodied various cultural characteristics, that is, if he or she was a law-abiding, upstanding member of the society, well mannered, respectful of authority, etc., then he or she would get ahead. For many first-generation immigrants, the portrayal of America as a place with numerous opportunities and its celebration of the self-made individual provided a favorable context in which hard work, sacrifice, and an emphasis on education yielded great dividends for themselves and their children. Thus, this philosophy and its American additions became prominent parts of both the familial narrative and expectations, which are passed on to the later generations.

Although scholars like Mary Waters and Philip Kasinitz have documented some West Indian immigrants as stating that there were distinct differences between themselves and African Americans, such statements were not noted among those I interviewed.[13] What was observed was a more subtle articulation of difference that was expressed in several ways. Within church life and worship services at the churches, much attention was given to affirming various aspects of immigrant life (wanting to better oneself, sacrifice, working hard, etc.) and West Indian culture (evidenced in the type of songs that were sung, the organizational structure they followed, and the language that was spoken, which was a mixture of English and Jamaican patois). By affirming these aspects of culture and life, these religious communities continued to demarcate their particular spaces as ones where immigrant life and West Indian culture was normative and prominent. As a result, although African Americans were not prevented from attending or joining the churches, the tenor was one that lent itself more toward the West Indian experience. As a pastor of one of the churches shared: "We had a few Americans, but they are not here at the moment."[14] From his interview, it also became evident that involvement/participation of African Americans in the ministry was sporadic since they "come and go." Given the level of sacrifice (financial, time, etc.) demanded within a growing ministry, having a group that "comes and goes" did not foster greater involvement in areas of leadership or other aspects of the ministry.

In discussing the renegotiation of ethnic identities by first-generation immigrants in New York, we should note that this occurs in tandem with the maintenance of some national identities. As a result, one of two primary ethnic identities can be articulated under certain circumstances. When interacting with the wider society, the collective black/West Indian identity is the one normally expressed. This is especially the case in regard to cultural events (West Indian Day parade), employment, political representation, etc. However, within the West Indian community, national identities may come to the fore.[15] One respondent, who is married to a Bajan/Barbadian, described the distinctions between Jamaicans and Barbadians as follows: "God help[ed] us that during the interim shortly after we were married in 1974 about three years or so, my daughter was about two, we purchase[d] our own home. We have that in Jamaica so it was not a big deal for me but no offence to Bajans, but they just didn't have that standard of living back then. Now it's a different scenario."[16]

The presence of national identities was also noted within the churches studied—these included: Vincentian, Barbadian, Trinidadian, Jamaican etc. Demographically, Jamaicans were the majority of the members in both congregations. This demographic majority fostered a dynamic whereby the Jamaican identities tended to dominate the others to the extent that the churches could be perceived as "Jamaican" churches. Within such a context, articulating another national identity could be difficult as one Vincentian expressed:

> I feel that a lot of the focus is on Jamaica rather than many countries. . . . It is a big step right now that they're going to St. Vincent [for short-term mission]. . . . They usually have an annual Vincentian cultural [show] where they try to raise money . . . to help in aid and medical supply in St. Vincent. A lot of people had complained that, why not [have] a Jamaican cultural show or something like that. And I'm feeling like, okay everywhere I go, I already know so much about the Jamaican culture, the food is always Jamaican food. I know how they speak, I know their music, even the bad. So it's just because . . . they want to be involved in everything.[17]

In the above quote, we notice the respondent's feelings of frustration at the attempts of the Jamaicans to dominate other nationalities and be involved in everything. According to this informant, this and similar feelings may contribute to the formation of other-dominant national identity churches—Barbadian, Guyanese, Trinidadian, etc. The reason being, that "people tend to go where they feel that their culture is usually more played out."[18]

London

When the respondents in London were asked about their ethnic identities they gave the following responses: black/West Indian; black/Caribbean; black/African, African, and Barbadian. What was significant about these responses was that the majority of the respondents ascribed to a hybrid identity expressed as a combination of black and some other ethnic identity. For many, this notion of "blackness" was developed in Britain in the 1960s in the context of British anti-black racism and partly due to the influence of the black power movement in the United States. According to Floya Anthias and Nira Yuval-Davis, two major criteria were used to define this concept. "First there is the notion of Blacks as sharing a common origin and culture and all that implies, and secondly, the notion of Blacks as sharing a common experience of racism and all that implies."[19] As a result of sharing this commonality, Asians, West Indians, and Africans were able to form a "united" coalition in order to speak to the issues they were facing. And it was within this forum that the concept black has taken on serious political undertones.

Coupled with the notion of commonality was also the issue of empowerment. This was expressed in the idea that as blacks they were able to not only speak with one voice but also facilitate certain changes that would benefit their communities. In the political arena this included: the push to eradicate the "stop and search" laws; the formation of organizations such as the Co-ordinating Committee Against Racial Discrimination and the Campaign Against Racial Discrimination (CARD); and the introduction of race-relations policies that benefited the black communities. In education it was seen in the emergence and growth of the supplementary and Saturday school program, and the continued fight for equality within the educational system.[20]

Thus, by embracing these particular identity conceptualizations, the first-generation participants highlighted the common features that they shared with other minorities and the forum this provided for their interaction with the larger society. It bears noting, however, that this collaboration was not limited to the political and educational arenas—it also found expression in the religious arena. Such collaborations were seen in having Afro-Caribbean, African, and Asian ministers as keynote speakers during the national convention of various black majority churches; coordinating prayer events like the Global Day of Prayer, London; and forming and participating in organizations like the National Church Leaders Forum (formerly the African Caribbean Evangelical Alliance), described as "a mechanism to articulate one voice for the Black Christian Movement in the United Kingdom."[21] However as the rest of their self-identification revealed, this collective unity was embraced only on a certain level, that is, only in interaction with the larger society. For within the black community itself, the other parts of their hybrid ethnic identities came to the fore.

Among the participants, the majority subscribed to a West Indian or Caribbean identity. According to Joe Aldred, by continuing to identify a group of people, many who are British citizens, "after where they have come from without reference to where they are, is to keep them in a permanent state of non-belonging, as 'foreigners.'"[22] While this statement may be true in terms of the wider society, it did not explain why these first-generation participants still adhered to their West Indian/Caribbean/African identities, even after living in Britain for over thirty years. The answers to this enquiry may lay in the response of one interviewee. She says: "My ethnic background . . . would be black. . . . Now I am also English, but it is [due to] my time of being here."[23] Here the participants' acceptance of an "English" identity only in terms of the length of her stay in Britain is noteworthy and calls us to interrogate some of the ideas that are associated with an English identity.

Historically, the term English has being linked with a sense of national belonging that was constructed in terms of an Anglo-Saxon ethnic consciousness—people sharing a common white heritage.[24] As a result it promoted an exclusive Englishness, one defined in terms of the concepts of blood, soil, and territory. Thus, England was perceived as a place for the English.[25] In the 1960s and 1970s, its opposition to "immigration and asylum, and general insularity and defensiveness" characterized this identity.[26] Thus, for many minority communities, the term English, as it relates to identity, was one that was seeped in racial undertones—calling attention to those who truly belonged and those who did not. For some, of the first-generation respondents, continuing to ascribe to a West Indian/Caribbean/African ethnic identity allowed them to root themselves in the culture and heritage of their homeland, a place where ethnically they are celebrated and nurtured. It also shed light on what they became, that is, they only became West Indian/Caribbean/African in the diaspora—prior to this, their primary identities were nationalistic.

Although their ethnic identity connected them to their homeland it was neither renegotiated nor lived out within that particular context. Instead its manifestation was within the British context, a place that had historically been hostile toward them.[27] It is in this regard that they took the features of their belongingness—their heritage and culture and used it to carve out a space of belonging within the British context. In this manner the renegotiation of their identity should not be typecast within a purely reactive framework. Instead, it needs to be perceived in a manner that acknowledges both the presence of the racism and discrimination that they experienced and the creative and instrumental ways they developed to thrive and live within such a context.

The remaining respondents described themselves in more nationalistic/regional fashion, African and Barbadian. What was significant about these two respondents was not only the manner in which they articulated their ethnic identity and the length of time they have resided within the London context, but also their interaction with their home context. Mary, a Ghanaian immigrant, describes herself in this manner:

> I usually say I am a child of God. . . . And apart from that I will say I am African. . . . And they will go forward and say, "Where are you from?" And I say, "I come from West Africa, [from] Ghana." . . . Then I'll say, "Ashanti." So they'll keep going on and on, and I will give the definite place where I, [where] my family come from, where I was born.[28]

As the above quotation revealed, one's birthplace or familial location, ethnic group, country, and region could all play a significant role in the process of one's identification. While each fashioned another layer of relating and identifying, it also combined with the others to make Mary the person that she was. Despite the orientation of her identities in various degrees toward Africa, Mary did not seem to have much contact with those back in Ghana. There were two specific times in which Ghana was mentioned in her interview—when she spoke about her identification and when she spoke about her written correspondence with her mother about wanting to become a radical, in other words, a politician who would help her people. In contrast, Mary spoke at length about the discrimination that she has experienced from both whites and blacks during her forty-two years residence in Britain. It is within this context that her African identities were being renegotiated. Mary stated:

> I was moved to the nurse's home [a residential facility for nurses]. . . . You encounter a lot of troubles from the sisters in the wards. . . . We have a lot of foreign people in the home and we were all together as a black people. We were together, when you come to any difficulty, we help one another. I must say you know the sisters were rough to us as a foreigner, . . . because we didn't have anywhere to go. They thought we were more or less like a slave and some of these sisters were so naïve, they didn't know much about the black people especially . . . when they hear that we have a different dialect. Because you know, when you come here you have an African accent and those who are born here got a different accent and that's why I never learned to change my accent because I wanted to be recognized as an African.[29]

Thus, for Mary, the renegotiation of her African identities allowed her to distinguish herself from the blacks born in Britain while simultaneously providing her with resources to live life in Britain. The desire to dissociate herself from the other blacks highlights some of the fission that exists within the black community. Although blacks of West Indian ancestry and those of African ancestry share a common ancestral origin, they were perceived, both by themselves and others, as having different cultures and histories, and thus existed as two separate ethnic groups. It is within this context that they competed for various social and economic advantages. In examining the friction that existed, one must acknowledge the role that certain stereotypes about each group played in the interaction among the groups. For some Africans, West Indians/Afro-Caribbeans were lazy and did not take full advantages of the opportunities they have been given, whereas to some West Indians/Afro-Caribbeans, the Africans were those who came to steal their jobs, and who reaped benefits without having to struggle for them.[30]

It is necessary to note that Mary's encounter with discrimination and racism fueled a desire to become a radical and also on some level anger with

God for allowing her people to be robbed by the whites. She expresses these sentiments as follows:

> When I see the things they rob us [of] because I come from a rich country where the resources are really in abundance. Then I came here and I saw that we are helping them to be [what] they are and we are poor. And anytime they speak, they speak against us, you know they call us . . . uncivilized. . . . How can [God] allow them to come and rob us? To make the nation as it is and we are poor and we are hungry. . . . To be honest, I wanted to be radical. . . . I wanted to be a politician you know. . . . To do what I can do within that scope to help my people.[31]

Her reconciliation with God and strength to continue living in Britain came from her mother's reply to her letter. Her mother said, "Listen God is God. He has a way to do it, just leave everything as it is and carry on what you are doing."[32] It is this belief that has enabled her to face the realities of life in Britain.

Like Mary's, June's identity was also oriented toward her homeland. June stated: "I'm proudly Barbadian. Yeah I prefer to say that I'm Barbadian, from the West Indies."[33] Unlike Mary, however, June had only lived in Britain for six years and was in constant contact with her family—especially her husband, who had been transferred back to Barbados. She stated that the initial decision to come to Britain was very difficult not only due to her job but also because she would be leaving her family for the first time.[34] Her primary reason for coming was to join her husband who was transferred to London by his employer. For June, her residence in Britain was temporary, "my reason for staying here . . . [is] because I have a particular goal. And that goal is to study more and to be of benefit to especially young people in the sense of church."[35] Thus, by maintaining a Barbadian identity, June continued to mark herself as the foreigner and a temporary resident in the wider British society while simultaneously remaining connected to the country to which she would return in the immediate future.

Religious identities

New York

Having examined some ways in which first-generation West Indian immigrants were renegotiating their ethnic identities, we will now investigate what types of religious identities were being perpetuated within the Pentecostal churches they attended. Two religious identities noted among the respondents were that of church leader and committed believer or saint. The most prominent however was that of saint. Within some Pentecostal circles, this identity is a product of several acts of grace—salvation, sanctification, and the baptism of the Holy Spirit. Following an individual's decision to accept Jesus as savior, that individual is expected to live a life that is holy and set apart unto God. It is within this context that the individual will experience the baptism of the Holy Spirit and thus be equipped for service to the world. During a sermon about prayer at a midweek service, a minister at Brooklyn church stated: "[God] wants to see our hearts transformed into a house of purity. [A] house purified and cleansed now [is] a house of healing, deliverance. [In this manner, the] church [can be] to the world what a hospital is to sick people."[36]

The saint identity, which has strong pietistic undertones, has traditionally been linked to a strict moral lifestyle, dependence on God in all aspects of one's lives, some levels of conservatism, minimal engagement in particular political and social activities (demonstrations, political actions focused on changing societal systems, partying, dancing, drinking etc.), and a high involvement/commitment to the church. All of these characteristics were observed among the respondents. For these saints, their relationship with Jesus Christ was a central element in their lives and a dominant feature of their religious identity. Thus, for them it was extremely important to live in a "holy" manner that would please God and communicate this identity. One informant articulated this as such:

> It is important to me personally, that I live and let the light shine as the word says. And somebody might wonder, "What is the light"? Somebody sees something that is different in you. There's something that is outstanding, there's something that somebody will always be able to see and that is what is important. Because people don't necessarily always want to hear you talk about God. . . . But even if they don't want to hear, if they can really look at you and say well she's talking about God and the way I see her act and what she does, no, how she dresses and things like they should be able to say, "Yeah! There is something different." I just trust God and pray and asked him to help me that I would live that life that will represent him.[37]

For some respondents, their dedication to pursuing and living a life that pleased God resulted in various blessings in their lives. For many, biblical precedence for this idea was provided by such scriptures like Deuteronomy 28 and 29 where obedience and commitment to God was seen as the prerequisite to the coming of blessings in the lives of adherents. Alternately, disobedience and lack of commitment resulted in bad things overtaking the adherents. According to one informant:

> We have a very faithful lot of folks. We see a lot of miracles right here. God has healed [the] sick, [people who had] stroke, [and] cancer. God has blessed his people tremendously. A lot of people [who] didn't [own] homes, bought their first. God has blessed them with homes. When I came here there wasn't that much cars, everybody have cars now. . . . Turns out you can say that God has been good to his people.[38]

The conservatism associated with the saint identity found its most notable expressions within the Pentecostal churches in matters of dress and in area of leadership. In regard to clothes, both genders were expected to dress in a modest manner. For the first-generation men this meant wearing a suit and tie to every service. For the women, this was equated to wearing a dress or a blouse and a skirt. For many first-generation women this also included wearing a hat or prayer cloth—a small circular piece of lace that is worn on one's head during church services. Theological justification for this practice was linked to scriptures like 1 Corinthians 11: 5-6, which admonishes women to have their heads covered during prayer. During my fieldwork, it was observed that there was some distinction in attire of the different generations. The majority of first-generation women in both Brooklyn churches wore hats and dresses or skirts that were several inches below the knee, while the men had short well-groomed haircuts, and wore suits and ties. In all, these articles of clothing were simultaneously conservative and formal in appearance and as such perpetuated the traditional West Indian sentiment of wearing one's best clothes to church. Among the immigrant children, there was the tendency to dress in a style that would be considered business casual—shirt and tie for young men, and a dress, or a blouse and a skirt for the young women. For these young women, the length of the dress or skirt was normally at the knee or slightly above it. In Beulah, most of the young women attended church with their heads uncovered. At Latter Rain Ministries in contrast, there was a mixture, with most young women wearing a prayer shawl and a minority having no head covering. One reason for the distinction in dress for the young women in both churches may have to do with the church leadership's particular interpretation of holiness. In Latter Rain Ministries, when the young women were serving on the choir or as ushers they were required to have on a prayer shawl. This was not the case in Beulah. Another reason may be the role of the pastor's children in the creating space for youth within key leadership positions in the church. In Latter Rain Ministries, this reality did not exist, while in Beulah, all of the pastors' children were in key positions and in these places they were spearheading the usage of technology in the services, the singing of contemporary gospel songs and other changes including what was seen as "appropriate" clothing for church. The place and role of the pastors' children will be discussed in more detail in Chapter 4.

Although the discussion concerning dress was a key issue of reflection and evaluation especially in regard to the second and third generation in both churches, it was more vocalized within Latter Rain Ministries. According to one respondent, Latter Rain Ministries was a place where they "believe in holiness." Therefore the issue of dress is highly important as she stated:

> Over the years I've been here, . . . the standard of you say, our adorning and the spirituality [has dropped]. You see a paradigm shift you know. No matter how you say [it], this is what the manual you know according to the scriptures say. It's still very lax and you know it's like oh well the anointing is over there and that person didn't have to do that, so why do we have to do that. We can get the anointing without wearing our hat or [by wearing] jewelry or [by not doing] certain little things that were real when I came here 30 plus years ago. I'm all for change but change for the better. I hate to know that something is going down, up yes, not down.[39]

For this respondent, laxity in dress among the youth was an indication of "something going down" in the church. This statement sheds light on an area of ongoing discussion and negotiation among the first generation, whose ideas of holiness and dress were shaped in the mid-twentieth century West Indian Pentecostal context (where ones' dress was perceived as an indication of ones' commitment to Jesus) and their children, whose ideas were being shaped in contemporary New York (where questions of outward appearance versus ones' heart condition are at the forefront of discussions).

Later in her interview this informant stated that despite this they had a fine bunch of young people within the church. She acknowledged that "they are not gonna be like us, they gonna do things differently but the main thing is to prepare [them for] faith [and] that's all I want, I mean that's the bottom line. I want to know that when I go to heaven they're there that's all."[40] Faith is presented here in an epistemological manner—seeking out knowledge. It is something that is learned and then expressed in ones' lifestyle. This preparation of faith was accomplished in several ways, namely: through the teaching given in Sunday school and the youth group; by preparing them for baptism; and by developing mentoring relationships with the young people. This was facilitated by the development of the concept of spiritual mother and father. The biblical mandate for such a relationship is given in the scriptures like Titus 2: 3-5 and Deut. 6: 6-7, that admonishes the elders and older women to teach the young men and women the ways of the Lord. Within this capacity, some of the first-generation men and women became models of masculinity and femininity, and the Christian lifestyle for the children and youth within the churches. Interestingly on many levels, the information conveyed to the young people by their mentors re-affirmed what was being taught by their parents. This included admonishing the young people to work hard, get a good education, and be committed in their service to the Lord.

For some first-generation women another feature of their religious identity was that of being a church leader. However, within this area a dichotomy existed in both churches. Although women were in leadership, and even in some key areas, the traditional male leadership roles were perpetuated. In Beulah, women functioned as the co-leader of the youth group, president of both the women's and evangelism ministries, minister of music, Sunday school teacher, licensed minister, secretary, and church treasurer. Coupled with these leadership positions various women in the church have been chosen to moderate and to preach at various Church services. However, within the denomination none of these women could become the senior minister/bishop of the church. As a result, no woman could hold any of the lead positions, and thus, had minimal input into the constitutional and/or significant decisions being made within the denomination. In terms of the ministry, the highest position that a woman could hold was that of a licensed minister. Within this capacity, a woman was authorized to preach and officiate during the services. However, she was not allowed to administer communion or baptize members since these activities can only be performed by an ordained minister, who within the denomination could only be a man. In Beulah Church, the senior minister's wife, who was also the co-founder of the church, was the only woman who holds this office. One informant, who has served in various leadership capacities, articulates the dynamic pertaining to leadership and the place of women within Pentecostal churches in the following manner:

> I realize that like in the secular world, in the business world that [there are] some places a woman is only allowed to go so much. So it doesn't matter her educational background, her qualification, [she's] not allowed to [have] certain roles. I think they call it the glass ceiling and I see some of that in the Pentecostal church as well.[41]

For this respondent the presence of the "glass ceiling" within the church, confirmed for her that although much change had been accomplished, there was still much to the done.

It is interesting to note that in Beulah, women's leadership especially in the ministerial areas—licensed minister, minister of music—was linked to the concept of calling, that is, an individual given a certain duty by God and is equipped by the Holy Spirit to accomplish that task within the church. As a result, it is believed that the women who occupied these positions did so only because they were called to serve in these capacities. It was this call that was discerned and affirmed in the licensing procedure. This process included: first being recommended by a local senior minister to the regional governing body; second successfully completing both the examinations and the oral defense about one's calling before a panel of senior ministers. In Beulah, the two women who held licenses were both related to the senior minister/bishop—they were his wife and daughter.

In Latter Rain Ministries, women also held various leadership positions. They were: missionaries, a key leader, president of the youth group and the women's ministry, choir directors, and leaders of the Sunday school. Although they occupied these positions that played a vital role in the church, they were noticeably absent from the key leadership positions. During fieldwork, I observed that at the Sunday morning and midweek services only men sat on the podium and preached.[42] Although women were allowed to moderate, this activity was more prominent during an evening service versus the Sunday morning service. Thus, within most Sunday morning services, visible female participation was focused on specific activities such as singing, Bible reading, ushering, and giving the announcements. Within Latter Rain Ministries' leadership structure only one female was present—Sister Grace. She was responsible for the majority of the official information that comes into and goes out of the ministry. She was also instrumental in planning and organizing the Annual Church Convention.

> Convention is not just coming together. It's coming together yes but reflecting on where we've been and where we're going. And not only that, but there must be a theme, God is saying something to us. . . . Since I became [a leader], I go to prayer and fasting [as] soon as the Christmas is over. And [I] start seeking the Lord as to what would he have us to do this year and what he wants to say to us. And it means hearing him, [getting] the scripture that he would have used to be the theme. Formulate a letter of invitation, and then to take it in to Bishop, and you know, meet his approval.[43]

As a missionary she has traveled to several other countries to initiate branches. She was also involved in the pastoral care ministry and home and hospital visitation. She took a chaplaincy course so that she could do her job in the ministry well. Unofficially, she was the go-to person for information on housing, jobs, immigration etc.[44] She was an intercessor, one of the primary mothers in the church and a stalwart member whose words carried a lot of weight. In all of these capacities, Sister Grace exerted tremendous influence within the church. During my fieldwork it was Sister Grace who introduced me to the congregation and who "granted" me access to respondents within the church. When Sister Grace was asked about her position in the leadership of the church she replied with two significant statements. First, she saw her positions within the church ministry in the context of her calling. In this manner she was very similar to the women in key leadership positions at Beulah. Second, because God called her to this ministry, she did not allow herself to be intimidated by anyone.

> Matthew 11:12 says, "the kingdom of God suffers violence and the violent have to take it by force." And I thank God that I'm not only a authoritative but I'm also a authoritarian and I'm aggressive. It wasn't always like that's cause when the Lord baptize me with the Holy Ghost I don't even think he know what was gonna happen with this one. . . . I give God all the honor, the glory, and the praise. But I refuse; I don't let anything intimidate me. It doesn't faze me.[45]

London

The religious identities expressed by the respondents within the London context were primarily that of the saint, and the child of God. The saint identity exhibited by many of the respondents was constructed through a process of othering—that is, the saint versus the sinner. The renegotiation of this identity within a growing secularized British context was especially significant for the respondents. When the West Indians arrived in Britain in the 1950s and 1960s, they believed that they were coming to a Christian nation. Instead they found one that was increasingly secular and understated in its religiosity.[46] In the years following the Second World War (1945–60), the churches in Britain underwent a period of reconstruction during which efforts were focused on rebuilding the physical structures, restoring flagging attendance and participation, and reviving the prewar institutions. The most symbolic representation of this sense of restoration was the Coronation of Elizabeth II in June 1953. Although these efforts were moderately successful, especially during the 1950s, they did not last. By the 1960s the churches were faced with the reality of becoming irrelevant within the society. In their pursuit to be relevant, "to be in rather than out of step with the world," the churches adopted a series of reforms largely modeled after the secular world.[47]

Faced with this secularized context, even within the churches, some of the immigrants drew upon on the saint religious identity that was formulated within their homelands to not only mark themselves as the "religious other," but also to resist "the pressures to adapt to British ways of thought."[48] During an interview an informant stated: "I got my background from home as a Christian. So I made it up in my mind [that] come what may when I come to this country nobody is gonna let me go apart, [go] astray. And I held onto my integrity and never let anybody push me."[49] For many of these respondents, their identity as a saint, that is, as the "religious other," was expressed in various mediums. One was as a member of a black-led or black majority church. This type of identification however is one that requires interrogation, for as Gerrie ter Haar concluded in the case of Africans in the Netherlands, the development of an alternate Christian identity as opposed to a universal one may serve the interests of Europeans rather than the immigrants.[50] This identity—West Indian Pentecostalism or Afro-Caribbean Christianity—as it was ascribed to the immigrants by the wider society served to highlight the distinctiveness between this expression of Christianity and what was perceived as "religious orthodoxy," that is, the theology and practices associated with the Western Christianity. Simultaneously, it continued to mark these particular Christian expressions and those who participate in these congregations as exotic and therefore not worthy of serious conversation and interaction. Both the distinctiveness and the exoticism that was associated with the immigrant churches' expressions of Christianity may result, as was the case in Britain, in the legitimate concerns raised by West Indian Christians about racism, prejudice, lack of welcome, etc., within the churches and society being dismissed as the musings of those who were ignorant of the way the system worked.

For many of the respondents, another medium through which the saint identity was communicated was by one's manner of dress that is, "looking like a Christian."

> I have heard, and it was a pretty common thing to say, you could look at the person and know that they're Christian. I don't know if it's quite possible. In the 1950's, early 60's to see a Christian [woman] wear a trousers suit would be almost demeaning and they would say, "Look at her!" Today that isn't an issue anymore. So the identity I'm talking about, . . . in the 1950's to see a lady in a female suit, you would feel that person [has gone] astray, today it is different.[51]

As this respondent notes, although certain changes had taken place in terms of dress, some people, especially the first-generation respondents, still felt that the "traditional" way of dressing was the right and holy way.

A third medium associated with the saint identity manifested by the respondents was a high level of involvement within the church. This involvement was conceptualized as being very committed to the things of the Lord—which was expressed in the sacrifice of one's time, money, and life in service to God. One informant described this commitment as follows:

> These are the days when I pray and say, "Lord, send the message for the hour that men and women will know that it's all about you." It is not half in the world, half in the church. Coming to the church and [not having] for the rest of the week that commitment, that connection to God, reading his word and praying. You've got to keep that in mind you know. There are people who are, you can see that they're committed but to me not fully, not half of the congregation as it were.[52]

What was noteworthy about these members was the manner in which they worked to build Kingsbridge NTCG Church and the NTCG denomination. Carol, a long standing member of Kingsbridge, described the members' commitment and sacrifice as follows:

> [We] rent halls and eventually we were in a Scout hall. And then the pastor [was] always look[ing] around and [he] saw this building [for sale]. . . . The members, we used to have to give our 50 pence, and £5 and £10. . . . It was in a state and the members, and the brethren, the different trades, the carpenters, the painter, and everybody and the ladies come every evening and cleanup. And everybody you know play[ed] their part.[53]

One respondent, who was instrumental in the establishment of several NTCG churches in the Midlands, also related his experience.

> Although I used to help others, in Coventry I was the chairman for the team that evangelized Coventry. So we would leave Birmingham where we lived and travel down in a car and we go from house to house. We see a door over there and we actually targeted black people. . . . And then you try and get . . . children for Sunday school. Then as soon as possible get a little school hall. And people would pay money for the little hall, sometimes out of our own pockets or the pockets of the group of people in the car.[54]

In embracing the religious identity of a child of God the respondents communicated a status of somebodiness and a relationship of belonging.[55] For many of them, this identity was especially important given the racialized and discriminatory environments in which they lived and worshipped. Being a child of God allowed them to "deal" with the discrimination and ill treatment knowing that in the end God would vindicate them. One respondent expressed this identity in the context of being harassed by someone at work. Her response in the face of this treatment was to make a declaration of her identity as a child of God. She stated:

> I would say I am a child of God you know. And the blood of Jesus Christ's dwell in me and his faith is in me and you are worried. It's not me you're seeing in the night or day. It's the spirit of God using my image to warn you that there's something drastic going to happen to you if you don't change your attitude towards me. . . . Two weeks later this woman was sacked.[56]

For three women, a major part of their religious identity was being a minister. The construction of this identity was especially significant for the two first-generation ministers, given the prohibition that exists within some Pentecostal churches regarding women in ministry. For one of the three, her ministerial identity was fashioned in the context of being a pastor's wife and very involved in church ministry. As a result of the ministerial identity, she enjoyed a certain level of independence, gained several opportunities to preach and be involved in ministry, and acquired a position from which she could address some of the pressing needs within the church. She stated: "I was a driver and I had my own car; he had his own car. So we drove some mornings, we both go out together and sometimes I will go different places [since] I might be preaching somewhere else." On one occasion, she went to a church to preach despite her husband's opposition. On that Sunday, her younger brother became a Christian as a result of her sermon. Although this informant did not give the impression during her interview that this behavior was the norm in her relationship with her husband, however it does highlight the conviction that in some cases when an individual is convinced of the leading of the Holy Spirit, then opposing one's husband was justified. Since her husband's retirement from ministry and subsequent death two years earlier, she has been involved in the preaching occasionally at Kingsbridge. During my fieldwork, she was at the planning stage of developing a ministry geared toward widows. According to her this was an important ministry because there are "*quite a lot of widows* in Kingsbridge church." She later stated:

> If you were to see people after they lost their husband, they're just depressed, stressed, held down. It's only the word of God that can really help. . . . I know this is definitely handed down to me from the Lord. And I will have to definitely do

it. That is something he wants me do now and I [am] going to do it. But I have to speak to [the senior pastor] about it and then you know get some, get some knowledge of how to start.[57]

For another who was the wife of a respondent, her religious identity was constructed in the context of being the pastor of a church. In this capacity she was able to preach, teach, and officiate at services. However, as her husband stated, she was not able to conduct communion or the baptismal services. Therefore although her ministry was validated, she was given a license and was the pastor of a church, it was her husband, the deacon, who was allowed to give communion and baptize the believers. It should be noted that his wife's identity as a minister was also firmly fixed within the concept of a calling. He stated:

[After] her mother died she went to Jamaica [for] the funeral. . . . When she came back she said, "Now my mom die I am going to move out to do something more for the Lord." We sat down . . . [and] she spoke with me with the pastor. . . . She spoke with him and came back. "Just go, just go and preach." And although you said go preach, if you've got the calling for preaching you can start even with your first neighbour you know. So she just start out like that. And then after that. . . they find that she's got a calling. . . . After a while she [had] to take some tests . . . [and they] give her a kind of lay license, lay preacher. Yes and that's where she started from until she get a little church.[58]

Manifestation of identities in the Pentecostal churches

So far in this chapter we have examined the ways in which West Indian immigrants in New York and London are renegotiating their ethnic and religious identities. In this section, we will analyze the manner in which these renegotiated identities are being demonstrated within the Pentecostal religious arena.

One of the dynamics that has been a driving force within Pentecostalism is the issue of empowerment. This was articulated within the belief that the baptism of the Holy Spirit was available to everyone, regardless of race, education, or gender. As a result many people who had been marginalized within the society could now become God's mouthpiece and in the process find a sense of dignity, empowerment, identity, and community.[59] For the first-generation immigrants in New York and London, this was also the case. The Pentecostal churches functioned as a place where they were leaders, the vessels of clay through whom God revealed himself. For many respondents empowerment was also linked to their re-creation of home. Thus within the churches in New York and London, many of the rituals were conducted in a manner that was similar to those found within Pentecostal churches in the West Indies. This re-creation of home however was indelibly connected with the formation of a spiritual family. This family was based on their common status as believers in Christ and thus children of God. This was a family that was there to encourage, support, love, and care for the immigrant as they navigated life within the metropolitan contexts. One informant relayed her experience in the following way:

> I was diagnosed with leukemia like six years ago. . . . When I found out, with church it took me a long time before I told anyone and when I finally did I think I told [a close church sister] and the pastor's wife. I wasn't going to tell people cause it was you know, just [didn't know] how to deal with it. In a way I remember I think the first time when I called the pastor's wife I remember [her saying that] they [would] call a day of fasting for me. I wasn't in church but a little bird told me, they asked everybody to fast. You know [from] the oldest to the youngest. . . . I remember . . . going back to the doctor and doing all of these tests and the doctors tell me that at the moment if they see any changes they would have to start putting me on medication. . . . So then they have me do like a bone marrow tests. . . . I think I must have went to about four or five specialists and all of them found the same thing. But after going to them like twice a month, then once a month to do all the test to see if there were any changes, there were no changes whether negative or positive. . . . So for the past six years nothing changed. But I know that . . . lot of prayers, and fastings have gone up for me. I know God did something. . . . I believe that God heal me.[60]

Although this informant was angry about her personal life being revealed to the members of the church she said, "[their reaction] made me see that the people were really concerned about me with the fasting. [So] going back to the question about the day of fasting I was happy that the brethren wanted to do that."[61] In this particular incident, a case of boundary violation nevertheless contributed to the formation of a family identity and the accompanying sense of belonging.

Another way in which the Pentecostal churches empowered migrants was by being a place where they are valued and celebrated. From the time of its development, the city has been seen by some people not only as the center for economic, political, and social activities but also a place of danger, squalor, and the "exotic locales of forbidden sensual delights."[62] Simultaneously the city was also a site of freedom, isolation, and continuous change. For as the German sociologist Georg Simmel noted, with the pursuit of the money economy within the city, there has emerged a "purely matter-of-fact attitude in the treatment of persons and things in which formal justice is often combined with an unrelenting hardness."[63] Thus there was the tendency for people's daily lives to be filled "with weighing, calculating, enumerating and the reduction of qualitative values to quantitative terms."[64] Within this quantitative environment, an individuals' worth was measured in terms of what one was able to produce or contribute to the society—which in turn was linked to one's education, race, gender etc. When West Indian migrants are evaluated using this form of measurement, many are deficient. It was within this context that Kingsbridge, Beulah, and Latter Rain Ministries provided a place of belonging, support, encouragement, and assistance for their members.

One group for whom this assistance was especially vital was the unauthorized. Within the United States, an individual's immigrant status is of primal importance. For many West Indians, it meant the difference between achieving the "American Dream" and the status that it produces versus being excluded from various levels of the society and in some cases subjected to exploitation for others' financial gain. By virtue of their unauthorized status, these immigrants were legally not permitted to work. As a result, most of the jobs that they procured are low-paying service jobs as nannies, home care attendants, cooks, and/or cashiers in various West Indian bakeries/restaurants, etc. In these positions, many immigrants did not have any benefits—health care, disability, sick days, vacation, etc. Instead, many of them were in positions where they could be exploited or abused by their employers and forced to work in appalling conditions.

For the unauthorized immigrants in New York, both Latter Rain Ministries and Beulah provided a place of belonging, a place where one's immigration status was a nonissue. Within both churches the undocumented person was seen first and foremost as a child of God and thus a member of the church family. The child of God identity was applicable to everyone, however given the vulnerability and potential for exploitation that can mark the lives of the unauthorized immigrant, having such a place of belonging and support was particularly significant. As a member of the church family, unauthorized immigrants are given various kinds of support and social care—information about jobs, housing, immigration, prayer support, some financial assistance, and in some cases, an opportunity to legalize their status. Within the churches, the unauthorized persons were not excluded from the ministry of the church, and thus have equal access to various leadership opportunities. These may include leadership in the Sunday school, choir, auxiliary ministries, deacons' board, administrative positions, and participating in the preaching ministry in the church.[65] According to one of the leaders at Beulah, "we [the church,] will embrace all of God's children who are undocumented. [In fact], we have some in our church right now."[66] In regard to the role that the church played in the lives of some of their undocumented members the same respondent stated:

> [The government] think that if you don't have certain papers, green card . . . you feel lost. But to me we're not here to deny anybody. . . . At one time we could have filed for them [the undocumented] through our church. . . . You have to consider the church, [and it's] financial ability. . . . You were not paying them actually but you could what you call give them some help. If you're not here legally you have [no] . . . right to work. . . . Some people, they get a little thing on the side, you call that "get it on the side." So we, we try our best to help [a] few people. . . . You have people that we file for and have gotten through now in our church and by right they're supposed to be [here], because that was the agreement that they would become full fledged members of that local church because since they are under the umbrella of that local church.[67]

The above quote highlights not only the process from the church leadership's standpoint but also calls attention to the loyalty that was expected from the undocumented migrant who was helped. However, as the above quote also indicated, this assistance did not automatically result in a lifelong loyalty to the church.

Another area in which the churches have helped to empower the first generation was encouraging them to pursue an education and to buy a home. This was conveyed primarily through the sermons and the influence of the senior minister, and implementing measures to celebrate the accomplishments of the members. In both Beulah and Kingsbridge, it was observed that whenever a member obtained a certificate or degree, a special ceremony was conducted during the Sunday morning service to celebrate these achievements. This included calling the individual to the front of the church and reading aloud the citation documented on the certificate or degree. Following this the individual would be presented with their certificate or degree by one of the ministers. Although such a ceremony was not noted within Latter Rain Ministries, they have designated one Sunday in June to celebrate all of the graduates within the church. They have also implemented a scholarship fund to provide some financial assistance to the young people within the congregation who are attending university.

One activity noted among West Indians immigrants, particularly among Christians, which encourages them to purchase homes, is a house dedication/ warming party. In this celebration, members from the church were invited to the new house to offer thanksgiving to God for the new home, request his protection and blessings for the inhabitants, and to eat and fellowship with fellow church members. Another forum that was used to encourage the members to pursue their education and home ownership was the sermon. For a minister, the Sunday sermon provided him with an important tool in influencing the members of a church. He stated:

> I said that as long as I'm here I don't want anybody to come back on the pulpit and decry education. We had very few nurses and only nursing was the thing here. . . . But since that, since I'm here, I believe a lot people have gone on to university, some who have gone to do their masters, you even have people were working on their doctorate, who have started. . . . So I am pleased from that point to see the number of people who are studying.[68]

Later in the same interview he also shared the following:

> I have watched people also buy their own houses. That's another thing that I believe in and talk [about] that people should come out of the rent house or lease or the tenancy places. You go into these tenant houses, you live there your full life paying week after week and when you're old you walk out and leave the house and you have nothing to show. So I supposed I have influenced people. I have at least helped people own their own house. And [a] lot of people here are house owners and the fact that house prices are going up it means that we can have something. Even if they haven't got their own savings they have a property.[69]

The encouragement in regard to home ownership is particular interesting given the West's critique of a market-based value system. For the immigrants in New York and London, home ownership is seen as a way of building financial stability so that immigrants can care for themselves in their later years, and possibly pass on something to their children when they die. With the US and UK social security benefits as they are currently, having alternative retirement funds have become a necessity. Historically, within the United States, this type of intergenerational transmission of wealth has been low within minority families, particularly that of blacks. As a result, blacks as a whole are at a disadvantage compared to whites when it comes to the economic, educational, and other opportunities they are able to offer to their children. In Britain, this intergenerational transmission of wealth occurred primarily among the titled gentry or upper classes. Given these realities, the pastors' encouragement in regard to home ownership should not be viewed as being complicit with the market-based value system but assisting his members in creating a new trajectory of financial stability that would be of benefit to them and their family in the years to come.[70]

As the above documentation indicated, many first-generation immigrants found their Pentecostal churches to be a place of acceptance, support, and empowerment. However, it bears noting that for others, these churches could also become places of disempowerment and marginalization. Sometimes the transformation process, whereby various West Indian cultural and religious features were transcribed into the new context in a manner that enabled first generation to recreate home, could also serve to make the churches places of exclusion. This was a dynamic observed in all three churches—Latter Rain Ministries, Beulah, and Kingsbridge. According to the sign posted outside of church building, Latter Rain Ministries is a place for all nations. However, a close examination of the church demographics revealed that its membership is primarily West Indian. Although Latter Rain Ministries was located in a section of Brooklyn that was 85.2 percent African American, this larger black population was not necessarily reflected in its membership.[71] During fieldwork it was also observed that both church entrances and church parking lot were gated. Although these gates were there for security purposes it does call us to question the type of image these padlocked gates presented to the surrounding community. Within Beulah, which was located in an area that had a smaller black population, this segment of the population was also noticeably absent. Some of the possible deterrents to African American involvement within these churches were: the stereotypes often perpetuated about them within the West Indian community, the lack of outreach to African Americans and the other ethnic groups that resided within the community; and the prominence of various West Indian religious and cultural elements within the churches.

Within Kingsbridge, the perpetuation of certain West Indian religious and cultural elements had resulted in the marginalization of several other ethnic groups, especially whites. According to one informant:

> We would like that when you come into this church it would reflect the community. It will reflect various cultures, it will reflect different nationalities and I think that's what we would like however I find that unless we take a few steps back that's gonna be very difficult to achieve. And we will have one or two Whites in the congregation but whether they stay, sometimes they stay for short period . . . but on a whole and it's predominantly a black community. And I don't think we're going to achieve this multicultural congregation unless we actually strategically look at the community, actually identify who is in our community, actually look at ways of bringing in, and we have to make changes.[72]

However this perspective about becoming a multicultural congregation is not readily shared by all of the members. According to one informant, the absence of whites was not due to the perpetuation of various West Indian ethnic and religious elements but instead to some whites coming and wanting "to take over [and] that sort of thing. They still have this superiority in them whereby they feel that they're superior and [do] not have to take instruction from us."[73] Thus for this informant, the cultural and religious dynamics evidenced in Kingsbridge allowed them to create an environment where they are not discriminated against due to the color of their skin. Given the historical and contemporary racial dynamics existing within Britain, having such a place of belonging continues to be of vital importance for many members of the black/West Indian community.

Having discussed the ways in which the Pentecostal churches function as places of empowerment, it is also necessary to discuss some of the performative and economic expressions found within the churches. This discussion is important because it give us a glimpse of the ways in which churches and these particular expressions enables the relocation of certain elements from the country of origin into the new context, which in turn facilitates a positive construction of meaning around different aspects of their lives as an immigrant. One of the most important expressions noted within all three churches is the role of music and songs. In the Praise and Worship format, songs and the accompanied music are perceived "as setting the stage for the rest of the service."[74] However by using the same hymnal that is used in the homeland and singing the same choruses, these songs and music also function as a transnational tie that connects the immigrants with their country of origin.

In immigrant's interaction with the host context, these songs and music expressed in the church may also function as

> a medium through which the migrant's culture and identities are celebrated and treated as the norm, and the migrants themselves are reminded of their identity as saints. . . . As saints they had access to the Trinity—Father, Son and Holy Spirit. Thus, where their race, gender and education might limit the positions they could hold within the wider society, in the religious community this is not the case. . . . As a result, the marginalized . . . can become God's mouthpiece, or a vessel used for his service. . . . For many West Indian migrants, this experience is an emotional watershed. It is from this place of empowerment that West Indian believers are able to declare with fervor and conviction:
>
> "Press along saints, press along in God's own way. Press along saints, press along in God's own way. Persecution we must face, trials and crosses in our way. For the hotter the battle, the sweeter the victory!"[75]

Therefore the same songs and music that connected the immigrant to their country of origin, also provided them with a way of navigating the realities of the new context. These songs and music thus also functioned as a vehicle of affirmation, empowerment, support, and hope. In turn it offered the immigrant a way of coping with the many difficulties that could accompany immigrant daily life while reminding them of the victory that was to come. Victory here could be interpreted to include both material and spiritual benefits.

Another expression observed particularly within the London context was the presence of a Rally—a Jamaican term for a church fundraising concert.[76] During the Rally, several churches with which Kingsbridge had an affiliation were invited and each was asked to give an item—that is, a song, a poem, or an instrumental presentation. Following each rendition, the audience was called upon to pay for the item. It bears noting that the price designated for each item varies depending on how much the audience was "moved" by the performance. "Moved" is used in this context instead of enjoyed because as Christians the assumption is that those who are performing are doing so under the anointing of the Holy Spirit. As the audience reacts to this performance, the Holy Spirit also moves among them. For some of these "moving" items, several individuals will engage in a standard Rally practice called fanning. During the performance several members of the audience would surround the performer and begin to fan them with paper money. When the performance ends, this money is then collected. This practice of fanning or spraying of money is not limited to the West Indian community, it also found in African context, especially during weddings and dances. At the end of the Rally, a representative from each team will come forward to declare the amount of money that team has gained. This portion of the program is very lively—filled with laughter, clapping, and comments stating that "next year this team will be the top team." Money raised in this Rally is normally allocated for the renovation work on the church building or some other church project. Thus in the Rally, one is able to note the ways in which various West Indian religious/ cultural elements have being relocated and re-positioned within the very fabric of immigrant religious expression.

As the immigrant navigates the terrains of the host context, he/she not only re-creates certain aspects of home but also adapts certain elements within his or her religious expressions. Two such expressions of adaptation were noted within the Brooklyn context. They were the presence of a religious enterprise and the emergence of an annual pastor's appreciation service. Religious enterprise was defined as the church's engagement in economic activity. Within its community Beulah functioned as not only a church but also as a landlord. By renting out apartments, the church gained an additional source of revenue, which enabled the church to pay off their mortgage and to become debt free in the eleven years after purchasing their building. For Latter Rain Ministries, the addition of the Manor, or church hall, to the main sanctuary, has provided it with a space that they were able to rent to other churches and people for various functions. The money gained from this venture was incorporated into the overall financial resources of the church. One of the things noted about New York is the lack of space. As a result, making optimal use of one's property is essential. In both of these examples of religious enterprise we see several ways in which the churches were utilizing their space for additional purposes that were beneficial to them.

Conclusion

For the first-generation immigrants the construction and the internalization processes whereby boundaries are legitimized and identities are articulated occur within a migration framework. Thus, it is their myriads of connections linking their localities of origin with those to which they migrate that helps them to forge a nexus from which emerges their "new" concept of the self and the other. For the first-generation West Indian immigrants examined in this chapter, this process involved using the ethnic and religious identities from their countries of origin to negotiate what it means to be a West Indian Pentecostal in a foreign land. For the immigrants in New York these ethnic identities include describing themselves either within nationalist or a black/West Indian-oriented rhetoric. Located within these identifications were the ideas of being the "model immigrant," who through hard work would achieve the "American Dream" and the distancing of oneself from the lifestyle associated with the lower income African American communities. In London, the identities being negotiated were in the hybrid formulation, with one part highlighting the notion of blackness that has its origins in the racial British society of the 1960s and the other ethnic, linking them to their country of origin. For the immigrants in both cities, the religious identities they were negotiating were around being a saint, a church leader, and a child of God, with questions about dress across generations, and the presence of the glass ceiling in regard to women being in leadership at the forefront of discussion. In carving out this space created by these identities, the immigrants call the host society to acknowledge their presence, not just as foreigners and thus the other but as viable and important segments of the society.

For many first-generation West Indian immigrants the immigrant church is vitally important. It is a place where they despite their immigration status are empowered, supported, and loved. However in this process of fulfilling these purposes, immigrant churches can also function as places of marginalization for both people inside and outside the churches. It will therefore be imperative for the first generation within the churches to reexamine the ways in which the church is being constructed. Such investigation will be essential especially in light of the emergence and the coming of age of the second, third, and later generations. Will these immigrant churches that have been places of acceptance and empowerment for the first generation continue to fulfill such functions for the immigrant children? It will also be important to investigate how these empowering elements found within the immigrant churches can be creatively translated into measures that facilitate the transformation of the wider communities. Answering these questions will serve to challenge the immigrant churches and their first-generation members in regard to both their definition of what constitutes church, and how they can continue to be a manifestation of Christ's body in the world. These and the questions surrounding the construction of identities among immigrant children form the basis of the chapter that follows.

4

Creating Space: Identity Construction Among West Indian Immigrant Youth

On forms I put African-American [laugh]. I'm a born American but I'm not American. My upbringing is, I would say definitely West Indian and West Indian is from my parent's background. . . . I was born here [Brooklyn, NY], I went to school here, I would say it's a mixture of both but it's mostly a lot of West Indian brought-upsy.

Second-generation male

For immigrant youth, the issue of identity is not always well-defined. As the above quote reveals, there is a measure of fluidity that underlies this process depending on what is required in any given circumstance. For this young man, on the forms that he had to complete for school, a job, etc., he chose African American. However, he immediately followed this statement by highlighting that although he was born American, he was not American. As a result of his upbringing he was West Indian. Thus, while he acknowledged that his identity was a mixture of American and West Indian, there was no doubt which of the two played the dominant role in his life. As he stated, "It's mostly a lot of West Indian brought-upsy."

Furthermore, when the identity discourse was applied to the religious immigrant youth, several dynamics had to be incorporated into the discussion—multiple cultures, religion, and youth.[1] Each of these factors, both in their singularity and amalgamation, had profound effects on the process through which boundaries were legitimized and allegiances were constructed, practiced, and directed in regard to the insider and the outsider.[2] According to Simon Coleman and Peter Collins, "Migrants engage in multiple cultural worlds that are dynamically intertwined and are thereby involved in complex processes of self-creation."[3] Among immigrant youth the accuracy of this statement becomes apparent when one considers the liminal position in which they exist. On the one hand, they are being shaped by the worldview, traditions, and practices of their parents' homeland and the host society. Alternatively, they are also actively engaged in a process of discovery that has various biological, psychological, cognitive, and social dimensions. According to Erik Erikson, the primary task of adolescence is identity development, one that is only complete "when the individual has subordinated his childhood identifications to a new kind of identification, achieved in absorbing sociability and in competitive apprenticeship with and among his age mates."[4] As adolescents and young adults navigate this terrain of self-understanding and discovery within the diaspora, one pivotal question they ask is: Who am I? Not just in relation to others but more specifically in terms of their reason for being.[5] In religion, they not only find a "natural medium for exploring these questions" but also another key resource for both identity formation and maintenance.[6] Given their liminality in relation to their parents and the society, as well as the "discovery" processes in which they are engaging it is necessary to investigate how West Indian immigrant youth are constructing and developing identities within the Pentecostal faith communities in which they and their families participate.

In this chapter, I argue that the immigrant faith communities function as a crucible in which several elements resulting in the construction of the immigrant youth's ethnic and religious identities converge and are fashioned into the concepts of self and the other, and the emergent practices that such conceptualizations embody in their lives are manifested both within these religious communities and the society at large. This chapter will be divided into three sections, each highlighting one aspect of the developmental processes in which immigrant youth are involved. The first section will discuss how they are interacting with the diasporan contexts. The second will detail the types of ethnic and religious identities being constructed by immigrant youth within these religious communities as a result of this interaction. The third highlights some features of the dialectic process in which they and the other members of the religious communities are engaged as they all seek to negotiate the societal terrains and live out their faith.

Dealing with home

The interaction between the immigrant youth and the home context is a complex encounter governed by and generating various concepts and attitudes about the self and the other, which in turn produce certain behavioral manifestations in the lives of those involved.[7] Within the sociological arena this encounter or meeting is described in terms of assimilation, which Robert E. Park and Ernest W. Burgess define as "a process of interpretation and fusion in which persons and groups acquire memories, sentiments, and attitudes of other persons or groups, and, by sharing their experience and history, are incorporated with them in a common cultural life."[8]

Although the assimilation theories discussed in this section deal specifically with the American context, they are also applicable to Britain. For within both contexts, the study of immigrants is normally conducted with the underlying assumption that assimilation into the dominant or core society is the prescribed trajectory. Such a mind-set can be problematic for, as stated in Chapter 3, some immigrants migrated with the intention of staying a short time in the host country. For this group, it was their continued connection to the country of origin and not assimilation into the host country that remained their primary focus. So even while they did what was needed to settle in that place, such as getting a job, having children, etc., a desire to eventually return remained. It was only later, after they had spent the majority of their lives in the diaspora, that many of them resolutely acknowledge that their "home" had become the host country (some others did return home). In New York and London, the desire to return home, primarily among the first generation, was evident from the perpetuation of the dream of acquiring a house "back home" upon retirement. While some of the later generations saw "back home" as a crucial part of their identities, for them it was not necessarily a place of eventual return.

Historically within the United States context, assimilation has been seen as following a straight-line trajectory, which resulted in identificational assimilation, that is, the development of a self-image that is wholly American. Although some scholars acknowledge that the characteristics of the post-1965 migrants are different in comparison to those of earlier migrants, they still assert that given time, these new migrants will also assimilate to this wholly American self-image that is based on the lives and values of white middle-class Americans.[9]

In *Assimilation in American Life*, Milton Gordon presents a typology of assimilation that serves to explicate some of the complexities involved within this process.[10] He is careful to note that the assimilation process is a matter of degree—in other words, each of the types or subprocesses may take place in varying degrees. The first subprocess of assimilation is cultural assimilation or acculturation and this takes place when the minority group arrives in the host society. During this subprocess, the cultural patterns of the minority group are changed to those of the host society.[11] The second subprocess is structural assimilation and intermarriage. In this stage the minority group is involved in large-scale entrance into cliques, clubs, and institutions of the host society on a primary group level.[12] Accompanying structural assimilation and intermarriage is the full involvement in the core society, which is albeit observed only in the absence of discrimination and prejudice toward the immigrants from members of the host society.

Gordon notes, however, that acculturation does not automatically lead to assimilation. In fact, he argues that in some cases "acculturation of the minority group may take place even when none of the other types of assimilation occurs simultaneously or later, and this condition of 'acculturation only' may continue indefinitely." For Gordon, the reasons for the "accommodation only" condition are twofold. One is spatial isolation or segregation in a rural context, as is the case of the American Indians on the reservations. The second is due to "marked discrimination . . . [that] succeeds in keeping vast numbers of the minority group deprived of educational and occupational opportunities and thus predestined to remain in a lower-class setting," as is the case with the African American lower-class population. Therefore, for Gordon, the pivotal stage in this process is structural assimilation because once it "has occurred, either simultaneously with or subsequent to acculturation, all of the other types of assimilation will naturally follow . . . like a row of tenpins bowled over in rapid succession by a well placed strike."[13]

When the straight-line assimilation theory is applied to children of white European immigrants who arrived in the United States prior to the 1920s, the predictions are confirmed—with each successive generation, the immigrant youth were more American, and experiencing greater social mobility and integration into the host society. For many of these white Americans, their ethnic identities as Irish, Italians, etc., became an optional, familial, or symbolic ethnicity, one which they could emphasize or subvert depending on the circumstances they were in.[14] It is worth noting that the majority of the European immigrant groups, that is, the Irish, Jews, and Italians, were at one time perceived by native-born whites as being racially distinct from them and were thus subjected to massive religious and racist theorizing at the height of the mass migration in the early twentieth century.[15] With time as these immigrant groups intermarried with other whites and moved up the socioeconomic ladder some of these distinctions faded.

With regard to the children of the post-1965 immigrants, however, this straight-line assimilation trajectory may not be their reality. Instead what scholars, such as Alejandro Portes, Rubén Rumbaut, and Min Zhou, have noted is that the integration of these new immigrant youth will likely be "segmented and take different pathways to adulthood, depending on a variety of conditions, contexts, vulnerabilities and resources."[16] An examination of the post-1965 immigrants reveals that these new immigrants constitute a diversity of ethnicities, classes, and national origins.[17] Some represent the most educated (Asian Indians and Taiwanese) and the least educated (Mexicans and Salvadorians) in the United States. The educational factor is particularly significant because of its impact on both the socioeconomic status and residential patterns of the immigrants. As a result, many Asian Indians are able to access various white-collar jobs and with it the salaries and benefits that enable them to fit securely into the middle class and live in the suburbs, while many Mexicans are relegated to the lower class, to unskilled and semiskilled jobs that provide little or no benefits, and to residences in socioeconomically deprived areas.[18] These diversities—ethnicities, classes, and national origins—among the parents combine with the new contexts to play a critical role in the assimilation trajectory for immigrant youths. As these new immigrant youth come of age, a primary question to consider is— Which sector within the host society will they assimilate into? The answer to this question depends on the pathway taken by immigrant youths. According to Portes and Zhou, there are several pathways available to them. One path may take immigrant youths along the relatively straight-line theory of assimilation into the society. A second may lead to "downward mobility and assimilation into the inner-city underclass" where abject poverty, high crime rates, and limited opportunities for educational or economic advancement may be the norm.[19] Still another path may result in the immigrant youth becoming socially mobile while deliberately preserving the values and interests of the immigrant community. Having acknowledged the possible pathways, we will investigate some of the factors influencing the immigrant youths' decision to choose one pathway over the others, bearing in mind that this choice may also determine the sector within society that they and their offspring will inhabit.

Context: Describing the place called home

There are several historical and social factors that influence the segment of society into which immigrant youth assimilate. Many of these, however, are connected by one major underlying theme—context. For many of these children, unlike their parents, their home is the present context in which they find themselves. It is *this* context that forms the reference point against which they measure all other places, including their parents' island homes. It is also *this* context that shapes how their parents engage with wider society, and sequentially determines how immigrant youth are nurtured and socialized at home. What then is the nature of the contexts in which the migrants and their children live? For the overwhelming majority of immigrant youth examined in this study both in the United States and the United Kingdom, their immediate context was urban— Brooklyn and London, respectively. The remaining respondents lived outside the New York City limits in Long Island or in areas outside of London. For many, their decision to move was due to the prohibitive cost of buying a house in the city. Although they had moved, they still commuted into the city several times a week to attend church, visit various family members, work, and engage in other auxiliary activities—shopping, hair care, etc. For these respondents as well, their formative years were spent within Brooklyn and London, and as such they provide valuable insight.

For the majority of West Indian immigrants who came to London and Brooklyn, the two primary determinants of their place of residence were the job market and family.[20] They went where their skills and labor were needed but also where they had family and social networks that could assist them in gaining access to these jobs and finding a place to live. In the majority of cases this was in the inner cities. One exception to this pattern was those migrants who entered the United States and the United Kingdom within a professional capacity, and for whom acquiring residences in the suburbs was a viable option.[21] In the United States, West Indian Immigrants made their homes among other minorities—especially among the African Americans. In Britain, however, the West Indian migrants lived among the larger white working-class populations. However, in both contexts, they encountered communities that were caught in a "debilitating cycle of economic poverty, psychological despair, and violence."[22] And it is these communities that were to play a formative role in the socialization and development of the immigrant youth in my study.

Immigrant youth in the United States are facing an economy that has been undergoing a series of dramatic changes since the 1950s. One change was the emergence of multinational corporations across various industries. Simultaneously, there was a movement toward a "free market" economy, which was believed to promote economic efficiency while maintaining the rights of the individual. One consequence of these changes has been the outsourcing of various manufacturing jobs from largely urban locations to other areas and/ or some developing countries. According to economist Bennett Harrison, this current trend among corporate management in various industries is an enduring one, focused on taking the "low-road" to achieving greater profitability, that is, increasing one's profit margin by decreasing the labor cost.[23] When job creation rates in the United States were examined between 1994 and 1997, (19,000 in high-wage fields versus 400,000 in retail stores), it was observed that with low-paying jobs, the desired aim of profitability was being achieved.[24]

Simultaneously, there were certain realities that continued to mark the ways in which the economy developed and how the immigrant youth participated within it. One was the coupling of high-wage jobs with college or advanced qualifications. As a result, those who lacked such qualifications had more difficulty finding a high-wage job. This became further exacerbated when one lacked a high school diploma or its equivalent. The second was the sense of entitlement that many immigrant youth developed as a result of being born in the United States. This was normally understood as having a guaranteed "right" to whatever they wanted. In some families where parents worked long hours, the parents sought to remedy their absence by giving their children everything. This remedy, however, served to further perpetuate the sense of entitlement among some immigrant youth. In the case of immigrant youth who lacked educational qualifications, there was also a lack of unwillingness to perform menial jobs as such jobs were perceived to be below them. The combined effect of these realities was that immigrant youth were confronted with a decrease in viable economic opportunities by which they could attain some form of economic security, a widening gap between educated high-wage earners and high school drop outs, and a mind-set that could potentially inhibit their economic progress—for in certain blue collar sectors (plumbing and electrical work) the "menial" job was the door to a thriving career.[25]

Having examined the economic changes that immigrant youth are facing in the United States, we will now turn our attention to the experiences of their counterparts in Britain. Beginning in the 1980s the British economy began experiencing some dramatic shifts. On the one hand, there was the expansion of industries focused on personal, protective, and professional services. Simultaneously the economy was also experiencing a decline in the food and drink, transport, textile and engineering, and telecommunications industries. The subsequent disappearance of these industries served to remove many of the ethnic minority population from the ranks of employed personnel. This development was particularly notable among West Indian males, who were concentrated in these declining industries and therefore were now susceptible to redundancy.[26] First-generation migrants, many of whom were close to retirement, were forced to pursue other avenues of employment. One avenue was self-employment. By investing their redundancy payments into their own businesses, some men and women were able to achieve social and economic mobility. For the others, redundancy produced a downward mobility that was discernible by low-paying jobs in a deregulated and relatively unskilled service sector that offered them negligible job security.[27]

For immigrant youth, especially males, the situation was dire since their entrance into the job market coincided with the decline in the very sectors that traditionally employed West Indians males. As a result, skill levels and qualifications became highly important. These developments were further exacerbated by the reality that many of these young men were entering the job market with fewer qualifications than their white counterparts.[28] For second-generation females in contrast, their prospects were slightly improved due to better academic performance.[29] Variance in educational achievement is also expressed along ethnic lines—with some Asians, particularly East Indians and Chinese, excelling more than Afro-Caribbean pupils. Within the employment sector, it was noted that although youth of West Indian ancestry were present in various managerial and professional occupations, young men were largely unrepresented. According to Richard Berthoud this underrepresentation was a direct result of their poor education outcomes, that is, lack of educational qualifications.[30]

Given the pivotal role that academic qualifications play in the job market in both contexts, it is essential to examine the status of the immigrant youth within the educational arena. In the United States, education and specifically "public education is seen as basic to [the] democratic political system, because it is both the main vehicle for equalizing opportunity in a diverse society and the major means by which the immigrant population is socialized into American values."[31] However, for some members of the society this equalizing opportunity never became a reality. Those most affected by this failure resided in the inner cities. Although children within these communities had access to free public education, the compound effect of various social, economic, and political issues, for a large percentage, undermined this access. In the United States, where one attends school is determined by one's place of residence, and therefore the problems affecting the surrounding neighborhoods also exert a tremendous influence over the schools located within their vicinity.[32] These realities were further exacerbated by the decrease in federal and/or state funding for public inner-city schools beginning in the 1980s.[33] Thus, in many school districts less money was allocated for each child in inner city schools versus those in the suburbs. However, the amount of money allocated for each student within a school district does not always tell the entire story. According to the United States Census Bureau, New York City is among the highest per student spending school districts in the country ($20,331).[34] Nevertheless, some of its schools that serve low-income students continue to face challenges related to overcrowding, lack of resources for academic supports and programs to address the social, familial, and other issues its students encountered on a daily basis. These dynamics, when combined, exerted immense strain on the system in a manner that some saw as hijacking the learning process. In his examination of schools in Hartford, Connecticut, Martin Carnoy observed that of the entire student body, 90 percent were African American and Puerto Rican, and came from the surrounding neighborhoods. Approximately 50 percent were also from families receiving income support from the government. When describing the situation that they face on a daily basis, one teacher said: "Few children learn to read at grade level in these schools, many have learning disabilities, and many complain of stomachaches, headaches, and other symptoms of hunger by midmorning." She concluded that the time and resources that should be used primarily for education had to be diverted as educators sought to address some of the more urgent needs of the student body, such as hunger.[35] The outcome for many of these students was a substandard education, high truancy and dropout rates, and minimal qualifications—all evidence of the hijacking of their learning process.

As John U. Ogbu notes, "In a disruptive urban environment caught between rising hopes and shrinking opportunities, younger members of native-born minorities have become increasingly skeptical about school achievement as a viable path to upward mobility and have thus responded to their bleak futures with resentment toward adult middle-class society and with rejection of mobility goals," such as getting a good education, desirable occupation, a good salary, and decent housing.[36] As an alternative, the wider society encouraged many of them to pursue sports and/or verbal and physical dueling.[37] Thus, two of the primary pathways to success presented by society to many inner-city minority youths were that of the athlete or the hip-hop artist. Academic success was rarely promoted as a primary pathway, since the much needed support systems to achieve this goal were oftentimes not provided within inner-city school districts. In recent years, the growth of the Charter school movement and increased academic support programs within inner-city neighborhoods have made the academic pathway a more viable option for inner-city youth. Since many of the West Indian immigrant youth attended these same inner-city schools, they entered an environment where students shaped each other's perception and expectations. The impact of this process on the immigrant youth, however, was directly related to the identities they constructed.

What was the educational situation of the children of West Indian immigrants in Britain? For the West Indian immigrants who went to Britain, education was perceived as one of the primary means through which their children would achieve recognition and status in the society, and as such, the majority of parents "[had] academic aspirations for their children."[38] And despite the injustices they encountered, many West Indian parents still felt that Britain offered their children limitless opportunities to improve themselves. However, when their children entered school, the reality only served to expose these ideals for the wishful dreams that they were—"the obstacles confronting the West Indian child in the British classroom [were] tremendous."[39] These obstacles came in the form of exclusion, lower expectations, the perpetuation of various stereotypes, and differential treatment toward minority children, especially black males. On the whole, many immigrant youth are excluded due to behavioral problems or for exhibiting culture-specific behaviors, that is, wearing various hairstyles or walking in what some considered an "inappropriate" manner. According to Richard Majors, "Teachers often label or view a Black child who demonstrates certain culture-specific behaviors as 'having an attitude problem' or even being 'ignorant' rather than characterizing the child as one who has pride, confidence and a positive self-esteem and cultural identity."[40]

When these perceptions were coupled with the ignorance or lack of cultural awareness or humility exhibited by many teachers toward immigrant youth, they resulted in some hostility between black pupils and their white teachers. These dynamics also created an environment in which many students, particularly black males, became the constant subject of differential treatment and were therefore "more likely than their White classmates to be disrespected, talked down to, over-monitored . . . and to have limited chances to tell their side of the story."[41] This differential treatment was not limited to the areas documented above; it was also visible in the lack of academic expectations that many teachers had for their minority students. One second-generation male respondent from London described his educational experience in the following manner:

> In terms of my school life I left school without any qualifications and I think for me school hadn't been a positive experience overall. . . . I was not really taking any qualifications when I left school. . . . When I first left school my teachers . . . were suggesting that I'd be a grave digger, so I don't think the [expectations]

were high of me in terms of just the school environment and at one point I was considering that as a career. . . . She [the respondent's mother] felt that I could do better than that if I keep pushing myself more and when I went to college . . . I was surprised when I actually got my qualifications.[42]

This respondent now works as a lecturer at a local institution of higher learning.

Within British society, the obstacles many immigrant youth confronted both in the job market and education were in actuality a visible part of a much deeper issue—racism. According to Robert Beckford, "A central feature of Black life in Britain has been ubiquitous racial oppression."[43] Ascribing an everyday perspective to racism was fundamental because it highlighted the process by which certain "everyday practices [became] part of the expected, of the unquestionable, and what [was] seen as normal by the dominant group."[44] Such an evaluation did not mean that this "informal" type of racism was harmless. In fact, the opposite was actually the case on two specific levels. One, these daily practices of injustice could produce various physical and mental health issues among those experiencing racism.[45] Two, by demonstrating how everyday racism existed not as a singular incident but as a complex structure, that is, "as interrelated instantiation of racism. . . . [Such that], expressions of racism in one particular social relation [were] related to all other racist practices."[46]

For many black males, there was an additional dimension—that of gendered racism. Within the legacy of historical and social constructions, "they [were] often demonized or positioned as a threat to the majority society."[47] When such stereotypes and public representations were combined with constructions of masculinity the result was the manifestation of racism along gender lines. Thus, for many second- and third-generation West Indians, particularly males, racial issues were a prominent part of their lives from which there seemed to be minimal respite.[48] One second-generation male respondent articulated the convergence of these dynamics in the following manner:

At times, I think for me at times it's been very frustrating. You encounter racism at every level of society, every institution and when you say what you see, you're deemed to have a chip on your shoulder in many different cases. And it seems to be a very common chip on the shoulder because a lot of people who look like me . . . have the same experiences.[49]

The perceived "chip on the shoulder" remark by whites in reaction to the second-generation's articulation of racism sought to shift the blame and place it squarely on the immigrant youth, who, due to some "cultural or genetic fault" was over-sensitive about certain issues and thus unable to function "properly"

within British society. As a result, very little attention was given to the role that
various socioeconomic, policing, political, and judiciary developments played in
facilitating the creation of a society[50] in which the immigrant youth, especially
the males, were continuously perceived as the "perpetual outsider" irrespective
of their status as British nationals.[51]

What impact did racism have in immigrant youth in the United States?
Historically, the United States has been known for its racism and discrimination
against several ethnic minorities.[52] With regard to racial distinction, Richard
Alba and Victor Nee argue that even when one considers the racial dynamics
found within the American society, some groups, such as Asians and light-
skinned Latinos may not be inhibited by racial distinctions and thus may follow
the straight-line assimilation process. Evidence for this is found in the relatively
high intermarriages among United States born Asian children to whites, which
Alba and Nee perceived to be an indicator of the Asians' acceptability to whites, as
well as the absence of a racial divide.[53] For the other groups however, it depended
on where they were situated in relation to those seen as phenotypically black.[54]

As West Indian immigrant youth come of age within the inner cities, they
were not only exposed to the socioeconomic and political disadvantage endemic
within their urban contexts but also to the racial and historical dynamics that
facilitated and perpetuated these conditions. In this context however, their
perception of and reaction to these racial experiences were more nuanced in
comparison to that of their British counterparts. The principal determinant of
where immigrant youth fell on the continuum concerning the issue of race was a
result of how closely they, as black youths, identified with the African American
community, and the class with which such association was established, that is,
the lower or the middle class. Such association was significant given that the
majority of immigrant youths, as stated earlier, were growing up within urban
communities and among African Americans who were in a lower socioeconomic
class. In the cases where immigrant youth were aligned with the perspectives
held by the African Americans in their neighborhoods, then they developed
oppositional views toward race and racial issues within the United States. Racial
tension and distancing was also perpetuated by some African Americans, who
perceived the West Indians immigrants in their neighborhoods who embodied
an ethnic identity as people who were unfairly benefiting from the societal
reforms they had won during the civil rights movement.

For the West Indian immigrants who identified with the middle-class African
American community, their views on racial issues ranged from apathetic to
moderate. One distinct characteristic of this association was the manner in

which they distanced themselves from African Americans in the lower socio-economic classes who they perceived to be overreacting or misrepresenting the black community in the media and the society at large. Thus, when asked about racism, one second-generation male responded, "Race, everyone says it's nothing but it's everything. It still is you know." When asked to clarify what he meant by this statement, the respondent spoke about fellow Americans "misrepresent us, they call each other 'n' words, and stuff like that. . . . It makes Blacks look bad, like [its] all about materialism and all about gang banging."[55] In response to the same question a second-generation female responded:

> Well, I am not really big on the race issue, . . . I don't really identify with race issues. Even this [report] in [the] news about the guy, the radio jockey, calling people whatever he call them. It's unfortunate, but I kind of think they kind of blew it out of proportion. I think we should grow up. People think like that all the time, he just happened to say it on air so that we hear it. . . . I don't get involved in discussions at work not because I don't know anything but I feel like I don't know enough about it.[56]

This continuum of views, apathetic to oppositional, was conceptualized and practiced in the context of the perception and experiences of racial discrimination and prejudice.[57] Dave, who immigrated from St. Vincent during his childhood stated, "I wasn't exposed to racist stuff until I came to America but I do feel that a lot of times Black Americans play it out in a way that they wanna make every white person wrong."[58] The presence of this dynamic was also noted in studies conducted among second-generation Jamaicans in Miami where three-quarters of the respondents reported experiences of racial-ethnic discrimination or the perception of such experiences.[59] However, in light of recent events in the United States involving black youth, especially males with regard to their interaction with the police and the wider society, there is the need for greater interrogation around how the West Indian immigrant community navigates race in America.

Constructing identities

Having briefly documented some of the salient features of home I will now discuss how immigrant children/youth are interacting with this context and the wider society. This assessment however, rests on one pivotal construct, identity. For it is this perception of self and the other that determines not only the pathway they will follow in the assimilation process, but also the types of signposts that will be erected to mark the way for future generations. In investigating this process however, I will also interrogate how the immigrant child/youth's participation in immigrant churches facilitated their identification. What are ethnic and religious identities being constructed within these religious arenas? This question is crucial given that these religious communities normally function as spaces where the first-generation ethnic/religious identities are maintained and negotiated. Since the immigrant youth are coming of age in an entirely different social context from their parents, the impact this has on their identity construction within these sacred arenas is worth exploring.

Brooklyn

Among the immigrant youth I interviewed in Brooklyn, the majority were constructing ethnic or hybrid/hyphenated ethnic identities that incorporated various elements of their parents' ethnic identification but along with certain characteristics emerging from their American upbringing. West Indian elements included working hard, striving for academic excellence, and showing respect for elders. For the males, these elements were linked with a particular definition of masculinity, that is, someone who was responsible, provided financially for one's family, and who would lead in making decisions. The American aspects included the acknowledgment of the child/youth's personhood and shifting the parent/child interaction from a monologue to a dialogue. This resulted in many families seeking alternate ways of disciplining the second generation and discontinuing the "be seen and not heard" practice that was normative within many West Indian families.

The identities they constructed were expressed as Jamerican (Jamaica/ American), Caribbean, black and Caribbean, African Jamaican, or multiracial. In the cases where the respondents described themselves as African American, they went on to clarify that although they were born in the United States, their upbringing was West Indian. One exception was a young man who stated: "I would say African-American. But most people would tell me that I'm Jamaican because they say, 'Oh I hear a Jamaican accent'. [Despite the accent] No, I would say I'm African American."[60] Although he held strongly to an African American identity, the interview revealed that while this identity had some oppositional undertones in the past, as he has grew older, it became flexible enough to allow him to incorporate the importance of hard work and education within its articulation.[61]

For another respondent, the question of self-identification was particularly difficult:

> Me, myself? I would say, this is very difficult because, I guess, I'm generalize[d] by my parents and, I guess, [by] everyone else. My parents would say that I'm a Yankee, they would say I'm American. Everyone else would say like I'm Jamaican. Me myself, I, to be honest I can't tell you. I don't know. I look at other races or other cultures and I see, like Asians, you see an Asian it doesn't matter if they're born here or not, they [would] still be considered an Asian. . . . So I don't tell people I'm Jamaican. I tell people my parents were born in Jamaica. You know I'm here but, it's kinda hard you know, still not the full-blooded American.[62]

The above quote uncovers the fluidity that accompanied the identification and self-identification of this young man. In his association with the wider society, his ethnic identity had prominence. However within West Indian circles, and particularly for his parents, it was his "American-ness" that was emphasized. In this regard, the identities he was constructing involved a negotiation between representation(s) and the context(s) he inhabited.

Since the majority of those I interviewed were constructing West Indian ethnic identities, what are some of the characteristics associated with this identification? According to Waters, ethnically identified immigrant youth exhibit the acceptance of

> their parents' and the wider society's negative portrayals of poor blacks and want[ing] to avoid any chance that they will be identified with them. They describe the culture and values of lower-class black Americans as including a lack of discipline, lack of a work ethic, laziness, bad child-rearing practices, and lack of respect for education. . . . [They also go to great lengths to] try to impress others that they are Jamaican or Haitian and most definitely *not* black American.[63]

For those interviewed, these characteristics held true. Many also held similar views to their parents in regard to hard work, education, respecting one's elders, and being a good citizen. However, in rejecting the stereotypical characterization associated with African American within a lower socioeconomic class, immigrant youth were faced with a dilemma. For unlike their parents who possessed various culturally identifying characteristics, such as an accent, the immigrant child/youth had no such markers. Thus, they are unable to draw the sharp distinction they desired between themselves and the African American community, with whom they were identified, by peers and the wider society. The result was the creation of a dual identity—the ethnic identity with which they self-identify, and the one prescribed by the wider society. According to Mary Waters, "This dual identity also exposes the second generation to a great deal of racism."[64] Because the wider society treated them as African Americans until they found out that they were *in fact* second-generation immigrants. Given these dynamics, many immigrant children/youth crafted specific ways emphasizing this identity—carrying nationalistic key chains, wearing particular cultural hairstyles and/or clothing, and listening to specific types of music, etc.[65] Choosing an ethnic identity also placed immigrant youth in a position where they were ostracized and ridiculed by their peers who, saw their good grades or speaking proper English as "acting white" (in slang—being an "oreo"). For second-generation males, in particular, this ridicule could also involve questioning their masculinity.[66] To cope with this ridicule, some immigrant youth, especially males, began "code switching," that is, when socializing with their friends they identified as African Americans, but at home, church, and around certain authority figures (teachers, elders, etc.) they switched to their ethnic identity.

Given what we have learned about ethnically identified immigrant youth, what were the experiences of their counterparts who chose an African American identity? Immigrant youths who self-identified as African American were placed in "conflict with their parents' generation, and most especially with their parents' understanding of American Blacks. Their assimilation into American culture [was] most definitely to Black America: they [spoke] Black English with their peers, listen[ed] to rap music, and they accept[ed] the peer culture of their Black American friends."[67] Linked with this African American identification was the practice of opposing their parents' ideas, most notably in reference to child-raising, achieving the immigrant dream, and views on race and urban life.[68] This "rebellion" by the children/youth was commonly met with the reassertion of parental authority, and fostered ongoing conflict within the family.

Mary Waters in her seminal work on second-generation West Indians concluded that those adopting an ethnic identity were primarily from a middle-class background, while those residing within the inner city adopted an African American identity.[69] In some settings (schools, neighborhoods, etc.) this conclusion was true. The exception was the identities exhibited within immigrant churches. Present within these churches was an element that could alter the identity construction process of inner-city youth. This element was the presence of a family. Complete with mothers, fathers, and "siblings, these churches gave 'adolescents access to adults other than their parents . . . [and provided] a sense of identity and belonging to the adolescents."[70] Limiting these relationships to mentoring or socialization overlooks the complexity these relationships engender. For immigrant youth from inner-city environments, these church "parents" provided various kinds of support, discipline, advice, emotional support, love, care, and perspectives on life. For those from single parent homes, it was their church "mother" or "father" who assisted them with their financial and other needs.[71] Although several members of the congregation functioned in this capacity in Latter Rain Ministries, it was the vice-president or president of the youth group who primarily inhabited this position. Evidence of this relationship was articulated in the way these individuals were addressed, as "mummy"/mother and daddy. One aspect of this particular relationship was regular communication between the "parents" and the "children." During my fieldwork it was common to hear several exchanges between the "father figure" and the youth, where the "father" asked the "youth" why they had not returned his phone call.[72]

For one respondent in particular, his definition of masculinity and leadership came from his father/son relationship with one of the men in the church:

> He was like my father, I would sit down and talk to him about [spiritual and personal] things, in fact sometimes I wouldn't have to talk to him he would talk to me about it. He was our youth president he was also the Sunday school teacher for the guys, the guys class. [In these classes] he used to talk to us like his kids. And not kids as in down to you, but as like his kids. He never minced words on what he was thinking at that time. . . . He would instill in us and always tell us that . . . whatever I give to you, you gotta impart to someone. . . . Right now I see myself doing a lot of what he has told me to do.[73]

Later in the interview, he shared that his "father" taught him to "be yourself, you can't be superman all the time, be yourself and show [others] sometimes that you're Clark Kent and use that as a way of strengthening them."[74] For this young man, his masculinity had to incorporate strength and vulnerability, responsibility, mentoring others, and being a "father figure" to other young men. This definition was in stark contrast to that expressed in many urban lower socioeconomic class African American communities where "in cultural terms, the prevalence of incarceration has made jail part of the symbolism of Black masculinity." Other features of urban African American masculinity included the image of the "gangsta" who was ruthless in his criminal activities but was still respected by everyone around him.[75] Within these communities, some of the older gang members were also seen as role models and the real protectors of the community in contrast to the police department. In this way, they functioned as the antithesis to the "man" and his establishment, traits that were valued and perpetuated.

Along with providing young men with an alternative construction of masculinity, religious communities also fostered the formation of a tight social network among their youth. The majority of my respondents were "born and raised" in the church. As a result, they had at their disposal a ready-made peer group with whom to socialize. One respondent described this phenomenon as follows:

> When I look around, the people I've known for twenty plus years, majority has come from this church. So these people I grew up with, these people I spent numerous hours with from sleepovers as young children to birthday parties to adult sharing in their weddings and stuff like that. So it's a community you know, and most of us would say, . . . it was an alternative, a safe haven for your parents versus having you playing with people from public school or playing with kids on the block or whatever. You made your community, your family and your church.[76]

Although this respondent was not sure if this type of community continued among the younger second-generation youth at the church, I found evidence revealing that this was still the case. According to a seventeen-year-old, "If you don't come to church you feel left out. . . . You look forward [to] us hanging out. [There will] be days when we won't have practice for quite a few Saturdays and when we get together we get in trouble a lot because we [didn't] get to see each other."[77] During fieldwork when asked to quantify the amount of time spent on their mobile phone with their friends from church versus those from school, the majority of immigrant youths responded that they spent most of their time talking to their friends from church. Further evidence of this tight knit peer group was observed every Sunday when most youths remained after the church service to hang out with each other.

In creating family and community, immigrant churches provided immigrant youth with a place to construct and maintain an ethnic identity. During my fieldwork, evidence of a fully developed African American identity was rarely found. The sole respondent who self-identified as African American exhibited few characteristics that many West Indian immigrants normally associated with African Americans in a lower socioeconomic class, namely being lazy or disrespectful of authority, etc. Given that my observation of this respondent was limited to church services, there was the possibility that his behavior may have been different within other contexts. However, when asked about this, he stated that at work he focused on accomplishing his job, being polite and friendly to the customers, and not getting involved in gossip or the other things that occurred. In terms of his behavior in the neighborhood, he stated that ever since he began attending the church he no longer hung out with the guys on the block, instead he was involved in reaching out to and mentoring neighborhood children, who he saw were getting involved with the wrong crowd. When his behavior was examined in light of the characteristics Mary Waters noted among the second generation who self-identified as African American, there was little congruence. In fact it seemed that this respondent was beginning to construct a more ethnically oriented identity. This young man's experience showed that in immigrant religious settings where an ethnic identity dominated, limited space was provided for the construction of nonethnic identities. In actuality, the space created was dedicated to the construction of alternative African American identities, those aligned with ethnic ones.[78]

Having outlined some of the ethnic identities constructed by immigrant youth in these religious communities, what are the religious identities emerging among them? For the majority of immigrant youth, one principal religious identity was the saint—an identity noted for conservatism in its beliefs, attire, practices, and apolitical engagement with society.[79] Adhering to the sharp definition, however, is problematic because it overlooks the ambiguity underlining this identification. For in addition to facilitating conservatism and an apolitical nature, this identity also provided some individuals with the tools to engage with society—especially the poor and marginalized.[80] For one respondent it was this identity that motivated her to organize a Thanksgiving Dinner for the poor and elderly, as well as become involved in the collection and distribution of clothes to people in the community. She explained, "I think for me it's a God given thing, where I have a drive to help people. Even at times I put myself out of the way, but never suffering because of it. So because God provides, I'm able to provide for others."[81]

Other features of the saint identity were, a strong emphasis on a dedication to Jesus Christ, modesty in dress, and holiness and morality in all aspects of one's lifestyle. In regard to dress, both the teenage girls and young women were asked to cover their heads and to refrain from wearing trousers to church. For one respondent, her involvement within the church became the impetus for adopting the habit of wearing a prayer cloth to church every Sunday, thus facilitating the formation of a certain aspect of her religious identity.

> Well sometimes I say come as you are but some people take it to an extent like the rule of the church is that you not supposed to wear any pants [trousers].

But sometime like on Saturday when you come to [choir] practice if you're coming from somewhere you tend to wear [trousers] and something like that. But you will have on [a] skirt with it. It doesn't make sense cause you know you have on pants. Like on Sundays, I see people coming to church in jeans . . . and it be skin tight, so like now, I see why pastor enforce wearing a skirt, because [the] skirt [is] a certain length and it won't be tight fitting. I see the purpose of it because there be people that don't normally come to church and don't know you, and would think stuff, and won't be paying attention to the message . . . and just be paying attention to you. So I see why they have certain rules and regulations about dressing inside the church.[82]

For this teenager, her participation in the choir had two outcomes: as the motivation for not wearing certain clothing (tight fitting skirt or trousers); and mediating her understanding of and acceptance of the church's rules surrounding dress. The change she narrated in the above quote highlighted that the process whereby youth embodied and exhibited certain beliefs and practices did not happen in a vacuum, but in those *intentional spaces* where they were woven into the fabric of the religious community. Within the church context, however, certain changes were also observed. In terms of adornment, girls and women within the congregation were now "allowed" to pierce their ears and process their hair. Among the young people there was greater liberty to talk about sex and other issues that they felt were pertinent to them. However, such discussions were normally conducted within the Friday night youth meetings. Therefore, while space was made for these discussions, designating them to the Friday youth group meetings kept these topics and the issues affecting the youth marginal in relation to the overall focus of the church. It will be interesting to see how this dynamic will change as the second generation become key leaders within the churches.

For many immigrant youth, their relationship with Jesus Christ also held a central place in their lives. Most acknowledged praying and asking for God's guidance whenever making decisions. For one respondent in particular, his relationship with Jesus Christ and the resultant call to pursue a music ministry produced some conflict with his mother.

It's not about not going to college, but the thing about it is that my mother [would] rather see me like do a trade, something more stable than music. Actually I do want to go to college for music and learn how to read notes and all that stuff, so that I can really compose music. . . . Right now I'm out of school. . . . But it's not that I don't plan on going to college. I have no problem with the education but it becomes a problem when you push your child in education instead of spirituality you know. And that's what I wanna make sure that I am doing, everything that I breathe, everything I do should work out to the fullness of God. So that's what I want to accomplish.[83]

The above quote uncovered a unique circumstance, where one's religious identity was seemingly in conflict with an ethnic identification (pursuing an education, and listening to/respecting one's parent). In the case, one of the underlying questions to be answered was: When a young person's religious and ethnic identities are in conflict, which takes primacy? For the young man quoted above, his religious identity was primary.

The prominence of the youth's relationship with Christ was also seen in the manner they interacted with those practices deemed to be sinful or worldly. According to the aspiring musician quoted above, "I don't plan on working with the Kirk Franklins[84] . . . because honestly I look at them and . . . some of the worldly stuff you dance to [is in] their music. I don't want that to happen. I wanted to be separate and holy unto God."[85] When dealing with sin in their lives, some immigrant youth took a militant stance against drinking, partying, premarital sex, smoking, etc. For them, sin hindered their growth in their relationship with Jesus Christ and had to be dealt with severely. Upon acknowledging its presence in their lives, many voluntarily disqualified themselves from participating in church ministry until their sin was dealt with. One respondent spoke about his process in this way:

Since I came back [from university] it took me awhile, it was about a year and a half until I came back in church [not attending church, but involvement in ministry]. It had to be a spiritual thing to empty out all the negative things that I took away [from university]. And you know I can honestly say I made a 180 from the days when I was in school and I changed all that. It was something I had to do, and [I] realize that you know, it was really hard leaving the wild life, the partying, the drinking, the hanging out and all that. So I would say that the road back, the road back was a hard one but my life has, I guess, transpired to be one of something that church I guess, the church would view as right. . . . [After] I came back [into the church], a year and a half after I came back from college, I felt it necessary for me to be part, be active within how the youth [committee] operate.[86]

For this young man, the church had moral authority concerning his life and thus was very significant in "dictating" what behaviors were "right."

The practices and articulation of the beliefs associated with the religious identities these immigrant youth constructed adds an overlooked dimension to the findings of Christian Smith and Melinda Denton in their study of American teenagers and religion. According to Smith and Denton, the religious life of the contemporary American youth is undergoing a transformation from the substance of historical religious traditions to a type of faith they term Moralistic Therapeutic Deism. Moralistic Therapeutic Deism is comprised of three central characteristics: a moralistic approach to life, providing therapeutic benefits to its adherents, and the belief in a God who exists and who created the world but who is not personally involved in people's lives.[87] The religious lives of immigrant youths provided a rare glimpse into the lives of youth who, while being shaped by the contemporary American context, were choosing to construct their religious identities in ways that aligned with the beliefs and practices that had been at the heart of Christianity historically, namely the centrality of Christ, salvation by faith, depravity of sin, the application of faith in all areas of life.

London

In the London context, the West Indian community inhabits a position that is similar to that of African Americans in the United States, in that they function as the comparable other for other ethnic groups. They also constitute the city's most inferior ethnic group. In this context, West Indian immigrant youth encounter "restricted employment opportunities, police discrimination, bad inner-city accommodation, inadequate education, [and] the whole cluster of forces emanating from white racialism."[88] Within the larger West Indian community, several identities were being constructed. These included one that oriented them toward their parents' island home, a black British identity that grounded them in their context, and one centered on avoidance, in which they downplayed the distinction between themselves and the wider white community.

Among my respondents, the majority were constructing an Afro-Caribbean/ black Caribbean, or black British identification. For those embracing an Afro-Caribbean/black Caribbean identity, this identity enabled them to root themselves in the heritage and culture of their parents and, by association, a community in which they are nurtured and accepted. According to one respondent:

> Generally speaking I'll [put] Black Caribbean [on the forms]. Before I used to write Black British but then I decided I didn't want to be Black British necessarily. I wanted to be Black Caribbean. So I tick Black Caribbean. [*Respondent was asked to give her definition of the term*]. That my parents are from the Caribbean and I feel that I'm still part of them, that I [am] wanted. If anyone['s] going to read the form, cause nine times out ten I wonder why they ask, anyway, but if

they wanted to look at it, I wanted them to know that I was a Black Caribbean person.[89]

It was noteworthy that the majority of second-generation females self-identified as Afro-Caribbean/black Caribbean. For those who self-identified as British or black British, they would also clarify that their identification also included a link to the Caribbean. One female articulated this nuance by stating: "Well, I'll say I am Black British. Probably [I] really have to, okay, I would say Black British as opposed to Black Caribbean really. But I would say I am full Black Caribbean, I'd say in a sense."[90] The "sense" this respondent referred to had to do with her cultural heritage through her parents and from her involvement in the black-led church. Later in the interview, this respondent spoke about the role several church members played in her development of certain behavioral traits, namely being disciplined and having good manners.

Among the third-generation respondents, aged nine to thirteen, the majority self-identified themselves as black British. However, for them, this identification was more an explanation of their nationality and their skin color than an interrogation of the factors that contribute to this construction. When asked why she held this identity, a third-generation respondent stated, "Because I live in England and I'm Black, [and because] my parents are Black."[91] For the older members of the second and third generation, constructing a black British identity included acknowledging Britain as their home. In this, they embraced what was perceived as "common" between themselves and whites, including language and literature and shared moral values. However this was done with an awareness of racism within British society and their overt reaction to its presence, further highlighting the societal factors that contributed to this particular identification.[92]

For second-generation males, the identities they constructed had strong political undertones and an overriding need to discover one's roots. These included: black British, a mix of black, African, British, and Caribbean; and black African. One respondent who self-identified as black British defined this identity as following:

By Black British, actually, me being Black is in terms of colour, British in terms of nationality. But the blackness also has for me a political element in that it just recognize[s] that my roots are not in this country. But I can see myself as British also. I haven't even been to the Caribbean although I have a wider understanding of the Caribbean from my home, but blackness refers to mainly to my colour, yeah.[93]

While a respondent who constructed a multiple hybrid identity—black, African, British, and Caribbean—explained his motivation behind this construction in the following words:

> Well, being Black [is] more about, not so much Caribbean, [but] just in terms of how, how I perceive myself to be and aah the British being the fact that I was born here. I don't call myself English, I call myself British. English seems to be more about people who are . . . indigenous to here, cause I don't know what that means, but people who have more of a rooted history here. In English you've got a lot of racist connotations attached to it. So those are the two and Caribbean is about from where my parents are from, that's about my ethnicity and African, well beyond just where my parents are from, but where I think I originated from as well.[94]

Still another respondent rejected all identification with Britain and the Caribbean. Instead he constructed an identity around the concepts of blackness and having an African origin.

> I suppose the African is more ancestral and it's more, for me, it's more rooted as opposed to Black Caribbean or Black British because I've kind of compartmentalized our existence within the continents as we've known it today, for example, so there's a Black continent as well. But by definition you can't have a Black British purely cause where [Britain] is situated in our world in a European segment, makes you know it does and generate Black people, whereas no more than Canada has aborigines, yeah. People are compartmentalized, you know, and the fact [that] some MPs say that, the fact that a horse is born in a pigsty doesn't make it a pig, it's still a horse and the fact that I'm born in white Europe with blue eyes and blond hair does not make me European. So from my personal perspective, you could say like I have done, Black, Black firstly and African next, that's it.[95]

All of the identities expressed by the respondents in the above quote were not static. They were fluid, undergoing various negotiations depending on the level of representation and interaction with the contexts in which they resided, worshipped, worked, and socialized. In *The Art of Being Black*, Claire Alexander highlighted an incident where she invited her main respondents for a thank you/farewell dinner. During the course of the evening, she noted: "Two distinct, and in some ways opposed, images of 'being Black', which are not related in any simple, unmediated way to external definitions, but to stances within and in relation to 'the Black community'." Thus, while all the respondents self-identified as black in relation to the wider society, within the West Indian community, this identity was subjected to different levels of interpretation and expressed in various forms.[96]

The political implication underlying the majority of the male respondents' identities were also a crucial feature. In this manner they were carving out spaces for belonging as they continued to interact with a society that historically has equated their community "with a 'culture' that is alien to, and inassimilable with, the British 'way of life'." As a result, the overruling ideology noted throughout British history was that an individual could not be both black and British. This produced a selective presentation of British history in which the presence and contributions of blacks prior to the docking of Windrush in 1949 was marginalized.[97] According to Claire Alexander, "Where nations are imagined as coterminous with ethnic, racial, or religious homogeneity, such an ideology imposes notions of absolute identities—an individual is either part of the imagined community, or is 'the Other': hyphenated or 'hybrid' identities transcend national boundaries and threaten social order."[98] Among the respondents, their identities threatened the particular construction that did not allot space for "the Other" while simultaneously transcending this construction to create an alternative in which "the Other" became a vital part of the social construction.

This theme of "being a threat" has exerted considerable influence on the manner in which the black communities were constructed and how the society responded to them. The validity of such themes, and the emergence of others, in the construction of identities among subsequent generations, is still to be determined. What will be similar is the profound influence that home, that is, the London context, will continue to play in their identification.[99]

One of the major critiques against the black majority churches in the United Kingdom has come from within their own ranks—specifically from among immigrant youth. Many argue that the church has failed to keep "pace with the modern, scientific, economic and political arguments that they relate to issues of life. While some openly reject the [church's] teachings as archaic, traditional and even mere Caribbean cultural taboos, there are others who earnestly seek guidance on matters of faith and practice."[100] Among those who rejected the church's teaching were many who sought out other alternatives, like Rastafarianism, or who left the church and Christian faith. For the immigrant youth who have remained, like my respondents, they sought to chart new pathways for their religious identities. Although the religious identity of the saint still rung true for many of the respondents, it was coupled with several modifications. For second-generation male respondents in particular, the political disengagement noted in some of their parents' religious identities was replaced by an increasing emphasis on engagement with various structures within the society.[101] According to one respondent:

> It is [a] long time we've spent telling ourselves that we can't mix the two. . . . You can't be Christians and politicians. And we've really fool[ed] ourselves into believing that. And we fooled ourselves into believing we can't be Christians and lawyers, which is rather rubbish. . . . And because we fooled ourselves that we can't be these things, [these positions] get filled by someone else. And other people that fill them are the non-Christians who can be lawyers and politicians and will be happy to tell you a lie. Whereas Christians should be filling these positions and upholding those principles and say I'm not going to move from this because this is what the word of God says. We will get back, but it's gonna take something very, very drastic and major you know.[102]

For this respondent and others like him, the articulation of his religious identity had grown to include public policy and service. Thus, the duty of the Christian was to bring the gospel to impact all areas of life, with no arena being exempt.

Although these immigrant youth, unlike their non-Christian counterparts would most likely not be engaged in violence, they were pursuing alternative ways of counteracting some of the negative perceptions of the community within the society. These ventures included the Saturday school and the play "Black Heroes." One respondent, who was actively involved in both activities, described them as follows:

> The Saturday school, it's really a school which is designed to support children aged seven to fourteen. And it started in 1997, as a means of supporting Black children in the community in schools. Although it's expanded beyond Black children now, we have lots of different children coming from different nationalities. . . . At the moment I'm working on . . . we are putting together a play called Black heroes. . . . That's a play which looks at a range of Black heroes, well Black people who people think, regard as being significant. It's people like Malcolm X, Martin Luther King and Mary Seacole and various other people throughout history. And it's a play whereby it tries to educate people about their lives. . . . There's an entertainer on one side, academics [on] the other side. . . . There's ministers as well of the gospel, who are on there as well, who are identified. And they're looking at trying to educate and raise self-esteem and also raise awareness in other communities, of the accomplishments that Black people have made. . . . I think I'd like to see the broader government taking on [this program] as a way of helping to raise self-esteem among Black children. And I think that is still a major issue.[103]

In the above quote we see another aspect of an expanded articulation of one's religious identity. One marked by the provision of supplementary educational programming and embracing the shared history and culture of the entire black diaspora (the United States, United Kingdom, and the Caribbean).

In terms of adornment, the statutes advocating the prohibition of wearing trousers and jewelry, processing one's hair, and wearing a prayer cloth during church services have changed. In this regard, the saint identity, expressed by females lost much of its association with adornment, and became more aligned with one's lifestyle, that is, the individual's relationship with Jesus Christ. A first-generation minister in discussing this change stated:

> It's kind of difficult to keep [that mindset] because Christianity is not so much [about what] people look like [but] who they are. . . . it was a pretty common thing to say you could look at the person and know that they're Christian. I don't know if it's quite possible. In the fifties, early sixties to see a Christian wear a pants suit, trousers suit would be almost demeaning and they would say, "look at her," today that isn't an issue anymore. So the identity I'm talking about, so in the fifties to see a lady in a female suit, you would feel that person astray, today it's different.[104]

As members of a Pentecostal religious community, respondents also upheld the authority of scripture as the Word of God. However, this belief was not practiced in the "do not question the bible" attitude held by many of their parents. Instead, respondents were diligently grappling with the tenets of their religious heritage and in the process sought to dissociate the cultural threads from the biblical ones. As one respondent articulated, "I think, . . . as we're growing and have grown so to speak, now we're in a different era where you can question things. You find out that Bible and tradition are two separate things and sometimes that becomes a little bit of a struggle, [it] seems to be a contradiction to some people."[105] The end result of distinguishing between core beliefs versus cultural traditions was greater flexibility in what "the" Christian pathway should look like.[106]

For two female respondents in particular, a prominent part of their religious identity was being a minister. This identity was particularly significant given the denominational prohibition on women serving in certain leadership capacities within the church—specifically as members of the pastor's council. The respondent who functioned in this role performed the same work as her male counterparts but was given the title of "advisor" on the pastor's council. Although she did not have a formal title like the men, she made it clear how atypical her "appointment" was and what it communicated about the congregation. She stated, "We are one of the churches that have kind of stepped out of the box to have women on leadership because generally speaking it's supposed to be ten men or twelve men: it all depends on the size of the congregation, but men only. So we've actually stepped out of the box by having women on it."[107]

The other respondent in leadership was the youth minister of the church. Two major challenges she experienced were finding her place in a male-dominated territory and having to negotiate the changes in relationship with people in the congregation who knew her as a child. She stated:

> I think, first of all as a woman it has presented some challenges because you have a lot of old school thoughts within the church, and you know at the beginning of my ministry, I didn't feel like I was particularly fitting into the protocol, because a lot of the words that the Lord would give me would . . . appear radical, but it was really because of the time that we're in and the people that we're speaking [to]. So I had to remind myself that, you know, God has given me a unique call and everybody's calling is different. And I had to learn to grow and appreciate that. I can't be fixed into a particular box. . . . I'm getting better at it now, I'm getting more confident with the voice of God and that's what I have to really strive [to do], to know his voice and that whatever he's set me to do I do it not because I'm necessarily comfortable but because I'm being obedient. But from a woman's point of view, it present[s] [challenges] . . . because sometimes I find in ministry that it seems like it's kind of a male dominated territory so you have to kind of come in not trying to prove who you are, but know who you are. Growing up here as a child and getting to this stage, sometimes people, you have some that appreciate the growth and the process and give that kind of respect and appreciation. . . . [And] you have others that will look at you and say, you know, whatever they want to call you. . . . And that you have to, you learn to live with that and [don't] take it personal you know, humble yourself, yeah.[108]

One important observation about these two women was the manner in which they functioned as role models for other women. In terms of their clothing, neither woman wore head coverings when they came to church or preached a sermon. On any given Sunday, both, like their male counterparts, would be seen performing various ministerial functions, like leading the intercessory prayer, praying during a child's dedication, etc. In terms of the seating arrangements during a Sunday service, the "advisor" to the pastor's council normally sat with the other members of the pastoral council and the senior pastor on the first pew. The youth minister sat in one of the pews immediately behind these ministers. In their interaction with their male counterparts and especially the senior minister, both were treated with respect and were highly regarded. During my fieldwork it was observed that the youth minister and another second-generation minister preached on more Sundays than the other ministers, including the senior minister. The other female respondents occupied those positions in which women have traditionally been involved—the Sunday school, the choir, women's ministries, etc. As a result, they did not have to negotiate the parameters of leadership in relation to their religious identities in a similar manner.

Appropriating their faith

Having discussed how immigrant youth in New York and London were interacting with home and constructing ethnic and religious identities as a result of this encounter, we will now examine the influences these processes were having on the religious communities in which they were involved. How were they appropriating their faith? What were the features of negotiation and construction as they and the first generation navigated the terrains of faith expressed in their theology and praxis? In this section, I argue that West Indian parents and immigrant churches both have a significant impact upon immigrant children and youth. However, this was multidimensional and at times contradictory, that is, an environment was created in which these immigrant youth were accepted, empowered, as well as marginalized and disempowered. Simultaneously, these immigrant youth were also exerting tremendous influences on the first generation and the religious communities as they reinforced certain beliefs and practices in matters of faith, while facilitating the reexamination and change of others.

For many of the immigrant youth in Brooklyn, their Pentecostal churches functioned as a place of acceptance and empowerment. It was a community of belonging—a place where they were known, reared, celebrated, disciplined, and counseled as "one of my children" by many of the adults. One respondent said this about the impact of the church community in her life. "I can say, to me, if you grow up in a church they are partially responsible for raising you. In a sense, so they play a big part in who you gonna grow up to be. So when you see me, like I'd say some people here, I'm similar to because we grew up here. We all grew up in the same church so our mindset is gonna be similar and things like that."[109] Coupled with the social, psychological, and emotional developments these institutions engendered within respondents, was the spiritual role they played in their lives. For the majority, these churches were their "home church"—the one in which they were "born and raised." As a result, they were one of the primary sites of their spiritual formation, and a place where they were introduced and nurtured in their faith in Jesus Christ.

The immigrant churches also functioned as a place of empowerment for many immigrant youth. It was where they acquired various leadership skills. In both of the churches, the majority of the respondents were involved in various ministries, including: Sunday school teachers, Praise and Worship leaders, ushers, youth choir members, youth leaders, ministers, and musicians. For one second-generation male, leadership training came as a result of having to officiate and organize various youth services.

> What evangelist [name withheld] used to do first was to give us, to start us to get bolder like giving a word [for the] youth service. So he'll [say to you] two weeks in advance, "so [name]" he used to do that to me all the time, "two weeks, you doing exhortation. Do it on whatever topic, you doing an exhortation." [His response was] "Oh my God!" . . . So you'll have to think of a topic, you've got [to] think of people who you gotta ask to come and bring forth your topic. [laugh] Oh gosh! That was the hardest thing to do but that was a stepping stone . . . it pushed me out there, it made me know how I have to present myself on that level.[110]

In giving youth, like this young man, total responsibility for these services, the churches created a space for the immigrant children and youth to gain various public speaking and leadership skills they could then transfer to their educational and employment contexts.

Incorporated within the process of empowerment was also the creation of an environment where the immigrant youth's religious calling could be discerned. For many of the young people in leadership in Latter Rain Ministries, this process was facilitated by the youth leaders, who would not only identify their calling but also provide safe places where their calling could be confirmed, tested, and practiced. During a group interview a youth leader, who was the second in command, described this procedure.[111]

> Youth leader: Pastor is there and then you have [the youth leader] underneath pastor. [The youth leader] could tell each and every one of you all where your calling is, because that's how you all know, isn't it?
> Teenager: Yeah she's around us more.
> Youth leader: She's the one who is around you all. She's the one who point out certain things and say okay [name] your calling is going to do praise and worship. So it is coming from the head, it might not directly come from the

pastor and that's why everybody gonna say it gotta come directly from pastor not all the time. If not pastor, somebody else, [the youth leader] might come to you and say okay brother [name] do this and you're like okay, and you be like because it's not coming from pastor you don't want to do it. That's what I'm saying it don't have to come from pastor for us to know our calling. [Teenagers respond: Yeah]. Somebody else who know, who may have discern, have certain discernment they will say this is what you're called to do.[112]

This discernment process was acknowledged by all of the second-generation respondents who served in a leadership capacity within Latter Rain. For some respondents, however, being chosen to serve in a certain ministry was a shock. Their acceptance was based on their understanding that their youth leader had discerned their calling. One member of the praise and worship team stated, "I got, I got chosen to do praise and worship. I was kind of shocked that [the youth president], she called and asked me to do it, like she asked me to be on the praise and worship team. I guess [she] notice that, that was my calling to do that."[113] As the above quote indicated, the discernment of the immigrant youth's calling did not come from the pastor but was facilitated by the youth leader who knew them. Thus the pastor's role became one of affirming what the youth leader had recognized in the youth's life.

For many second-generation immigrants in London, the church also functioned as a place of acceptance and empowerment. It was here that they received the training that enabled them to later serve as members of the pastor's council, coordinator of the Saturday school Program, Sunday school teachers, choir director, member of the ladies' ministry board, etc. According to one respondent, the church provided her with various skills that she later utilized in various religious and secular settings. Two specific skills that she acquired were public speaking and the ability to relate to people across several generations. She stated, "When you're out maybe in a secular job or outside of this church community, you realize that you're able to do certain things but then you think, 'Well where did I get that training?' It maybe was from the church."[114] This empowerment feature of the church was particularly significant for the young man who had been encouraged by his teacher to become a gravedigger. He stated:

> I think I've gained confidence maybe from doing things in church that perhaps I didn't have in school, having the opportunity. Being pushed to do things a little bit more in church more than I was being pushed in school has given me perhaps more confidence. And I feel more confident when in terms of public speaking and communicating with groups of people.[115]

This quote underscores how pivotal the empowerment dynamic remains for young black males in Britain. In a society where they are expected to underperform or be involved in gang and criminal activities, the provision of opportunities to engage in and acquires various leadership skills is very significant.

Intricately connected with this empowerment feature was the church's role as a place for support and guidance. This was certainly the experience of many of the respondents. According to one young woman, "Church more or less has played a big, big role in terms of people giving me directions, and setting an example for us. Especially the older people in the church they more [or less helped to] curb me you know. Sometimes I would be naughty. They sa[id] things out of love but you didn't see it at that young age . . . [but] as you grow older I see why they said [that] to me."[116]

As this group of immigrant children and youth was growing up, the majority of their close friends were from the church. As such the church became their primary site for peer socializationm, formation, and affirmation. For some members of the third generation, the church was a "safe space"[117] to socialize, receive academic assistance, and gain black role models (black heroes) who were different from those presented by society. The beneficiaries of this "safe space" and the resulting programs were from the church and the wider community. As families from possibly different neighborhoods, socioeconomic backgrounds, and religious experiences interacted, it created the potential for the development of relationships that might not have occurred. Through a mentoring program, "people [in the church] who [were] trained in particular areas of work such as teachers or accountants or ministers, . . . give support to other people, younger people coming up in the church." Although the other programs like career days, Saturday school,[118] and youth club were open to the young people from the church, most of the recipients were from the community. A mother of one of youth club attendees shared how happy she was to have a "safe space" where her son could go on a Friday night to socialize. The provision of this safe space was seminal due to the violence that occurred in the surrounding areas.[119]

While these churches functioned as places of acceptance and empowerment, for some immigrant youth they were also places of marginalization and disempowerment. In the churches in Brooklyn, where various West Indian religious and cultural traditions were given a prominent position, little space was made for immigrant youth to adopt an African American identity or engender certain changes within the church structures. In fact, within this context, the leaders and many first-generation immigrants normally perceived such measures as acts of disrespect or "rebellion." Although none of the respondents conformed totally to the characteristics Mary Waters associated with an African American identity, there was one individual whose identity included the engagement of community youth using a socially conscious lens.[120] During the group interview, it was interesting to observe how both the youth leader and other respondents interpreted this respondent's divergent views. In most of the responses, particularly those of the youth leader, his views were construed as him "misunderstanding" what was being discussed. Thus, his perspective on the church's lack of outreach to young people within the community, a ministry which he believed needed to be addressed and approved by the senior pastor, was interpreted as him failing to understand that everyone should be actively engaged in fulfilling their God-given roles and not wait on the pastor to do things.[121] From my observations of this and other immigrant congregations in New York, this teenager's view was insightful given the critical role that the leadership played in shaping and directing the ministry of the church, among its members and within the community.[122]

Another consequence of the maintenance of various cultural and religious traditions within the Pentecostal churches in Brooklyn was the creation of a worship context that some American-born children found boring or irrelevant. This included, thirty minutes to an hour of lecture-style sermons, limited references to the issues youth encountered in their daily lives, the absence of their opinion in decisions about the different aspects of regular worship, etc. During fieldwork, I observed a number of behaviors among several immigrant youth that communicated this reality. These behaviors included texting and/or playing games on mobile phones, talking with peers, sleeping, and doodling during the Sunday service, etc. For many of these young people, their church attendance was mandated by their families. One phrase I heard frequently during fieldwork and my membership within an immigrant church was "as long as you live in this house you will have to attend church." Strict enforcement of this perspective by parents normally resulted in some children and youth turning away from the faith altogether after they left their parents' homes.[123]

Another way in which these religious communities can marginalize or disempower the youth in their midst was by failing to adequately prepare them to engage with society. In their desire to provide youths with a protective and supportive space for constructing their identities, parents and church leaders also created a sheltered environment that did not adequately prepare many youths for certain social realities they would encounter upon leaving home. According to one respondent:

> So when I went away to school [university] and was living there, it was like out of the protection of like church and home and where I was really raised. I wasn't exactly living; I wasn't reinforcing anything that I learned here. . . . Again coming out of, not having grown up with, say you know, a lesbian or a homosexual here and just having [it] in your face constantly and all those new ideas they present in the classroom and you know and challenge what you know. We never had those kind[s] of discussions here to say, okay when you go away to school you gonna maybe come up against this, or cults on campus will try to draw you.[124]

Thus, for this respondent, the lack of preparation around what she would encounter in college left her ill-equipped to address the alternative religious views and understandings of sexual orientation and gender identification. This precipitated a crisis of faith resulting in her living differently, for a period of time, from how she was raised. Although she eventually returned to the norms and values transmitted by her parents and the church, this was not normative for all immigrant youths, who could find themselves alienated and adrift from their parents and the church as a result of their crisis of faith.

Within the London context, a major critique of the church by young people has been its perceived failure to engage with the "real" issues that they faced within the society. As the second generation was growing up in the 1970s and 1980s many parents were unaware or chose to overlook many of the racial dynamics that their children were facing. Thus many of their children came to see their parents and the church as providing very little space for their perspectives—many of which are focused on implementing systematic changes within the church and the wider society. The result was the exodus of several immigrant youth from the churches and their involvement in other religious groups, like Rastafari and other forms of active engagement with the society.[125] Those who remained used the tools they had gained to slowly bring about changes within the church. For some of these youth, however, the church continued to function at various times as a place of disempowerment and marginalization. Like their United States counterparts, many were ill prepared to face life away from home. Another area of marginalization came in the form of the pressure placed on pastors' children. According to one respondent:

> [There] was a lot of pressure, a great deal of pressure. And I suppose it's hard to articulate it perfectly, but to sum it up you pretty much were highlighted and pinpointed most times and it was incumbent upon you to be really responsible

in terms of the faith. Some of it was fine, you could just deal with it. But it was when it became difficult [that] you kind of thought, "Well, aah this is a bit difficult, this is a bit, it infringes on who you're as a person and in terms of your development". In particular I think of the church as [being] very strong on no makeup and no jewelry at the time. And when I was growing up, at the age of fourteen [or] thereabouts you wanted to experiment a little bit. [But] in fact you can't do that, you're [the] pastor's daughter, you can't do that. And I just thought, "Oh I can't wait until I'm old enough I can just leave, you know."[126]

As the immigrant youth were coming of age in Brooklyn and London they were challenging their religious communities to reexamine and modify both their beliefs and practices. However, this was more pronounced in the London church in comparison to those in Brooklyn. There were several factors for this difference: namely the types of identities being constructed, the demographics within the churches, and the receptivity among the first generation, especially among the leadership, in regard to the proposed changes.

As a result of constructing ethnic and religious identities similar to those of their parents, the immigrant youth in Brooklyn accepted many of the West Indian cultural and religious traditions. In both Latter Rain and Beulah, the worship service, liturgy, administrative structure, and religious tenor were organized in a fashion reminiscent of the churches' West Indian heritage.[127] Thus, the hymns sung during various church services were from the Redemption hymnal or an equivalent hymnal, and many of the choruses are West Indian in origin.[128] In terms of demographics, the Brooklyn churches are primarily first generation and as a result the re-creation of West Indian religious practices was very prominent. In fact for some members, it was this "re-creation" that motivated them to join the church. This demographic feature continued to be a permanent characteristic of the churches because of the ongoing influx of new West Indian immigrants, both legal and illegal, to the city. Within Latter Rain, this generational dominance was translated into the absence of immigrant youth in key leadership positions. Despite these dynamics, in the areas where they were present, namely in the youth group, youth choir, praise and worship group, and the Sunday school, they were fostering change. Within the youth group they were ensuring that sexual issues were discussed and students were more adequately prepared for university. These conversations included sharing with the young people about the realities of university life and helping them to develop strategies to deal with them.

In Beulah Church, there were three immigrant youth in key leadership positions—a deacon, the youth/associate minister, and the music minister. In these capacities, these immigrant youth were involved in preaching, leading praise and worship, coordinating the Sunday services, etc., activities that developed their leadership skills. What was significant, however, was that two of the three individuals were the pastor's children. When the church was started in 1998, it consisted of only the senior pastor and his family. Thus, it was necessary for his children to be involved in various ministries. Although the church has more members, the level of participation among the pastor's children has remained the same. Some of the other immigrant youth, however, were beginning to challenge this form of leadership to create an environment in which more young people had access to leadership roles and the training opportunities they provided. One issue highlighted by this challenge was the fact that members of one family, normally the pastor's family, held the majority of the key positions and thus became the "designated" successors in that ministry. The manner in which the leadership of Beulah handles this challenge will be critical, and in some ways may become one of the determining factors of future immigrant youth engagement, participation, and commitment to the church and matters of faith.

Negotiating change

For the churches in Brooklyn, two major challenges that they will face as the immigrant youth mature are relevance and creating space. How will they make the Christian faith that is now so embodied in West Indian cultural and religious traditions relevant to the "disinterested" American-born children, particularly those who are constructing modified or non-West Indian ethnic and religious identities? How will certain aspects of the liturgy—the use of hymns and lecture-style sermons—intersect with their media-dominated learning style? How will these churches create spaces of belonging for the immigrant youth? Will room be made for their perspectives, especially those that may necessitate major changes in the life of the church? For these churches in particular the challenges posed by the immigrant youth will determine the future of the church's existence. For unless the Christian faith is made relevant and spaces of belonging continue to be created, many immigrant youth may not find it worthwhile to remain in these churches.

For the immigrant youth in London, the construction of hybrid identities was coupled with championing measures that were producing major liturgical and structural changes within the church. Concurrently, the churches were undergoing a demographic shift from a first-generation membership to a primarily second- and third-generation one.[129] Although the majority of the senior pastors in the denomination were first generation, many of the other leadership positions were occupied by immigrant youths. This exerted a tremendous impact upon the church's ministries at the local level. In Kingsbridge in particular, the immigrant youth's presence in key leadership positions was linked to the willingness of the senior minister to see the church change in order to be relevant to its membership and to the community. He states, "When I came here [to Kingsbridge], the Jamaican culture or sub-culture was very strong and it dominated the others . . . from [a] leadership position [I] had to help to change that."[130] This was accomplished by insisting that the members speak English and not their native dialects. As a result of the collaboration between the immigrant youth and the first generation—particularly the senior minister— many of the West Indian cultural and religious traditions in the church were replaced by more contemporary expressions of faith.[131] Thus, the church hymnal and pew Bible have been replaced with contemporary choruses, and Bible verses projected onto an overhead screen and two television monitors.[132] There was also a change in religious dictum concerning dress, whereby women were no longer prevented from sitting on the rostrum and leading worship while wearing trousers, or preaching with their heads uncovered. Another major change was having women in key ministerial positions.

As the third generation comes of age in Kingsbridge, their presence and absence provided first- and second-generations church leaders with a unique opportunity to continue to grapple with matters of belief and practice. Having experienced the exodus of their children and their peers from the church, they were working to ensure that the church remained relevant to the third generation. As they knew from past experience, failure to do so could result in another "exodus." One major area in which they were grappling with matters of belief and practice was in terms of dress, specifically what constituted "proper" church attire. Some of the questions being asked were: Are jeans and trainers (sneakers) appropriate to wear? Where in the Bible does it say that you have to wear your Sunday "best" to church? Another area had to do with the format and time of the services: Would a later time be more convenient? Is the lecture-style sermon format the most effective way of communicating the gospel to a generation of young people whose learning style is overwhelmingly shaped by media and other technologies?

As immigrant youth who were once members of the church have been killed by guns or incarcerated, the church leadership at Kingsbridge has also had to reexamine their stance on issues related to gun violence and outreach to people in the penal institutions. This has resulted in a thriving prison outreach ministry coordinated by a member who was also chaplain in one of the city's prisons. The church's interaction with gun violence was twofold. One, there was the implementation of an antigun crime initiative called "Not one more drop of Blood." Through this initiative the church developed an ongoing relationship with the police to discuss crime in the area and measures to reduce it. The church also organized various marches and campaigns that highlighted the prominence of crime in the black community and called for its reduction. Two, the church was one of the few churches in the area that conducted funerals for those killed as a result of gun violence. According to one of the ministers, this was a tangible way for the church to establish contact with and support the families and the young people affected by gun crime.[133]

Conclusion

The role and impact of the religious communities within the lives of West Indian immigrant youth cannot be understated. As they grow into adulthood, they are facing a diversified trajectory in terms of their integration within their home societies. For many West Indian immigrant youth, their black phenotype, has resulted in the projected straight-line assimilation being replaced by downward mobility and possible incorporation into the ethnic minority underclass. It is within this context that the West Indian Pentecostal churches provided them with the social, ethnic, and religious tools needed to construct their identities and navigate the realities within the "home" context. For those in Brooklyn, this was accomplished by providing an environment that fostered the construction of West Indian ethnic and religious identities. This created an alternative pathway for socioeconomic mobility and integration into middle-class society. In London by contrast, the juxtaposition of the contextual realities with the cultural features within the religious communities resulted in the immigrant youth constructing hybrid identities. Although these identities incorporated elements of both (culture and context), they were wholly distinct and thus able to critique these elements. In the political undertones noted in some of their identification, as well as the prominence of issues concerning roots/belonging, the immigrant youth were simultaneously calling the society to reexamine those structures that continued to oppress and marginalize minorities and the religious communities to be more relevant within the society. In this manner, the immigrant youth used components from both environments to chart a new course of integration and engagement within the larger society.

As the immigrant churches in Brooklyn become more established within their urban context it will be important for them to begin to reevaluate their praxis. For in creating a space where the West Indian ethnic and religious identities are normative, they were not only "distancing" themselves from the wider community, but also marginalizing some of the immigrant youth in their midst. For these young people, this experience may result in their eventual exodus from their religious communities. It is in this regard that the London churches have something to offer to the Brooklyn congregations. Having experienced the exodus of the second generation, they could testify to the necessity of engaging with their youth around the issues they deemed relevant and the wider community to facilitate the continuous growth of the church and the transference of the Christian faith to the next generation.

For the West Indian Pentecostal churches in both contexts, the coming decades will be decisive ones as a "new" kind of immigrant youth come of age. In the London context, these will be the younger members of the third generation and the emerging fourth generation. Within the New York City context this group will consist of members of the second generation who are currently children or in their early teens and the developing third generation. These immigrant youth will be those who have "grown up" on various multimedia and advanced technologies that have accompanied globalization—the internet, mobile smart phones, portable media players, etc. For many of these children and youth, information is received through video clips and sound bites, and they expect to "have a say" in the decisions (parental and otherwise) concerning their lives. For these children and youth, the current liturgical and cultural norms—expressed in the forms of the one-hour lecture-styled sermons, head coverings, the prohibition on wearing casual clothes to church, and the unwillingness to discuss certain issues from the pulpit—may not help in effectively articulating Christian beliefs in a twenty-first century context. What will constitute viable forms of ministry for this generation? How will these churches engage with the society and these immigrant children and youth? These are crucial questions and answering them may require these religious communities to critically reevaluate who they are, for at its heart, this engagement will call for a fresh approach to the incarnation of their theology and praxis.

In this chapter and the previous one, I have focused on the identity portion of the tapestry. In both, I have argued that the color and diversity of the strands exhibited were influenced by the contexts in which West Indian immigrants (first, 1.5, second, and third) resided. In these spaces, they were presented with a variety of patterns to follow when adding to the tapestry. One was to reclaim what was constructed in Chapter 1 and bring it into the new home context. Another was to construct something new that had no resemblance to what came before. The final option was to take what was previously constructed within the lands of origin and combine it with strands from the new context to produce something that was a mixture of both. As these two chapters have argued, each of these patterns were perceived by the immigrants and others as processes of continuation or disruption. Regardless of how the patterns were perceived, their overall contribution to the tapestry cannot be denied, for in the blending and disruptions the tapestry was made and with it the story of the West Indian Pentecostal in the diaspora was created.

Led by the Spirit: Mission within West Indian Pentecostal Churches

Go ye therefore, and teach all nations, baptizing them in the name of the Father, and of the Son, and of the Holy Ghost: Teaching them to observe all things whatsoever I have commanded you: and, lo, I am with you always, even unto the end of the world.

Amen. (Matthew 28:19-20, KJV)

In examining Christianity, one notes the profound link that exists between its expansion and human migration. In the biblical text and in books about the history of Christianity one finds numerous examples of people who migrated to new contexts and formed settled communities through which various religious beliefs were practiced and disseminated. According to Andrew Walls, the migration exhibited within the biblical text can be categorized into two types: punitive or redemptive. Punitive migration, a kind of forced migration, occurs due to some kind of wrongdoing, and thus is marked by dislocation and deprivation. Redemptive migration, in contrast, emerges out of a call—a divine mandate to leave or go. Although this migration also produces a loss of home, it is voluntary in nature.[1] For many contemporary migrants, the impetus for their relocation is due to forces beyond their control (various socioeconomic and political developments, persecution, slavery, etc.); for others, their migration is a voluntary response to a divine mandate.[2] These two distinctions cannot be treated as mutually exclusive, however, for in certain cases both can play a pivotal role in the decision to migrate. One arena in which the convergence of these distinctions is observed is within immigrant religious communities in the diaspora.

In recent years there has been a plethora of discourses about the demographic shift—from the North to the South—within Christianity, to the extent that scholars predict that the beliefs and practices expressed within the southern continents may have a greater influence than those expressed in the West on the Christianity typical of the twenty-first century.[3] Coinciding with this emergence of Christianity as a non-Western religion has been the proliferation of various global and local forces aimed at uniting the world into one global community—marked by the increasing permeability of nation-state boundaries to the movement of people, goods, and ideas, and where ebbs and flows in one area directly impacts those in other areas.[4] It is within this globalizing context that we observe a dramatic surge in the post-1960s global migration from the South to the more developed nations of the North. As stated in Chapter 2, the impetus for migration is multifaceted, and includes: economics, sociopolitical dynamics, historical linkages, familial dynamics, etc. Accompanying this global movement is the emergence of non-Western Christianity in the North. As many of these immigrants relocated, they carried with them not only a vibrant Christianity fashioned within and excavated from the experiences and developments of their homeland, but also what they perceived to be a divine mandate to re-evangelize the North. For many non-Western Christians, the North has historically been the bulwark of Christianity. However, as nations in the North become increasingly secularized and pluralistic, this is no longer the reality. This new reality is what these Christians are seeking to change. Although questions abound about the validity of this "reverse mission," its presence provides us with a glimpse into a contemporary development that could profoundly impact Christian belief and practice in the twenty-first century.

In this chapter I will investigate how West Indian migrants are conceptualizing and practicing mission within Pentecostal churches in New York and London. Prior to accomplishing this task, I will give a brief overview of Pentecostalism and some of the mission models. I will also discuss how Pentecostalism and these specific models fit within the West Indian religious landscape that fashioned the faith taken by these immigrants into the diaspora. Some questions addressed in this chapter are: How are these religious communities conceptualizing and practicing mission? How do issues of identification influence these processes? How is the West Indian immigrants' perception of a divine mandate translated into various mission-oriented activities both within the immigrant church and the wider community? What are some of the challenges that this conceptualization and practice of mission pose for the immigrant Pentecostal churches and the wider society? In answering these questions, I will seek to highlight which of the strands discussed in Chapter 2 remain the same, which are modified, and which emerge primarily from the new context.

Pentecostalism and mission

In recent years, there has been some debate among Pentecostalism scholars about the theological and geographical origins of the movement.[5] Some scholars, particularly David Allen, traced the origin of the movement to Edward Irving and the Catholic Apostolic Church of 1832.[6] For some scholars, priority is given to Charles F. Parham and the outpouring of the Holy Spirit in Topeka Kansas in 1901,[7] while others give reference to the African American preacher William Seymour and the Azusa Street Revival that took place in Los Angeles in 1906.[8] Still for several others, the Pentecostalism movement can "call not man … father" since it was due to a sovereign move of God.[9] For Brumback, "The absence of a progenitor of our own Movement [is the indicator] that this mighty revival was begotten by an extraordinary outpouring of the Holy Spirit."[10] According to Robert Anderson, the task of finding a distinctive geographical location for the origin of the movement is in itself problematic since similar revivals were also experienced in Wales, India, Egypt, China, Germany, Australia, and New Zealand around the same time as the Azusa Street Revival.[11] The quest for a singular place of origin becomes even more challenging given the myriad theological strands that have contributed to what Pentecostalism has become. As a result, some scholars have argued that although any number of factors can be identified as contributing to the emergence of Pentecostalism, particular attention should be given to the theological factors from which the movement drew its energy.[12] However, this focus can itself be problematic because as Edith Blumhofer argues in regard to Azusa Street, the giving of priority of position to any place or theological factor may result in making "the historiography of Pentecostalism surprisingly contentious because adherents generally embrace a particular version of the revival's story and [thus] engage parts of its legacy rather [than] the whole."[13] Such criticism requires particular attention given the current prominence and influence of Pentecostalism within world Christianity.[14] Having acknowledged this note of caution, it is required to state that given the focus of this research it will be necessary to locate this discussion within the events of Azusa Street and American Pentecostalism; after all, these constitute the origins of the Pentecostalism manifested both within the West Indies and the diaspora.[15]

Having briefly discussed the origins of Pentecostalism, we can now examine some of the mission models that were exhibited within the movement. Particular attention will be given to three models emerging from the Azusa Street Revival since it forms the trajectory by which Pentecostalism came to the West Indies. These are the work of the Holy Spirit, eschatological beliefs, and the legacy of black spirituality.

For several scholars, the work of the Holy Spirit constitutes Pentecostals' most strategic and influential model because it facilitated the rediscovery of the indispensable role of the spirit as power-for-mission and the importance of the miraculous and numinous within any mission strategy or model.[16] One site of rediscovery was the Azusa Street Revival that occurred in Los Angeles California, from April 1906 to about 1915. Led by the African American preacher, William J. Seymour, this revival was characterized by dynamic worship services, racial integration, speaking in tongues, and ecstatic spiritual experiences accompanied by miracles and the work of the Holy Spirit.[17] Within the Azusa Street Revival, the work of the Holy Spirit was articulated in the concept of the baptism of the Holy Spirit and evidenced by speaking in tongues or glossolalia.[18] For some, this baptism indicated that an individual was "ordained" and equipped with the gifts of the spirit thus enabling them to fulfill the divine task that they were given.[19] Intricately linked with this baptism was the illumination and indwelling of Holy Spirit. Whereas external factors (socioeconomic, and political contexts, upbringing, etc.) were thought to exert a certain amount of influence upon an individual, the Holy Spirit was seen to have more influence "because, [by] dwelling within, [the Spirit could] get to the very center of one's thinking and emotions, and lead one into all truth."[20] In terms of the development of the Christian life, it was also believed that the Holy Spirit "guides the believers from spiritual birth to maturity."[21] Central to one's maturity was the sanctification process, in which the Holy Spirit facilitated the ongoing changing of one's heart and mind to seek after the things of God. As a result of this baptism and the subsequent sanctification process, believers who were previously marginalized and excluded due to their lack of education, social status or race, now found themselves empowered and equipped for ministry. In this manner they were inaugurating a new Pentecost, and with it a new movement within the Church.

Closely linked with the baptism of the Holy Spirit was the second model— eschatological beliefs. Throughout most of church history, eschatology, or the theology of last things, has been a topic of ongoing debate, friction, and great speculation. For many Christians, eschatology invites them into a discussion of finding a balance between the "already," "the not yet," and the Second Advent of Christ.[22] For the believers at Azusa, the issue of the last days became an area of seminal importance and a major impetus for their missionary strategy. As a result of the baptism of the Holy Spirit, these Pentecostals believed that they were living in the last days and it was their duty to prepare the world for Jesus' return. For many of them, glossolalia, or speaking in tongues, was initially thought to be xenoglossa, that is, speaking a "real" foreign language that was previously unknown to the speaker.[23] Thus, speaking in tongues was perceived as a means of God miraculously "equipping them to make known to every tribe and nation the urgent news that the Last Days were at hand."[24]

Speaking in tongues was also believed to be a sign in several others ways. To the universal Church, it was a sign "of the restoration of the 'early rain' of apostolic power and gifts being restored in a 'latter rain' for missionary activity."[25] In regard to the unbeliever, speaking in tongues was interpreted as being "equivalent to prophecy,"[26] and thus capable of facilitating conviction within the unbeliever when it was spoken in their presence. For some believers, it was evidence that they had received the baptism of the Holy Spirit, had gifts for ministry, and were a part of the bride of Christ.[27] This baptism, however, was not to make the world morally, politically, and socially just. No, this empowerment was for evangelization—so that the nations would hear the gospel. With the Second Advent believed to be at hand, the participants at Azusa saw themselves as God's agents, as those God would use to usher in its inauguration. In *The Everlasting Gospel*, Faupel confirms the significance of eschatology to the missionary thrust found in the early days of the movement. He states:

> The United States certainly was not the extent of the Azusa vision. Whereas Parham seemed intent on the evangelization of the North American continent before heading overseas, adherents from Los Angeles began thinking in global terms from the outset. . . . Sensing the nearness of the return of Christ, workers feeling called to the foreign field were reluctant to wait for Parham's appearance on the scene. When Parham sent word that his coming would be delayed, a number decided to set out on their own.[28]

Being convinced that the new Pentecost had come in their midst and the imminent return of Christ was fast approaching, several of the participants at Azusa Street were sent out with the Pentecostal message.[29] The urgency to carry the message to others was seen not only in those who were officially commissioned by Azusa Street, but also in many others who came in contact with the revival at Azusa and who felt called to go and give witness to their experience.[30] Even the "recent migrants to Los Angeles who were converted to the new movement returned to their hometowns, impelled by a belief common among the early Pentecostals that they had an obligation to bear witness of their experience to their friends and relatives."[31]

The third model noted within Pentecostalism and specifically the Azusa Street Revival is the legacy of black spirituality. This spirituality has its origin in the lives of the slaves who were forcibly taken from Africa and brought to the Americas.[32] Within this context, the slaves took various elements of the Christianity presented to them by the whites and their African religious heritage to produce a "tertium quid"—a religion distinctively different from its main contributors and one that emphasized the numinous in personal and public forms of worship, narrative theology, oral liturgy, and maximum participation in many aspects of the religious community.[33] According to Cheryl Jones, the "oral-narrative dynamic allows for the Christian 'story' to be integrated with life experiences. It gives a 'voice' to every believer inasmuch as it is the responsibility of everyone to participate in the telling of his or her experience."[34] Within such a framework, both theology and belief are forged in the context of the faith community and the lived experiences of its participants. Associated with the narrativity of theology was an oral liturgy, of which one key element was that every member was a full participant. Jones states, "Such a liturgy bridges the gap between laity and professional."[35] The result was equality within the body of Christ, and the restoration of belief of the priesthood of all believers.[36]

The dynamics built into the revival at Azusa Street served many functions in the lives of the participants. It brought to prominence the concept of wholeness found in black spirituality as well as ecstatic worship—using one's entire body and emotions in the act of worship—that is, singing, clapping, dancing, etc. According to Faupel, "[Parham, due to] his experience at Topeka, . . . sought to strip [the movement of] the excessive demonstrations of emotion [the Pentecostal] message tended to evoke."[37] For Seymour, however, drawing upon his black heritage, these emotional expressions had tremendous value and were encouraged. Along with the emotional expressions, Seymour also "believed Spirit-baptism to be part of the atoning work of Christ."[38] This atoning work was not limited to the proclamation or even speaking in tongues. The fullness of the atonement of Christ was modeled in lives that reflected a return to wholeness—"the human family, pure and happy."[39] Since the baptism of the Holy Spirit was available to everyone, regardless of race, education, or gender, anyone could be used to communicate God's message. Thus, Pentecostalism provided its adherents with a space to speak, a place where their voices would not be muted due to lack of education, gender, race, or social standing. As a result many who had been marginalized within the society found a sense of dignity, empowerment, identity, and community.[40]

Pentecostalism within the West Indies

As noted previously, what constitutes being West Indian today is the product of the interactions between various cultures over many centuries. One prominent feature involved in this was religion and, in this regard, Pentecostalism's advent within the West Indian religious landscape is a continuation of a process in which the islands have been involved for centuries. Using the models of mission discussed above, this section will investigate how the Pentecostal movement entered and was transformed within the West Indian context. The scope of this discussion will focus primarily on Pentecostalism within Jamaica because it is the origin for the majority of adherents in the churches studied in New York and London.

When Pentecostalism arrived in the West Indies in 1909, it found a religious landscape able to accommodate many of its beliefs and practices. It is noteworthy that the first Pentecostal "missionaries" to the West Indies were Rebecca and Edmund Barr, black Bahamians, who upon receiving the Pentecostal experience in Florida returned to their homeland to share the message.[41] Therefore, from its inception, we are provided with a glimpse into the trajectory and the character that Pentecostalism would take in its integration into the West Indian religious landscape. First, it highlights the role that blacks would play within the movement. For, while it was primarily white missionaries who introduced Pentecostalism, it was the indigenous preachers who disseminated it among the masses.[42] As shown in Chapter 1, this was not new—indigenous preachers were also employed in the Christianization of the slaves. Second, it roots the movement within the black religious experience. Although Austin-Broos is correct in arguing that the Holiness CoG, which arrived on the island in 1908, served as a "theological forerunner," it did not constitute the basic framework that enabled Pentecostalism to be inserted and to thrive within the Jamaican religious landscape.[43] That position was occupied by Revivalism. For, as Barry Chevannes argues, Revivalism facilitated the creation of a space in which Pentecostalism could be incorporated into the Jamaican religious landscape and as a result "one is tempted to argue [that] Myalism has once more shed its garb and is now wearing Pentecostal clothes."[44]

Revivalism, an indigenous Jamaican religion, was the product of the fusion of Myalism and Christianity.[45] Myalism, an Afro-Jamaican religion practiced during colonial rule, incorporated various African religious elements, such as "a dance ritual, an initiatory rite tradition, and a pharmacopeia for herbal and spiritual healing,"[46] as well as a Christian cosmology and the revering of biblical personalities. The Christian elements mentioned above were incorporated in an orientation that gave primacy of place to experiencing "God or the Holy Spirit in the body during worship services. [T]his was demonstrated in ecstatic emotional displays."[47] The Christianity of Myal adherents was not focused on receiving an abstract forgiveness of sin or cultivating a moral life in the European mode, instead their faith was deployed "for the healing of personal and community ills," both of which had physical and spiritual dimensions.[48] The incorporation of these Christian elements into Myalism was a product of the influence of George Liele and Moses Baker, African American Baptists, who brought the gospel to the free and enslaved blacks of Jamaica.[49] It was this movement that became the Native Baptists.

Drawing on the above elements, Revivalism was constructed in a manner in which spirit possession constituted one of its key features. According to Barry Chevannes, "Spirit possession is a sign that one already has a special relationship with the particular identified spirit."[50] This is a spirit associated with either the Holy Spirit or a benevolent spirit within the African-derived pantheon. This experience of being spirit possessed normally occurred within the context of ecstatic worship and culminates in trances, glossolalia, prophecies, and healing.[51] However, as George Simpson notes, for some practitioners—specifically those playing the roles of the "leader," "captain," or "mother," spirit possession could also occur outside of this context.[52] For the Revivalist, "the ideal life is life in the spirit," for it was in the spiritual realm—that an individual would ultimately gain victory over sin.[53] Thus, it is believed that "the Holy Spirit cleanses and redeems the believer, an act later celebrated by a baptismal rite."[54] Associated with this lifestyle was also the idea of empowering possession—the possession of the spirit (the Holy Spirit) would result in that individual being empowered to fulfill certain tasks. These include: conducting healing, communicating with the spirit (primarily through dreams), fulfilling a call to ministry, having the ability to pray; engagement in evangelism; and performing various leadership roles within the meetings.[55] In this articulation of "life in the spirit" one also found the concept of holiness. According to a Revivalist preacher, "Some people can't get the spirit because they are not clean. They are not pure; they have not lived the right way."[56]

The type of Christianity integrated within Revivalism was that of the Native Baptists, who adhered to a literal interpretation of the Bible, oral theology, and liturgy, to belief in the inspiration of the Holy Spirit, and to baptism by immersion. According to Kortwright Davis, Caribbean culture in general—and Jamaican culture in particular—is primarily an oral one.[57] This feature is also noted within its folk or indigenous religions, of which Revivialism is an example. As a result, the "preference in this religious context is for narrative styles of communicating truths about the faith, as opposed to dogmatic, didactic, philosophical teaching styles."[58] Ultimately, this created an environment where theologizing was not limited to the activities conducted in "holy places"—the church or seminaries. Instead, theology was found in the experiences of everyday life (in the home, the field, and the street) and was an activity in which everyone could participate regardless of their educational qualification or economic status.[59]

When Pentecostalism arrived it found a space already prepared for its inception—primarily due to the significant parallels that existed between it and Revivialism. The importance of the work of the Holy Spirit in the believer's life found its contemporary in Revivialism's beliefs about spirit possession. Likewise, the narrativity of theology, orality of liturgy, and expressive worship emerging from Pentecostalism's legacy of black spirituality found a mirror image in West Indian spirituality and the practices within Revivialism. Similar to the eschatological beliefs expressed within Pentecostalism was Revivialism's belief that after death the soul of an individual returns to God for judgment.[60] Thus, as Pentecostalism located common elements within Revivialism that enabled its insertion, it also encountered a dynamic new society that called for its transformation. In what ways was Pentecostalism reformulated within the Jamaican context? Using the three-mission models discussed previously we will investigate some of the ways Pentecostalism was reformulated.

According to Noel Leo Erskine, one of the most fundamental questions asked within the Jamaican religious context is: "What must we do to be saved?"[61] As a result, the central issue for many people is how to obtain freedom or salvation from sin, which "the church maintains [to be] the root cause of poverty, crime, and social and economic injustice."[62] Simultaneously, as a result of the legacy of slavery and the abject poverty that ravages various sectors of the society, many people have come to "feel cursed and condemned."[63] Erskine states that "Jamaicans often characterize themselves as living with a sense of worthlessness and refer to their marginal existence as the consequence of God's punishment."[64] Within Pentecostalism this characterization of sin is further interpreted to encompass the world—which is believed to be under the devil's rule and therefore evil. For Pentecostals in Jamaica, the singular solution to this problem was salvation—repenting and accepting Jesus as one's personal savior. One of the marks of one's salvation was baptism—both by water immersion and by the

Holy Spirit. The water baptism by immersion, which to many converts was the sign of their commitment to Christ, was also perceived as having a re-creative effect, in that the sins from their past would be eradicated and they could begin a life free from sin and its effects. Pentecostalism's provision of an opportunity to acquire a new life was attractive to many blacks for whom the presence of sin and its perceived effects—poverty, socioeconomic injustice etc.—dominated various aspects of their lives.

Once converted, the believer was expected to live a sanctified life and abstain from the practices of the world. The primary facilitator of this process was the Holy Spirit, who was perceived to indwell or possess the sanctified believer. The distinctive expression signifying that an individual was sanctified and baptized by the Holy Spirit was speaking in tongues. Accompanying one's experience of spirit baptism were strict moral requirements that were complemented by a eudemonic fervor. So while dancing, singing, and engaging in activities associated with a worldly lifestyle were prohibited within the believers' daily lives, in the church, these elements were transformed into spiritually acceptable forms of celebration and expression. As Austin-Broos argues, "The focus of Pentecostalism on personal salvation and interior experience manifested in embodied and highly portable forms of speaking in tongues and ritual dancing matched in religious terms [the] economic individuation" that characterizes the Jamaican economic sphere.[65] That is, Pentecostalism's focus on individual salvation was aligned with a similar work of individualization also occurring in the economic realm within society. As a result, the significance of the baptism of the Holy Spirit was not only associated with empowerment issues, but also with its function of serving as a distinctive marker that denoted that an individual was saved and sanctified.

Thus, in a context where sin was associated with poverty/crime/injustice, Pentecostalism's engagement with the society was conducted on the level of the individual—how the individual could be transformed and re-created as a result of salvation in Jesus Christ. This orientation toward individual transformation was seen in the movements' focus on evangelism, which was articulated in several ways: by believers distributing evangelistic printed materials and witnessing; and in the church by having altar calls during the services and conducting open-air crusades. In these formats, it was believed that the sin problem and the associated effects would be addressed. Evangelism, however, was not restricted to any context, boundary, or time and because it was conducted within the realm of daily life all activities became opportunities to save a soul. Therefore, mundane activities like going to work, the market, or the beauty salon underwent a conversion process to become divine moments filled with the expectancy of the salvation of an unsaved person and the resulting transformation of that individual and possibly their family.

As discussed previously, throughout Jamaica's religious history certain branches of the church have functioned for its populace as a place for alternative representation, especially for the marginalized. During slavery and in the early years of emancipation, this position was occupied by the Moravian, Methodist, and Baptist denominations as they allied with the slaves in their fight for emancipation, economic independence, and justice. However, in the subsequent years, these denominations were faced with diminishing attendance among their membership. Although the Great Revival of 1860 resulted in new converts being incorporated into the churches, it also resulted in the resurgence/emergence of several African-derived (like Obeah) and Afro-Christian religions (Revivalism, Kumina, etc.). Underlying both the growth of the African-derived/Afro-Christian religions and the diminished attendance within the denominational churches was the conviction among many blacks that their former allies were now aligned with the ruling elite and the overall system. For "clergy from Britain who had once been radicals became clergy endorsing the colonial way, and the denominational churches in Jamaica, albeit as they grew in independence, became missionary training grounds for foreign clergy rather than sites of critical theology."[66] Thus, an area that historically had been one of critical engagement about the society was co-opted to support the colonial system.

When Pentecostalism entered the Jamaican religious arena it did so as a movement greatly influenced by its black spirituality legacy and as a movement catering to the needs of the marginalized and disempowered. Simultaneously, it entered through the door of Revivalism, a religious movement that was anti-status quo in its beliefs, practices, and adherents. Where did Pentecostalism fit within the Jamaican religious spectrum? Pentecostalism found its home in an intermediate position between the denominational churches and the Afro-Christian religious groups. Due to its focus on the indwelling of the Holy Spirit and expressive worship, Pentecostalism was perceived by some of the denominational churches and the populace to be very similar to the Afro-Christian religions. In catering to the underlying needs of a large portion of the blacks underclass, Pentecostalism gave them another means of dealing with their sin problem through conversion. It offered them a new identity as a saint, someone who was an example for the society around them, and provided them with numerous opportunities for empowerment—through leadership, teaching, preaching etc. Pentecostalism also granted its adherents a means of reattaining status within society—the adherents were not just members of an African-type religion (members of such religions did not enjoy much credibility), instead they were members of American denominations that had a certain level of credibility. However, the Pentecostalism movement was also aligned with the denominational churches in their nonpolitical stance and preservation of the status quo. As Pentecostalism grew, this alignment was to generate another level of respectability and acceptance within the society. For unlike other indigenous religions like Rastafari, which openly critiqued social and corporate injustices and called for change, Pentecostalism focused on liberating the individual from sin while perpetuating an otherworldly or compensatory mind-set which looks "to a time when its practitioners will transcend their current circumstances in a new role in the world as ritually felicitous beings."[67] This mind-set, which was also taught and practiced during slavery, told believers to orient their lives toward heaven, the place where they would be rewarded, and to be, as they awaited that reward, hardworking and moral individuals who obeyed the authority that God had placed over them.[68]

As Pentecostalism became a part of the Jamaican religious landscape, eschatology continued to play a significant role in its growth. For many of the sanctified believers, it became the constant reminder to live holy lives—for the second coming could occur at any time. The impending return of Jesus also became the impetus to engage in evangelism. However, this evangelism was primarily focused on local and regional contexts with very little attention being given to perpetuating the global thrust that had accompanied early Pentecostalism or the missionary ventures to Africa by emancipated slaves.[69] The two major mission trajectories that represent the exception to this focus are evangelism to the United Kingdom and to the United States—the focus of this book. One possible reason for the development of a local/regional focus is the pervasiveness of the dependency syndrome within the Jamaican and Caribbean contexts. The regions' socioeconomic and political vitality is not only heavily influenced by agents outside of the region, but also, within the religious arena, the decisions, funding, and structures of some organizations come from the headquarters located elsewhere. One consequence of this dependency is that it undermines self-initiative and the overall development of the local church to the extent that mission is perceived to be "what rich Europeans and North Americans did in the poor 'third world'."[70] This premise is currently undergoing some changes, however, as some Christians interrogate what it means to be involved in the missio dei—mission of God.

Mission within the diaspora

So far this chapter has briefly documented some ways in which mission was conceptualized and practiced within Jamaican Pentecostalism. In this section we will analyze an ongoing development in the discourse on mission within Jamaican Pentecostalism—the relocation of West Indian/Jamaican Pentecostals to New York and London. How are these "new" carriers of Pentecostalism conceiving and practicing mission within the diaspora? In the United States context this question is especially informative because on one level this relocation could be perceived as Pentecostalism returning to the shores from which it went forth to change the world.

On an organizational level, all three of the churches—Latter Rain, Beulah, and Kingsbridge—involved in this research conceived mission as being within the framework of the Great Commission:

> Go ye therefore, and teach all nations, baptizing them in the name of the Father, and of the Son, and of the Holy Ghost: teaching them to observe all things whatsoever I have commanded you: and, lo, I am with you always, even unto the end of the world. Amen. (Matthew 28:19-20, KJV)

For these churches the focal points in this passage were: go, teach all nations, and baptize them in the name of the Trinity—three activities that were seen to be intricately tied to evangelism and the winning of souls. Several forms of evangelism were associated with this conceptualization of mission, namely personal, public, local, and international. Within the churches, mission as evangelism was communicated through two main forums—literary and oral. Therefore, in the weekly bulletins, in the visitor's welcome booklet, and on the church's websites, visitors were told and the members were reminded that the primary aim of the church was evangelism. According to its website, Latter Rain Ministries was "a growing ministry with [a] focus on winning lost souls for Jesus Christ."[71] For Kingsbridge, winning souls was combined with a focus on discipleship, with the aim that the church members will "Win and Disciple others."[72] In the oral format, mission as evangelism was communicated through various parts of the liturgy—the hymns and choruses, the sermons, and other parts of the service. One common feature noted during the services in all three churches was the altar call.[73] This was an invitation during the service to nonbelievers to make a decision to accept Jesus Christ as their personal savior. What was noteworthy about this invitation was not only its position within the liturgy but also what it communicated to those who were present during the service.

The altar call, a concluding element within the service, had three parts—the invitation or appeal, prayer time, and celebration/counseling. During the invitation, worshippers were reminded of the depravity of humankind, their need for a savior, and the atoning sacrifice of Jesus Christ. It concluded with a plea to the nonbeliever to leave the life of sin and come to the altar and accept Jesus Christ.[74] In some cases, the altar call would also include a call to the believer to recommit herself or himself to living faithfully for Christ. During the prayer time, those at the altar were led in reciting the sinner's prayer.[75] Following this prayer there was a time of celebration. This included thanking God for the new converts and counseling—the latter involved taking the new converts into another room where they received instructions on how to grow in their "new" faith and discipleship.[76] A respondent communicated the importance of this part of the Sunday service in the following manner:

> I love when they do an altar call. If they don't do an altar call on a Sunday morning I don't feel happy, I go home and feel that coming to church was a waste of time. But if they have altar call and one soul come, I feel more happy than anything, so winning souls is the most important thing.[77]

Thus, through features in the weekly service life such as the altar call, both the nonbelievers and believers are given an opportunity to evaluate their lives and, if needed, begin anew.

At the root of this conceptualization of mission as evangelism were several beliefs originating from within Jamaican Pentecostalism—namely an emphasis on salvation and its links with the baptism of the Holy Spirit and eschatology. Thus, the perception of the world as depraved and under the leadership of the devil continued to occupy a prominent position within the theology, liturgy, and life of the church and its members. In the churches, members were admonished to remain separate from the world. For the churches the only solution to this problem of humanity was salvation in Jesus Christ. Thus, for those who were saved—signified by the baptism of the Holy Spirit—it was their duty to go out and try to win others to Christ. The addition of the belief in the imminent return of Jesus Christ added urgency to the mission, propelling the believer to go out into wider society to encourage sinners to come to Christ and thus be saved from eternal damnation. Thus, through the sermons, hymns, and the altar call, believers were reminded of the divine mandate that they had been given, and the eternal significance that is associated with them fulfilling that mandate. One by-product of this conceptualization of mission as evangelism could be the perpetuation of an otherworldly and nonpolitical mind-set among many of the believers within the churches. Therefore, the focus was on maintaining their separation from the "bad" world, walking the straight and narrow so that they would be ready when Jesus returned and go with him to heaven. However, associated with this focus of separation is the need to see the "lost" being saved so that they too can go to heaven. So although a separation is maintained from the evil world, it is frequently traversed in order to evangelize.

Having discussed how mission was conceptualized from an organizational perspective we will examine how individual members were conceiving mission. For the majority of the first-generation immigrants in New York and London, mission was also conceived in terms of evangelism—winning souls. For one respondent in New York, the "mission is souls . . . winning [those] who [are] lost at any cost. That is the vision that [the senior minister] has and I've caught it ever since I came here."[78] For this respondent and many others at Latter Rain, this phrase, "winning the lost at any cost," constituted the mission statement or modus operandi not only of the church in Brooklyn but of the ministry in all of its locations. In London, a similar conception of mission was expressed. According to one respondent who was a deacon and a member of the pastor's council in Kingsbridge, the mission was "to win souls." He further stated, "I suppose for Christ . . . the main agenda was for souls."[79] One dynamic noted in this respondent's responses was the level of commitment he perceived to be associated with such a conceptualization. The work of winning souls was something that an individual had to be very committed to, probably even at the cost of one's family or one's life.

> [As] a Christian your main objective is for souls. And if you have your family and just [stay with] your family [all] the time you won't please God because sometimes you have to leave them and go. I've heard about many ministers that leave their families and go, go preach. Not that they don't love them but they've got a calling to go. I remember my first wife [now deceased] who was an evangelist, I'm sick in bed and she just cover me up and said, "Okay I going out." She gave me my meal, I got my bath and she put me in bed. Some people would say my wife is sick or my husband is sick I can't come out, but Jesus said leave them [and] go. Cause you are leaving him or her in the care of the Lord.[80]

For some respondents, like this deacon, biblical justification for such a belief could be found in scriptures like Luke 14: 26-27, which they interpreted as admonishing them to make their love of Jesus and acts of service a primary priority in their lives even before their family and themselves.

Among the immigrant children in New York and London, the conceptualization of mission as evangelism was also prominent. A second-generation respondent in London stated: "You can't separate the mission of [Kingsbridge] from that of the Bible which is you know the great commission but I, personally I think it's to expand the church. It is to sow the seeds of love and so that others would come to know Christ."[81] In Latter Rain Ministries this sentiment was also expressed in the following manner: "Our mission and sole mission and purpose is to win souls. If you done anything else well you're not doing what you're supposed to be doing cause my thing is that it all about winning souls."[82] Following this respondent's statements concerning mission, the other members of the group were asked for their opinions on mission. The majority agreed with the statement that this respondent had made.

However, in both contexts, some immigrant children were interrogating and critically examining such a conceptualization. One respondent articulated this in the following manner:

> To be honest I don't know. The official mission, I don't know. I could say that my pastor has stressed. What he says is souls . . . souls for the Lord. I mean I can take from that whatever I want. I don't know. Things that I've noticed don't equal to what I've heard. . . . I mean souls for the Lord that's all good, that's all fine, but it has to start somewhere and I don't know if it's starting in the right place. I don't know if we're starting in the right place. We've been on this block in this church for probably 30 years but nobody from this block comes to this church except for handful of people. . . . I don't think all nations [are] here. I don't see a percentage here from other nations. I do see a large amount of Caribbean people and I guess the way I'd take all nations is that everyone is welcome and I agree with that.[83]

For this respondent, if souls were so important, then the question that should be asked was why were members of other nationalities so noticeably absent. Although this respondent was able to accept the redefining of "all nations" on the church sign to mean that all nations were welcome, one still noted the underlying struggle to find a conceptualization that allowed for the synthesis of what was stated and what was practiced.

Within the London context, the interrogation by second-generation leaders and lay members was expressed in two forms: advocating for greater community involvement, as well as acknowledging the need for change in the meaning of mission within the church. Two respondents communicated these perspectives as follows:

> I see our mission really to meet the needs of the local community. I mean there are some people that [see it as] having TV ministries and all that sort of thing which I think is good. But for me it's meeting the needs of the local people and

been involved in community activities and community initiatives. Being aware of the issues that are relating to people within the local community whether that be things like gun crime, single parent families, drug abuse. On the local level being a centre for people where they can come to for help and support.[84]

I think this church as itself is looking for soul winning and a journey from birth to heaven. And in that journey trying to fulfill a positive lifestyle and morals, high standards, discipline. I think it's that journey getting toward heaven that's their mission, it is the mission of the church. The changes now I find is that the journey has changed significantly from when I was growing up. It was a particular road that we went on and it was quite a narrow road and we stayed on that road then you just look for it and you got there. Whereas now it seems as if the road has very, various roads coming off of it, but we're all still ending up with the same place. . . . [Before] you took on whatever your parents told you and . . . you just took it on without questioning cause we weren't allowed to question. . . . We found [that a lot of] what they were saying . . . was tradition, culture, rather than Biblical. As we're growing and have grown so to speak, now we're in a different era where your question things. You find out that Bible and tradition are two separate things and sometimes that becomes a little bit of a struggle, seems to be a contradiction to some people but that's the differences.[85]

For these two respondents, the mission of the church was to meet the needs of the local community, evangelism—evidenced in winning souls—and providing a pathway for people to journey to heaven. For the second respondent, this pathway which was formerly very narrow and marked by believing all that were told by her parents, had now broadened to include several pathways that allowed the individual to separate what was biblical from what was cultural tradition.

Thus, among the immigrant children in both contexts, we note that some reconceptualization of mission as evangelism was emerging. The significance of this development not only in the churches but also in their engagement with the wider society is a topic for further study and examination. In the section that follows, I will address some of the possible causes for this reconceptualization as well as discuss some of the missional practices occurring within the immigrant family and the Pentecostal churches.

In both the New York and London contexts, mission was practiced in a manner that was similar to the Jamaican/West Indian context, that is, focused primarily on evangelism, and local in its outlook. However, this similarity was exhibited in different degrees within the two contexts. There are several reasons for the degree of differences. One was the experiences that West Indian immigrants had in their diaspora contexts. The second was the variation that existed in the types of ethnic identities that West Indian families were renegotiating and constructing.

The third was the contexts themselves, which had a distinct history in both their development and interaction with immigrants.

In New York, continuation was seen in the perpetuation of personal and public forms of evangelism, namely hospital and prison visitations, street and public transportation evangelism, and occasionally open-air evangelistic meetings. Among some believers, engagement in both public and personal forms of evangelism was perceived as one of the main signifiers that an individual was a committed Christian. Simultaneously, for some members, a distinction was made between what was considered to be every believer's divine mandate to evangelize—normally seen as personal evangelism and the public forms which was the duty of those who were called to evangelize. During a group interview, one respondent stated, "Personally I'm not good at evangelizing. I am not the kind of person who's willing to get up and say okay let me go out there and preach on the bus. . . . I'm not that kind of person but if there [was a] push from here or somewhere I would do it."[86] The response from the vice president of the youth group, was "then that's not your calling. You have to walk in your calling. You cannot walk out of your calling. Okay you see because you are a Praise and Worship leader you can't say well I'm going to do evangelism. No you stick to what God call you to do."[87]

In terms of public evangelism, due to the demographic composition of the Brownsville and Flatlands sections of Brooklyn, this form of evangelism was normally geared toward fellow West Indians and other minorities. Although both Latter Rain and Beulah were involved in public evangelism there remained some difference in the forms that it took. In Beulah, the primary form of public evangelism involved members of the church's evangelism team going to high pedestrian areas like major intersections, subways, and bus stops, and to shopping malls, to preach and distribute evangelistic literature. For Beulah, this was quite important because these activities were incorporated into a church report that was submitted to the denominational headquarters.[88] Public evangelism for Latter Rain took the form of hospital and home visitations conducted by deacons and missionaries. Although both churches conducted open-air evangelism, this was infrequent. The reasons given for this irregularity was the difficulty associated with acquiring a permit from the police, the large amount of paperwork, and the large amount of work that accompanied organizing and having such an event.

Among the West Indian respondents in London, evangelism was predominantly articulated in terms of the personal evangelization of members of the black community. Although the focusing of evangelization within the black community, beginning in the 1960s and onward, was influenced by the antisocial and noise pollution laws of the day, it was primarily due to the discriminatory treatment immigrants received from the larger white community. One respondent who was involved in planting NTCG churches stated: "We actually targeted black people because on some white [people] doors, if you knock you would be insulted. . . . I'm not saying all of them were the same. But [as] the saying [states] once bitten twice shy."[89] Thus, within the London context, new converts were primarily "won" to Christ through the personal relationships that were established between themselves and the believers. In these relationships, the believer became a source of support and assistance—offering a listening ear, counsel, advice, and prayer—for the unconverted whenever they were encountering difficulty in their lives. For one respondent, her coming to Kingsbridge Church and her subsequent salvation were a result of the support and prayers that she received from a believer. She states:

> I really struggle[d] [with] these Pentecostal people. [laughs]. "Oh Lord!" She [the believer] said: "Come, come to my church. Come and visit my church." It took about four years for me to yield. . . . The struggle in my workplace was getting intensive. So one day I say, "Well, I will go with you." But all the time she comes [to church services] and ask prayer for me, so one day I said "I'll go with you." I came.[90]

One particular dynamic noted in both contexts in regard to personal evangelism was the gender specificity that was involved; women were encouraged to develop friendships with other women and men with men. In terms of public evangelism, sometimes this distinction was removed since this type of evangelism was conducted in public places and in teams. However, in certain contexts, like house visitation, evangelism was normally conducted by mixed gender groups or along gender lines. Respondents stated that these precautions were followed to protect church members and nonbelievers, and to prevent evangelistic work from suffering a loss to its reputation.

Another way that the practice of mission was reminiscent of home was in regard to the scope that evangelism took within the churches—that is, local evangelism. What changed in both contexts however was the manner in which "local" was defined. Whereas in the Jamaican context, "local" evangelism was defined in largely spatial terms, within the diaspora, this term took on some cultural appropriations. "Thus 'local' evangelism also [came] to signify evangelism specifically to members of the West Indian community who may or may not live in your spatially 'local' community."[91] Although this nuanced definition of the term "local" was exemplified by all three churches, here too there was some variation. On one level, Latter Rain Ministries embodied an international focus. According to the signboard on the church, it was "For All Nations." With eight branches in three countries and with continuing involvement in various mission trips to the Caribbean, the ministry may evidently seem to have an international scope. However, upon a closer investigation of the demographic composition within the branches and the targeted population on these mission trips it was noted that the majority were West Indians. Therefore although Latter Rain Ministries was international in its scope, it was still "local" within a cultural and ethnic sense. In Beulah too, it was this cultural/ethnic definition of "local" that was seen. Therefore, although the church was located within an area with a fair amount of minorities, the congregation was predominantly West Indian—many of whom travel from other communities in Brooklyn, as well as from Queens and Long Island to attend the church. One reason for the emergence of the cultural/ ethnic definition of local evangelism was the maintenance of various West Indian ethnic and religious identities that served to continuously link the immigrants to their islands of origin while simultaneously distinguishing them from the larger African American population among whom they lived and worked.

Although the redefinition of "local" evangelism to incorporate the ethnic/ cultural dynamic was also noted in London, it was not as prominent. For as the immigrant children—the second generation as well as later generations—came of age they were facilitating a process in which the term "local" was reclaiming much of its spatial/locational definition. The main catalysts of this change were the construction of black British identities among the immigrant children, their ascendance to various leadership positions within the churches, and their critical examination of how the church should function within its local special context both now and in the future. As a result of these developments, Kingsbridge was becoming a place where various members of the wider community were present, welcomed, and supported. One tangible manner in which Kingsbridge communicated this was by being one of the churches that conducted funerals for the young people from the community who were killed as a result of gun-related violence. According to one of the ministers, Kingsbridge did this as a way of caring for the community and offering support to the grieving families. What was notable in this situation was that in many cases both the family members of the deceased and many of those attending the funeral may not have had any prior contact with the church.

Kingsbridge had also implemented two programs that catered to the needs of people within the community—a Friday Youth Club and a community project for pensioners. Although the Brent County Council currently funded both programs, they were housed within the church buildings. The implications resulting from this relationship was complex. On one hand, Kingsbridge may gain a certain level of visibility among the members of Parliament, the law enforcement officers, and within the community as a result of being perceived as the "face" of these community ventures. However, this visibility may also result in the church undergoing greater scrutiny in terms of its finances and allocation of other resources. Concurrently, this relationship also fostered an environment in which both the leaders and members of Kingsbridge continued to interrogate the church's role in politics and the wider society. These community ventures were further complemented by several changes within the church geared toward making the church more welcoming to people who were not from a West Indian background. These included: prohibition on the use of patois in the services; implementation of more contemporary styles of worship—the use of multimedia technologies, in place of hymnbooks and pew Bibles, in the services; and removal of the restrictions that were placed on women's apparel, especially those related to trousers and head coverings.

One area where the churches in New York City and London were practicing mission in a different manner was in their use of multimedia and other kinds of technologies in their ministry. Through the Internet, Latter Rain and Kingsbridge could provide the gospel message to a wider audience, establish communication, and became a place of support and spiritual nurture for the wider public. On Kingsbridge's webpage, a visitor was able to download Sunday messages, sign up for weekly bulletins sent via electronic mail, and submit prayer requests. For all three churches, the role that multimedia technologies played in disseminating the gospel was indispensable. In Latter Rain, the use of multimedia was primarily seen in the recording and dispensing of sermons on compact discs. The move toward incorporating technology was not new. The sanctuary in the church was already equipped to facilitate the use of technologies. According to one respondent, "When . . . Bishop was erecting the new sanctuary . . . the wires were run already, everything was put in the ceiling. So the vision was there, [when this] all happened back in 2000, that we would use technology to get the gospel out."[92] In Beulah multimedia technologies were primarily used during the portions of the service that were under the leadership of the immigrant children, that is, during praise and worship and when the pastor's son was preaching.

In Kingsbridge by contrast, multimedia had become an essential feature in the Sunday service as overhead projectors and television screens replaced the hymnals and the pew Bibles. The projection of the service has also enabled worshippers in the balcony and the back of the church to see with greater clarity what was happening up front during the service.

Within the churches in New York, interaction with the community was conceived in terms of being a place of spiritual guidance and engaging in benevolent ministry. When respondents from both churches were asked about the church's involvement in the community, the majority of the responses were about the prayer meetings and/or the benevolent ministries (food and clothing distribution, and visiting the sick and prisoners) that the churches were performing. One respondent who was a deacon of one of the churches stated:

> We give things out, but we can't campaign near to us if other people campaign too, [because] people forget which person [is from which] outreach ministries. Also over at [name withheld] Hospital a lot of people come over to our service, to a prayer meeting here . . . three days from eleven to one o'clock Monday, Wednesday and Friday. It's a good [thing] and everything is done to feed them physically and spiritually and it's an outreach ministry.[93]

For one respondent the church's lack of engagement in the "practical" side of ministry was due to lack of space and also because a need for such a ministry did not exist in the surrounding community.

> You might see that [as a] practical way to help community with food and all these other things, to have a soup kitchen. Well we don't have the sort of convenience right now. . . . You know you live in some area and you find that this is not one area that people gravitate to. . . . You know they're not too hungry. . . . We're all of those are things [having a soup kitchen]. We discuss and we think of the practicality of it, do we have enough room? Then you need to know you have people who should be able to serve in those areas so there [you] are. I mean if I have the ability that I could do this. . . . There're some things that right now I, I realize that we got to [do]. . . . We probably can extend ourselves a bit more . . . in the sense of the verbal, you know verbal expression of the word you know and evangelism. . . . Of course that will entail people going and talking with people and people investing into people lives and relationship.[94]

In London Kingbridge's mission engagement included being involved within the community. This was in the form of the community projects that were documented earlier and the inauguration of an anticrime initiative called "Not one more drop of Blood." Through this venture, leaders in the church met periodically with the police about crime in the area and organized marches and campaigns geared toward highlighting the prominence of crime in the black community while calling for its reduction. Coupled with these initiatives, various church leaders participated in joint church meetings where they discussed some of the pertinent issues occurring within the community and drafted several documents that were then presented to leaders within the community. Finally, although members are not told which political party they should support, they were encouraged to become involved in the political process, especially by becoming members of the council boards.

Challenges for mission within the diaspora

Having examined some of the ways in which mission was being conceptualized and practiced within the diaspora, it was also necessary to consider some of the challenges associated with the conceptualization of mission as evangelism and the practices that accompany such a formulation.

One telling critique that has been leveled against Pentecostalism in general and these specific immigrant congregations in particular was their focus on the spiritual at the expense of being socially responsible and actively engaged within the socioeconomic and political contexts in which they are located.[95] Pentecostal theologian Edwin Villafañe notes, "While it is true that Pentecostalism has been recognized as a powerful force in evangelism, world missions, church growth and spirituality, it is equally true that their services and prophetic voices against sinful social structures and on behalf of social justice have been missing."[96] The exception in some cases would be the global emergence of Progressive Pentecostalism, where a holistic approach is taken in regard to the gospel and ministry and as a result of which Pentecostals are engaging in various social and political activities alongside their commitment to a belief in the coming kingdom of God.[97] It is unfortunate that this kind of holistic social engagement has often been absent within Pentecostalism within the region and in the diaspora. As documented earlier, Pentecostalism emerged in historical contexts where many Christians did not question the status quo. Instead, they focused primarily on issues related to their spirituality and being respectable, hardworking, law-abiding citizens. When the immigrants relocated to various diaspora contexts and began to establish churches, it was this religious heritage that became the substratum from which ministry and mission was and continues to be articulated.

One challenge for the churches will be the rediscovery of the prophetic voices within their West Indian Christian heritage. These are the prophetic voices of their ancestors who reinterpreted the gospel taught by the missionaries and white elite to produce a liberating force that transformed them from chattel slaves to children of God, entitled to freedom and liberty. It was also those elements within

West Indian culture that refused to be acquiesced or Westernized at the expense of the full humanity of the individual. In rediscovering this religious past, the churches will need to come to terms with how they have been shaped and what factors have resulted in their emergence. They will also need to acknowledge and interrogate the various ways in which Pentecostalism, both within the West Indies and in the diaspora contexts, has been and continues to be purged of these prophetic voices in its desire to attain respectability within the society. This will in turn assist them in reclaiming those parts of their heritage they have been taught to dismiss and degrade—the celebration of "blackness" seen in Afro-Christian religions like Revivalism and the social critique noted in other religious movements like Rastafari.[98]

Rediscovering their activist heritage will also challenge immigrant Pentecostal churches to re-interrogate exactly what the great commission means. Is it just to evangelize or is it also to see people and society transformed as they encounter the liberating presence of Christ?[99] For churches in New York especially, this may mean reevaluating the perceived ethnic and cultural barriers that continue to separate them from those within their communities and then taking steps to be a place where others are "welcomed" not only physically but culturally and religiously as well. For Kingsbridge, the challenge will be to sustain and further develop social engagement in a manner that it becomes the responsibility of all its members. Another aspect of this rediscovery will be acknowledging the ways in which Pentecostalism has facilitated America's ongoing spiritual and cultural hegemony within the region. For Kingsbridge and Beulah this is particularly important because although their local and regional leadership is black, at the denominational level the leadership that governs them is primarily Caucasian and American.[100] Although Latter Rain does not have this denominational dynamic, there is still a need to ask if it is creating a framework whereby the particular conceptualization and practice of mission emerging in the Brooklyn/New York context is then treated as normative for the branches in the other countries.

Another challenge posed for the immigrant churches is the place of the immigrant children. One phrase that was periodically heard during my fieldwork was, "a church without young people is a dead church." As the immigrant families continue to settle in the diaspora and their children construct identities heavily influenced by their contemporary context, it will be important for the churches to begin to revisit both their belief and practices concerning mission. For as the Pentecostal churches in London reveal, the perception of the world and its systems as mostly evil and the subsequent withdrawal into sacred spaces may have served to alienate many young people both within and outside of the church. For many of church youths the movement into silos and the church's failure to seriously engage what blacks were experiencing within the society made it irrelevant, that is, unable to speak into their experience as black youth. As a result many left the church for other movements like Rastafari or no religious association.[101] For those outside the church there was continued disengagement with organized religion. For some scholars, this lack of religious association and disengagement signifies that the immigrant children have assimilated within the wider British culture. However, accepting this viewpoint carte blanche would be to render these young people and especially those who left the church voiceless, unable to critique the church about the ways it alienates others. As these developments have occurred the leadership of the NTCG have become more responsive to needs of their youth. They have organized several programs focused on having a dialogue with young people about their concerns and how those concerns can be addressed; moreover, as a denomination the NTCG is also continuing to interrogate how the church can be more welcoming and nurturing for young people.

It is in this regard that the Pentecostal churches in London present the immigrant churches in New York with a window into the future. For both churches in New York it will be imperative to grapple with how to live out the reality of being a "child of God"—not in a manner that maintains the "us" versus "them" dichotomy but instead creates a place/space for meaningful interaction between individuals inside and outside the church. It is in this venture that the immigrant children may be the church's most valuable resource. They may be the ones who will spearhead the process of extricating tradition from orthodoxy and who seek to find various modes of articulation that facilitate the inception of religious beliefs and practices within contemporary contexts. Two areas in which this extricating process will be meaningful are in worship and leadership. What will constitute "meaningful" worship within the Diasporan contexts, both now and in the future? In the area of leadership, how can the contextual issues within the host society inform church life and ministry in a manner that enables the church to cooperate with other Christian communities as well as give a listening ear to what "non-Christians have to offer and to criticize?"[102]

The immigrant congregations in NYC and London also exist within a period of dynamic changes within world Christianity—changes which have made the rhetoric of reverse mission a staple within academic discourse. Reverse mission or mission in the reverse examines the spiritual dimension which accompanies and influences the movement of Christians primarily from the non-Western world to the West. For many of these immigrants, this spiritual dimension is communicated in terms of having a divine commission to reinvigorate or re-Christianize the increasingly secularized nations to which they owe their Christian heritage.[103] Associated with this term is an ideology which, "if taken seriously—would turn the traditional relationship between African-European, not to mention the responsibility that go with it, on its head."[104] For, on the one hand, "reverse mission" calls into question many of the stereotypes that Westerners have of non-Westerners; on the other, it also facilitates a reorientation of the axis of association between the West and the majority world, so that the non-Western nations now become the center and the West the periphery.

Although migrant communities have helped to revitalize church attendance in certain places, further interrogation of the pervasiveness of this revitalization in terms of the host communities is required. Is the revitalization interpreted primarily in the overall statistical increase in the amount of people attending church or in charting a change in the religious practices of the nonmigrant population? Associated with this process is the ongoing transformation of the relationships that exist between the Christians of the non-Western and Western world. For as Lesslie Newbigin states, "We need their [the non-Western Christians] witness to correct ours [the Western Christians], as indeed they need ours to correct theirs. . . . For they have been far more aware of the danger of syncretism, of an illegitimate alliance with false elements in their culture, than we have been. But whether it is we or they, we imperatively need one another if we are to be faithful witnesses to Christ."[105]

The challenge therefore for the West Indian immigrant churches in New York and London is to discover where they fit in this process. What can they learn from and contribute to the ongoing debate about interaction with the host society? In this regard, there is also the need for greater interaction and cooperation between immigrant and other minority churches. This interaction—specifically between African American, and African and West Indian immigrants—will demand that they critically examine the causes for the disunity that has persisted between them. How can their common heritage—as believers who have an African ancestry—become a means of overcoming divisive issues and a means of facilitating the emergence of forums of collaboration?

Conclusion

In the coming years, it is projected that the face and practices of world Christianity will continue to undergo profound changes. However, unlike in the twentieth century, the driving forces behind these changes will be emanating from non-Western Christian contexts. One arena in which these changes will be manifested is in the emergence and growth of non-Western Christian communities in the Western nations. For as many of the non-Western immigrants relocated to the developed countries, they carried with them not only a vibrant Christian faith fashioned within and excavated from the experiences and developments of their homeland, but also what they perceived to be a divine mandate to re-evangelize the North. Armed with this divine mandate and with a religion able to cross boundaries, immigrant churches are finding creative ways to carving to conceptualize and practice mission. For West Indian immigrant churches, this is accomplished by drawing upon a West Indian Pentecostal heritage fashioned from the reformulation of American Pentecostalism within an Afro-Christian framework that is then inserted into the regional religious landscape. As a result, mission, as it is conceived and practiced by these Pentecostal immigrant churches, is primarily evangelistic and focused on redeeming a fallen world to its creator. Simultaneously, however, these immigrant churches are also undergoing various changes as various "agents" from inside and outside of the churches are challenging their current conceptualization and practice of mission.

Within the churches, this challenge is primarily embodied in the immigrant children. Born and raised in the diaspora, these immigrant children desire to see the church become a place where exclusive cultural traditions make room for active engagement with contemporary contexts and a rediscovery of the prophetic elements of the West Indian religious past. Outside of the church, this challenge is seen in the drive toward greater cooperation between various immigrant churches, for example, between West Indians and Africans, and the host churches. For as Andrew Walls correctly asserts, we need each other in order to be the body of Christ in the world.[106] Given the challenges that are arising and the current academic discourse on reverse mission and its impact or lack thereof on the host churches, it is warranted to say that the years ahead may be ones of questioning for these West Indian immigrant communities as they continue to seek to be led by the spirit in the contemporary contexts in which they exist.

In adding this final portion to the tapestry, I have highlighted that while West Indian Pentecostal churches are drawing on those strands that were created in the West Indies, some of those strands are undergoing major changes, and new ones are being added. Pivotal in the addition of these new strands, however, are the challenges that are arising within these religious communities from the immigrant youth and the wider society.

Conclusion: Living their Faith

If religion is to flourish, the needs and conditions, the fears, the anxieties, the hopes and aspirations to which it is addressed must be real in the experience of the believer.

C. Eric Lincoln, *Race, Religion and the Continuing American Dilemma*
(New York: Hill & Wang, 1999 [1984]), 61

It has been argued throughout this book that to perceive immigrant religious communities as existing primarily as colonies or inward-looking communities is problematic. First, by adhering to such a perspective, one may continue to perpetuate the identification of these religious communities within the wider society as foreign entities whose value is quantified only in relation to their deviation from the ascribed norms of the society. In doing this, one may run the risk of overlooking the ways in which the host society also contributes to the creation and proliferation of these perceived "insular" organizations. Second, such conclusions fail to seriously consider the importance of these religious communities within the lives of immigrants. For as this book and the above-mentioned quote by C. Eric Lincoln indicate, these religious institutions thrived because they addressed many of the felt needs of the immigrants. In the process, they became places that facilitated the immigrants' adaptation to the host society while simultaneously maintaining various transnational ties with their home country.

By highlighting these particular issues, this book has sought not only to analyze an ongoing development within world Christianity, but also to address several areas that have been largely neglected in the academic discourses within the United States and Britain. For although several scholars are engaged in examining how faith communities are influencing the post-1965 migrants to the United States, their attention is predominantly focused on Hispanics, Asians, and Africans—the ethnic groups that constitute the largest percentage of recent migrants.[1] As a result, the impact of faith communities on West Indian migrants has been largely neglected.[2] Within the British context by contrast, several scholars have investigated and documented the role that faith communities play within the West Indian population.[3] However, the majority of the studies have been centered on the experiences of the first generation with minimal attention given to the influence of these faith communities among later generations.[4]

Throughout this book, the examination of immigrant faith communities was conducted within the context of three Pentecostal churches in which some West Indian migrants in Brooklyn and London participated and was centered on two themes: One, the manner in which these religious communities facilitated the construction and renegotiation of ethnic and religious identities among three generations of West Indian migrants; two, the role these communities played within the conceptualization and practice of mission within global and local contexts. In order to analyze these two themes however, it was necessary to address two preliminary areas. The first was to briefly review the process by which various ethnic and religious identities were formulated within the West Indian context. This reexamination, documented in Chapter 1, highlighted the multiplicity of the players involved and some of the factors that have made these identities a reality. Thus, when the Africans, British, Spanish, Americans, and other nationalities interacted within the framework of slavery, colonization, and Christianization, the result were several West Indian ethnic and religious identities. Central to these identities was a characterization marked by cultural and religious dynamism, as well as an aptitude toward survival and adaptation in the midst of adversity. As these specific features of the ethnic and religious identities became embedded within the ethno-cultural and religious DNA of the West Indian population, they provided the foundation for the interaction between the immigrants and their new context.

The second issue explored was the factors that have contributed to the relocation of the migrants and the emergence of the immigrant Pentecostal churches. In Chapter 2, it was argued that when investigating migration, immigrants, and the related faith communities, room has to be given for a diversity of perspectives. In this regard, this chapter sought to critique the dominance of the economic rhetoric—that is, push-pull model—within the empirical studies on West Indian migration, by highlighting the role that the historical economic interaction between the West Indies and other countries, the proliferation of certain images, immigration laws, and the family played within the migration process. It is only in examining all of these factors that one gains an adequate picture of why many West Indian immigrants chose to migrate. In discussing the emergence of the West Indian faith communities, a multidimensional approach was also critical, particularly while studying the roles both the host context and the immigrants' backgrounds and histories played in this process. This was because immigrant faith communities, like other social organizations, were actively involved in a process where they were simultaneously influencing and been influenced by the context in which they were located.[5] Thus, when West Indian immigrants encountered various discriminatory ideologies, structures, and practices within the American and British societies that were directed toward the minority populations among whom they were classified, they utilized their ethnic and religious resources to create spaces of belonging, empowerment, and survival. This took the forms of ethnic enclaves and social organizations—specifically, religious communities. This chapter also highlighted the ways that the host context contributed to the formation and maintenance of various transnational ties. In this regard this chapter served to document some of the ways in which migrants were able to articulate what it meant to be a West Indian Pentecostal in a foreign land. As a result, West Indians were also able to correct negative stereotypes, while also articulating their position as sojourners in a foreign land.

In Chapters 3 through 5, the two major themes of this research, identity and mission, were considered. Particular attention was given to the role Pentecostal communities played in West Indian migrants' engagement with these themes. Chapter 3 illustrated the manner in which these faith communities fulfilled a multiplicity of functions within the lives of the first generation. In the perpetuation of the rituals and religious beliefs from the home context, the first generation found a place where their West Indian culture and values are celebrated and treated as normative. In the circle of believers, they found a family that was ready to support them in various forms—socially, financially, legally, etc. These faith communities also provided a space where their ethnic and religious identities were renegotiated. This chapter also demonstrated how the construction and the internalization processes whereby boundaries are legitimized and identities are articulated among first-generation migrants occurred within a migration framework. For the first-generation West Indian immigrants examined in this chapter, these processes involved using the ethnic and religious identities from their countries of origin to negotiate what it meant to be a West Indian Pentecostal in a foreign land. As a result of carving out this unique space the first generation continued to call the host society to acknowledge their presence, not just as foreigners and thus the other but also as a viable and important segment of the society.

Chapter 4 argued that the role religious communities play in the lives of West Indian immigrant children cannot be understated. For in a context where ethnic minority youths were facing a diversity of trajectories in terms of their integration within the host society, including downward mobility and incorporation into the ethnic minority underclass, religious communities provided them with many of the social and religious tools needed to navigate the terrains of adolescence and young adulthood. In the Brooklyn context, this was demonstrated by fostering the construction of West Indian-oriented ethnic and religious identities. Thus, the immigrant children and youth were able to develop an alternate pathway toward social and economic mobility and integration into middle-class African American society. In London, the combination of the contextual and cultural features within the religious communities resulted in the construction of hybrid identities among immigrant youth that not only incorporate elements of both features but also critique them as well. Thus, located within many of these identities was the prominence of issues relating to roots and belonging and the need to actively engage with the structures and systems within the host society. In this manner the immigrant youth called on society to reexamine those structures that continued to oppress and marginalize minorities, and asked the religious communities to be more relevant, giving sufficient consideration to the issues influencing their lives. Within this chapter the intergenerational critique of the West Indian Pentecostal church was given particular attention. This attention was aimed at investigating some of the ways in which these institutions empowered and disempowered children/young people and to discuss some of the ways in which the children and young people are challenging the church in terms of its worship, organizational structure, and rituals.

Chapter 5, which focused on the term mission, sought to highlight some of the dynamics that have accompanied the well-documented demographic shift in world Christianity, particularly the emergence and proliferation of non-Western Christian communities in Western nations. For, as many immigrants relocated to the developed countries, they carried with them not only a vibrant Christian faith fashioned within and excavated from the experiences and developments of their homeland, but also what they perceived to be a divine mandate to re-evangelize the North. Armed with this supernatural authorization and a religion that is able to traverse national boundaries, these faith communities were engaged in a process where their conception and practice of mission was undergoing dramatic changes. For the West Indian religious communities, the Pentecostal heritage, fashioned from the reformulation of American Pentecostalism within an Afro-Caribbean Christian framework, has not only resulted in their mission being conceived and practiced as evangelism, but also as social engagement with the wider society.[6] This chapter also demonstrated how some of these faith communities functioned as sites where global and local forces exerted influence upon the conceptualization and practice of mission within the host context. Thus, while mission activities may be global—that is, initiated within several national contexts—they may be centered on a particular immigrant population. Religious beliefs and practices that were local to the home context were translated to the global contexts of the host societies. As a result, the terms global and local became more nuanced. Simultaneously, this translational process also became one of dynamism and constant negotiation—as the faith communities functioned as sites where ideas emanating from the home and host society were able to critique and influence each of those contexts.

In conducting this research, I have sought to undertake an examination of Pentecostal churches among West Indian migrants in New York City and London, in the hope that it will encourage further discussion about the manner in which Christianity is being appropriated by various religious traditions within contemporary contexts. In striving to fulfill this goal, I will conclude this chapter by highlighting some of the areas in which further academic research is warranted.

One area requiring additional research is youth, religion, and globalization. As the world becomes an increasingly connected unit, the significance of religion has not diminished; instead, it has become a crucial marker of identity, a space for social and cultural formation as well as a medium through which various traditional practices and beliefs are reappropriated. Coinciding with these developments is the dramatic demographic shift in the center of gravity of world Christianity, from Western countries to non-Western ones. As a result, most of the world's youth reside in the very areas where Christianity has the majority of its adherents.[7] Therefore, if we are to understand Christianity within contemporary contexts and speculate about what its practices and process will be in the twenty-first century, we will need to focus our attention on the religious lives of young people. As a generation, youth constitute the frontline in terms of cultural and social change.[8] It is their engagement with Christianity, its ideas, and institutions that will reveal not only the future expressions of religious beliefs and practices, but also the extent to which it will be resilient, innovative, and adaptable in relation to wider global, social, and cultural developments. Within this framework, it will be necessary to investigate how youth are appropriating faith in a variety of contexts—giving particular attention to those areas that have not garnered much research within academic discourse, that is, the non-Western world and the diasporan contexts. Another question that will need to be addressed is: How are youth in Africa, Asia, and Latin America appropriating their Christianity in terms of global developments and their local ethno-cultural and religious dynamics?[9] Although this research has highlighted some of the ways in which some second and third generation West Indian children are appropriating faith and challenging the doctrines, rituals, and organizational structures of immigrant faith communities, it was focused on churches within a Pentecostal tradition. Therefore additional research is needed to explore how West Indian immigrant children are appropriating faith within mainline churches as well as in other diasporan contexts, for example Canada. Finally, in exploring the relationship between youth, religion, and globalization, attention needs to be given to the role that media, the internet, and other forms of technology play within this interaction.

Another area requiring further research is the immigrant church in diasporan and global contexts. As this research has revealed, this institution is pivotal in the lives of many immigrants. Given its prominence, it will be imperative to investigate how these institutions are assisting their members to navigate some of the issues and realities that accompany immigrant life, such as marriage, gender politics within the home, and the presence of female clergy. Associated with this area is the interrogation of the manner in which these immigrant faith communities can be seen to represent the frontlines of a possible theological and power shift within world Christianity. Even as these churches become inserted within the fabric of the host community, they are exhibiting dynamic financial strength as they raise funds to purchase their church buildings and other commercial properties.[10] In this regard, some of these immigrant churches are debunking some of the stereotypes that have persisted about non-Western people and their financial status. Alternatively, many of these immigrant faith communities are interacting with the host communities from a perception of orthodox Christianity that is constructed with a non-Western framework. By so doing there is the reemergence of the "cultural variety and plurality of idioms [that] were inscribed [within] the original character of Christianity."[11] The implications of this reemergence and the growing financial strength of contemporary immigrant faith communities within the diasporan and global contexts, on the future of world Christianity, is an area that will require further research. Some questions to explore are: How are the religious landscapes in New York and London changing as a result of the diversity of expressions within Christianity and the financial independence of immigrant churches? What are the theologies that are now emerging as a result of this diversity within world

Christianity and the immigrant experience? How do they enrich the overall texture of Christianity on a global scale?

Central in the future studies of youth and religion, and immigrant faith communities in the diaspora, will be the way in which immigrant youth and their parents and grandparents are living their faith, that is, how their faith influences all aspects of their lives. As this book reveals, it is in this space where ethnic and religious identities are negotiated and/or constructed, mission is conceptualized and practiced, and generations of immigrants are drawing on their histories, cultures, etc., to inform and challenge the wider socioeconomic, political, and religious contexts in which they live, work, and worship.

Postscript: Engaging the Field

The insider-outsider debate has received a fair treatment in scholarly literature across disciplines.[1] With the flourishing of research by native ethnographers—immigrants or members of other groups conducting research within their own communities—this debate remains an important area of discussion.[2] For the critics of insider research, this approach is seen as "lacking critical distance and [the] objective stance necessary for effective scholarship."[3] This critique is countered with the argument that while outsiders have critical distance, they lack the cultural and "contextual understanding of the community."[4] In what follows I discuss how I engaged with the insider/outsider debate and the impact it had on my fieldwork and research as a whole.

I am a female Jamaican/American who is a member of a transnational family that has ties to several nations—Jamaica, Trinidad, Canada, the United States, and Britain.[5] Some relatives and I have been members of West Indian immigrant churches similar to those being examined in this book. Given the above realities, negotiating the insider/outsider dynamic and the accompanying issues were an ever-present aspect of my fieldwork. On one level, I approached this study as an insider, in that there was certain cultural understanding and experiences that I had in common with the informants. Simultaneously, I was an outsider on another level—I was an ethnographic researcher who was interacting with immigrants and religious communities, the majority of whose members I had little or no prior relationship with. In conducting this study, it became clear that my role as insider/outsider was frequently situational, "depending on the prevailing social, political and cultural values of a given social [and religious] context."[6] Two areas in which this was apparent were gaining access and positionality, and obtaining credible information.

In all three churches gaining access took on various nuances. Principal in gaining access was obtaining permission to conduct fieldwork. This necessitated meeting with the senior pastors of the churches to share a little about my own background and research aim, about how I became interested in the topic I wanted to study, and to give them a brief summary of my research proposal. Following these meetings, I received the administrative consent needed to proceed. Although these meetings all produced the same outcome—permission to proceed with fieldwork—there were certain details that highlighted various aspects of my insider/outsider status.

In the case of Latter Rain Ministries in Brooklyn, administrative permission was obtained twice—initially in July 2006 when I was given preliminary approval and introduced to the congregation as someone who would be returning in 2007 to conduct research, and again in February 2007 when I began fieldwork. Upon my arrival in February 2007 to commence fieldwork, my outsider status was brought to the fore. For although I now had final approval from the senior pastor to conduct fieldwork I still needed to engage directly with one of the key leaders in the church who functioned as a gatekeeper to access informants. This leader determined my level of access in that she reintroduced me to the congregation as a researcher, gave me the telephone numbers of the leaders to contact, arranged a group interview with the teens and young people, and suggested some people for me to interview. Within the group interview another gatekeeper was present— the vice president of the youth group. This group was preselected and included those teens and young people who were observed to be very active within the church. This was balanced by also interviewing some of the young people not included in this group. It bears noting that both times I was introduced to the congregation my insider/outside status was highlighted, for while I was introduced as a Jamaican and a Christian (an insider), it was in the context of a researcher who was studying the congregation (thus an outsider).

With regard to Beulah Church, although I received permission from the senior minister to conduct research, I was never formally introduced to the congregation. My introductions to the members were on an individual rather than communal basis and were brokered in two ways—through relatives who were leaders in the church and informally by some of the leaders who knew that I was doing research on the congregation. As a result, for some people I was seen as an insider—the relative of church leaders whom they loved and respected— while for others I was positioned in an in-between space, neither an outsider nor an insider. For these people while I had received the approval of the pastor and the leadership, they were not sure where to place me, or my research within the overall schema of the "way things were" in the church.

In Kingsbridge Church in London, administrative approval was accompanied by three events that pointed to an overlap between my insider and outsider status. First, I was asked by the senior minister how many informants I would need for the study. Second, in the process of being formally introduced as a researcher to the congregation by the senior minister, he remarked, "she is one of ours," and therefore members were encouraged to assist me as much as possible.

Third, the acting secretary was asked to compile a list of members who were willing to be interviewed and to give the list to me. Later on in the fieldwork as I became aware of certain gaps, both the senior minister and leaders were very cooperative in assisting me in rectifying this.

Thus, in the context where I was most conscious of my outsider status—I was not as familiar with the British context as I was with the American context. I was growing in my knowledge of church life on England, and I had not had any prior meetings or connections with this church. I was treated in a manner that moved me from the outsider end of the insider/outsider spectrum to somewhere in between, the researcher who is "one of ours." In contrast, what was most surprising for me in regard to the churches in Brooklyn was how much my outsider status factored into my interaction with the leadership and members of the congregations. In many ways I had thought that my familiarity with the context and prior contact with churches before commencing fieldwork, would have placed me closer to the insider side of the spectrum. Finding myself somewhere in between an insider and an outsider in Brooklyn and London contexts highlighted the need of adjusting my fieldwork timeline to give more time to participating in services and becoming familiar with the congregation before conducting interviews (two and half months in Brooklyn and about three weeks in London). It also facilitated my ongoing examination and critical reflection on the dynamics underlying and resulting from the shifts in my position as an insider/outsider.

In obtaining credible information, I started my interviews with the members and leaders who were recommended either by the gatekeeper at Latter Rain or the senior pastor at Kingsbridge. In the case of Latter Rain, I decided that given the gatekeeper's significant role in the church, it was important to include her in the study. In this manner, she would become more familiar with what I was doing, thus enabling me to interact more freely and interview those who were not previously recommended. Adjusting my fieldwork timeline to give more time to familiarize with the congregation was also important in ensuring that I would receive credible information. This also allowed me access to people who were not on the recommended lists. Including their input in the research was vital in ensuring a balance in perspectives. In the cases where I conducted a group interview, I would follow-up with several individual interviews so that I could ask additional questions about what had been shared.

Another practice that fostered the collection of credible information and assisted in my becoming familiar with the congregation was attending the midweek, youth, and other services. At Kingsbridge I made it my weekly practice to attend the Monday fasting and prayer meetings. As one of the few young people in attendance I got the opportunity to pray with, interact, and build relationships with the older members of the congregation. These meetings also provided an opportunity where I was seen as a fellow believer, who prayed with them about their children, their ailments, their daily lives, and other prayer needs. These moments provided me with their perspectives on West Indian life in London and created an openness and willingness to speak with me and participate in my research.

Of the three churches, Beulah was the one that required the most self-reflection and analysis in regard to obtaining credible information. As stated previously, I had relatives who had been and were members of this church. At the same time, I was staying with these relatives during the course of my fieldwork. While this arrangement allowed me to be close to both research sites, these realities added another dimension to the information that I became privy to, both from relatives and from members. At times I wondered if I was being told the information because I was the relative of a member or as a researcher. I also had to consider what was the motive behind what I was being told. Was I seen as a power broker who would somehow validate a certain position from what was shared? Added to this, the recommendations for people to interview primarily came from the members. As the fieldwork progressed I became more aware of the various groups within the church and their allegiances. Given the complexity that governed the Brooklyn context, my self-reflection on the dynamics that were at play, and in order not to have the data collected co-opted to support a certain position, I decided that it would be best for the integrity of the research to use this church as a secondary study site and make Latter Rain, the other Brooklyn church, and Kingsbridge the primary ones.

As a West Indian immigrant studying other West Indian immigrants, I am considered as an insider.[7] However as I have shown above, my identification as an insider/outsider within the religious communities that I studied was not predetermined or static. Instead, it changed and fluctuated as a result of the particularities within the local communities, the nature of the research, actions taken over the course of the fieldwork, and having to navigate certain familial relations and dynamics. As I found myself on different points on the insider/outsider spectrum it became crucial to continually engage in self-reflection and critical analysis on what I was observing and hearing, to pay attention to what was spoken/unspoken, power structures, and other features governing the religious community in order to preserve the integrity of my fieldwork and the overall research project.

Notes

Introduction

1 David A. Roozen, William McKinney and Jackson W. Carroll, *Varieties of Religious Presence: Mission in Public Life* (Cleveland: The Pilgrim Press, 1984), 4–15.

2 Within the rural context, many residents related to others based on their parish or county associations. Once immigrants moved to the diaspora, the competing parish or county distinctions lost much of their salience as the immigrants adjusted to life and the accompanying common experiences within their new contexts.

3 Steph Lawler, *Identity: Sociological Perspectives* (Cambridge: Polity Press, 2008), 2.

4 Ibid., 3.

5 Mary Waters, *Believing Identities: West Indian Immigrant Dream and American Realities* (New York: Russell Sage, 1999), 47.

6 Stuart Hall, "Introduction: Who needs 'Identity'?" in *Questions of Cultural Identity*, ed. Stuart Hall and Paul du Gray (London: Sage Publications, 1996), 4–5.

7 Neither of these processes is unified or complete but is ongoing, changing in light of the realities encountered within the society.

8 Hall, "Who Needs Identity?," 4.

9 David Bosch, *Transforming Mission: Paradigm Shifts in Theology of Mission* (Maryknoll: Orbis Books, 1998), 392.

10 Ray S. Anderson, ed., *Theological Foundations for Ministry* (Grand Rapids: Eerdmans, 1979), 544–5.

11 This was normally conducted within a Western constructed framework.

12 As a result of these critiques, especially in the non-Western contexts, evangelism (proclamation and discipleship) was reformulated within a holistic framework, one in which the "proclamation [was] not merely for 'spiritual' solace but for practical impacts in the real world." Ken Gnanakan, "To proclaim the Good News of the Kingdom (i)," in *Mission in the Twenty-first Century*, ed. Andrew Walls and Cathy Ross (London: Darton, Longman and Todd, 2008), 6; Stephen B. Bevans and Roger Schroeder, *Constants in Context: A Theology of Mission for Today* (Maryknoll: Orbis Books, 2004), 239–80.

13 Michael W. Foley and Dean R. Hoge, *Religion and the New Immigrants: How Faith Communities Form Our Newest Citizens* (New York: Oxford University Press, 2007); Jacob K. Olupona and Regina Gemignani, eds, *African Immigrant Religions in America* (New York: New York University Press, 2007); Gerrie ter Haar, ed.,

Strangers and Sojourners: Religious Communities in the Diaspora (Leuven: Peeters, 1998). For West Indians in the America and Britain, this context was a racial one, governed by the proliferation of several discriminatory stereotypes about minorities, especially those of African descent.

14 Foley and Hoge, *New Immigrants,* 10.

15 Ibid.

16 John A. Arthur, *The African Diaspora in the United States and Europe: The Ghanaian Experience* (Aldershot: Ashgate Publishing, 2008), 101–2.

17 Minette Marrin, "Should we limit immigrants to Europeans?" *The Sunday Times,* June 17, 2007, accessed October 9, 2008, http://www.timesonline.co.uk/tol/comment/columnists/minette_marrin/article1942934.ece; Ruben Navarrette Jr., "Commentary: Immigrants melting into the pot as usual," *CNN Politics. Com,* May 27, 2008, accessed October 9, 2008, http://edition.cnn.com/2008/POLITICS/05/27/navarette.may.27/index.html.

18 Nicole Rodriguez Toulis, *Believing Identity: Pentecostalism and the Mediation of Jamaican Ethnicity and Gender in England* (Oxford: Berg, 1997), 2.

19 These were typically constructed within an Anglo-Saxon middle-class framework.

20 Mary C. Waters, "Ethnic and Racial Identities of Second-Generation Black Immigrants in New York City," *International Migration Review* 28, no. 4, (1994): 804.

21 Paul A. Pomerville, *The Third Force in Missions* (Peabody: Hendrickson Publishers, 1985), xi.

22 In order to maintain the confidentiality of this research, pseudonyms will be used for informants and the churches. Throughout this book, the two churches will be designated as Latter Rain Ministries and Beulah Church, and the church in London will be Kingsbridge Church.

23 In the New York City context, very few third-generation informants were available because the immigrant population is predominantly first and second generation.

24 An immigrant was designated as 1.5 if they migrated to the host country before or during their early teenage years. Ruben G. Rumbaut and Kenji Ima, *The Adaptation of Southeast Asian Refugee Youth: A Comparative Study* (Washington, DC: U.S. Office of Refugee Resettlement, 1998), 1–2.

25 This included three males and eight females.

Chapter 1

1 Hugh Thomas, *The Slave Trade: The History of the Atlantic Slave Trade: 1440–1870* (London: Papermac, 1998 [1997]), 11.

2 Manuel Castells, *The Information Age: Economy, Society, Culture,* vol. 2 The Power of Identity (Oxford: Blackwell Publishing, 2004 [1997]), 7.

3 Orlando Patterson, *The Sociology of Slavery* (London: Macgibbon & Kee Ltd, 1967), 9.

4 The people of the West Indian islands are predominantly of African descent and consequently comprised the majority of the immigrants in the diaspora. Although there are many East Indians in Trinidad and Tobago, and Guyana, their numerical presence among the immigrants is small.

5 Justo L. González, foreword to *A Violent Evangelism: The Political and Religious Conquest of the Americas*, by Luis N. Rivera (Louisville: Westminster/John Knox Press, 1992), ix.

6 "The Bull Inter Caetera (Alexander VI.). May 4, 1493," in *European Treaties bearing on the History of the United States and its Dependencies to 1648*, ed. Frances Gardiner Davenport (Washington, DC: Carnegie Institution of Washington, 1917), 77.

7 Samuel Eliot Morison and Maurico Obregón, *The Caribbean as Columbus Saw it* (Boston: Little, Brown and Company: 1964), 19.

8 Samuel Eliot Morison, *Admiral of the Ocean: A Life of Christopher Columbus* (Boston: Little, Brown and Company: 1942), 229.

9 Ibid., 13.

10 De Orbe Novo, *The Eight Decades of Peter Martyr D'Anghera*, trans. Francis Augustus MacNutt, vol. 1 (New York: Burt Franklin, 1970 [1912]), 63.

11 Patrick Hylton, *The Role of Religion in Caribbean History* (Kearney: Morris Publishing, 2002), 156–7; Jayme A. Sokolow, *The Great Encounter: Native Peoples and European Settlers in the Americas, 1492-1800* (London: M.E. Sharpe, 2003), 212–13.

12 Lewis Hanke, *Aristotle and the American Indians* (Chicago: Henry Regnery Company, 1959), 13.

13 Anthony Pagden, *The Fall of Natural Man: The American Indian and the Origins of Comparative Ethnology* (New York: Cambridge University Press, 1982), 23.

14 Ibid., 24.

15 Ondina E. Gonzalez and Justo L. Gonzalez, *Christianity in Latin America: A History* (New York: Cambridge University Press, 2008), 43.

16 Pagden, *The Fall of Natural Man*, 104.

17 Ibid., 29.

18 For more information on the encomienda system, see: Rivera, *A Violent Evangelism*, 113–31.

19 Ibid., 126.

20 Bartolomé de Las Casas, *A Short Account of the Destruction of the Indies* (New York: Penguin Books, 1992), 11.

21 William M. Denevan, introduction to *The Native Population of the Americas in* 1492, ed. William M. Denevan (Madison: The University of Wisconsin Press, 1976), 5.

22 Rivera, *A Violent Evangelism*, 176.

23 "500 years of Indigenous Resistance," *Oh-Toh-Kin* 1, no. 1, (winter/spring 1992), accessed March 2004, http://www.dickshovel.com/500.html.

24 Noël Deerr, *History of Sugar* (London: Chapman and Hall Ltd., 1949), 116.

25 J. W. Purseglove, *Tropical Crops: Monocotyledons* (London: Longman Group Ltd., 1974), 607.

26 Peter Sharpe, *Sugar Cane: Past and Present*, accessed October 10, 2007, http://www.siu.edu/~ebl/leaflets/sugar.htm.

27 Rivera, *A Violent Evangelism*, 181.

28 Ibid.

29 Ibid., 182.

30 James Walvin, *Making the Black Atlantic: Britain and the African Diaspora* (London: Cassell, 2000), 13–21.

31 Philip Sherlock and Hazel Bennett, *The Story of the Jamaican People* (Kingston: Ian Randle Publishers Limited, 1998), 79.

32 Ibid., 81.

33 The word Maroon is derived from the Spanish word *cimarrón*, the root of which is *cima* meaning peak, summit, or top. Originally it referred to domestic cattle that had escaped into the mountains. Over time it was used exclusively for runaway slaves. Richard Price, ed. *Maroon Societies* (New York: Anchor Books, 1973), 1 n. 1.

34 Michael Craton, *Testing the Chains: Resistance to Slavery in the British West Indies* (Ithaca: Cornell University Press, 1982), 61.

35 Eric Williams, *Capitalism and Slavery* (London: Andre Deutsch Limited, 1964), 51–84, 98–107; Geoff Palmer, *The Enlightenment Abolished* (Penicuik: Henry Publishing, 2007), 22–38.

36 See Colin Kidd's discussion on how the curse of Ham was perceived by many United States Southerners and some of their contemporary commentators to be "a divine sanction for race slavery." Colin Kidd, *The Forging of Races: Race and Scripture in the Protestant Atlantic World, 1600–2000* (Cambridge: Cambridge University Press, 2006), 139–41.

37 Twagilimana Aimable, *The Debris of Ham* (New York: University Press of America, 2003), 41.

38 See James Walvin, *Black and White: The Negro and English Society 1555–1945* (London: Allen Lane The Penguin Press, 1973); Cornel West, *Prophesy Deliverance/ An Afro-American Revolutionary Christianity* (Philadelphia: Westminster Press, 1982), 55–61.

39 Samuel Yeboah, *The Ideology of Racism* (London: Hanslib Publishing Limited, 1988), 44–5.

40 Eric Williams, *From Columbus to Castro* (London: Andre Deutsch Ltd., 1970), 112.

41 The majority were exiled to the West Indies as a result of various measures instituted by Oliver Cromwell. David Stevenson, "Cromwell, Scotland and

Ireland," in *Oliver Cromwell and the English Revolution,* ed. John Morrill (London: Longman, 1990), 166–7.

42 Richard Bean, *The British Trans-Atlantic Slave Trade, 1650–1775* (Michigan: University Microfilms, 1971), 103–4; and Williams *Capitalism and Slavery,* 13–19.

43 Donna Essix, *Brief History of Jamaica,* accessed February 2005, http://www. jamaicans.com/info/brief.htm.

44 Ibid.

45 Thomas *The Slave Trade,* 555.

46 Ibid., 355. In the case of the Dahomeys, once the slave trade began, it was maintained by the succeeding generations of royalty. King Agaja's involvement was followed by that of his son King Tegbesu and his grandson King Kpengla.

47 Ibid., 187.

48 R. B. Sheridan, "The Wealth of Jamaica in the Eighteenth Century," *The Economic History Review* 18, no. 2 (1965): 304.

49 Patterson, *The Sociology of Slavery,* 38.

50 David Watts, *The West Indies: Patterns of Development, Culture and Environmental change since 1492* (New York: Cambridge University Press, 1990 [1987]), 359.

51 Patterson, *The Sociology of Slavery,* 39, 41.

52 Ibid., 42.

53 Ibid., 41, 159.

54 Ibid., 43.

55 Watts, *The West Indies,* 355

56 Ibid.

57 Patterson, *The Sociology of Slavery,* 44.

58 Ibid., 137; Watts, *The West Indies,* 365

59 Charles Johnson and Patricia Smith, *Africans in America* (New York: Harcourt Brace & Company, 1998), 63.

60 Patterson, *The Sociology of Slavery,* 82.

61 Eric Williams, "Capitalism and Slavery," in *Caribbean Slave Society and Economy,* ed. Hilary Beckers and Verene Shepherd (Kingston: Ian Randle Publishers Limited, 1991), 121.

62 Sidonie Smith, *Where I'm Bound: Patterns of Slavery and Freedom in Black American Autobiography* (Westport: Greenwood Press, 1974), 13.

63 Richard D. E. Burton, *Afro-Creole: Power, Opposition, and Play in the Caribbean* (Ithaca: Cornell University Press, 1997), 49.

64 Craton, *Testing the Chains,* 36. Stella Dadzie, "Searching for the Invisible Woman; Slavery and Resistance in Jamaica," *Race and Class* 32, no. 2 (1990): 21–38.

65 Jack P. Geene, "Society and Economy in the British Caribbean during the Seventeenth and Eighteenth Century," *The American Historical Review* 79, no. 5 (1974): 1505.

66 Patterson, *The Sociology of Slavery*, 174–81.

67 Craton, *Testing the Chains*, 25.

68 Patterson, *The Sociology of Slavery*, 180.

69 Within the Ghanaian context this word has another spelling—Ananse.

70 Marcia Davidson, "Anancy Introduction" *Jamaican Culture*, accessed September 19, 2013, http://www.jamaicans.com/culture/anansi/anancy_intro.shtml.

71 Patterson, *The Sociology of Slavery*, 253.

72 Burton, *Afro-Creole*, 65.

73 Upon signing the treaty with the British in 1740, the Maroons became "British" agents who would hunt down slaves and return them to the plantations. As a result, the numbers of runaways in Jamaica slightly decreased.

74 Craton, *Testing the Chains*, 61.

75 Elsa V. Goveia, *Slave Society in the British Leeward Islands* (Forge Village: Murray Printing Company, 1969 [1965]), 258.

76 Ibid., 255–7.

77 Patterson, *The Sociology of Slavery*, 264.

78 Ibid.

79 Ibid., 266.

80 Price, *Maroon Societies*, 233. The slaves who were taken were eventually incorporated into Maroon society.

81 Patterson, *The Sociology of Slavery*, 270.

82 Ibid.

83 Sherlock and Bennett, *The Jamaican People*, 140–1.

84 Craton, *Testing the Chains*, 99.

85 Ibid., 99–158.

86 Ibid., 244–5.

87 Sherlock and Bennett, *The Jamaican People*, 142.

88 Shirley Gordon, *God Almighty Make Me Free: Christianity in Preemancipation Jamaica* (Bloomington: Indiana University Press, 1996), 97.

89 Craton, *Testing the Chains*, 291. There is some discrepancy concerning the number of slaves involved in the rebellion. According to Sherlock and Bennett, the number of slaves involved were probably 20,000, of whom 207 were killed and over 500 executed. Sherlock and Bennett, *The Jamaican People*, 273.

90 Ibid.

91 Patrick Bryan, "The White Minority in Jamaica at the end of the Nineteenth Century," in *The White Minority in the Caribbean*, ed. Johnson Howard and Watson Karl (Kingston: Ian Randle Publishers, 1998), 120.

92 This internalization created an aversion within "civilized" blacks toward their fellow blacks who they saw as "uncivilized" and backward.

93   Keith Hunte, "Protestantism and Slavery in the British Caribbean," in *Christianity in the Caribbean: Essays on Church History*, ed. Armando Lampe (Kingston: University of West Indies Press, 2001), 91.

94   Ibid. 87.

95   Ibid. 96–7. Arthur Charles Dayfoot, *The Shaping of the West Indian Church, 1942–1962* (Gainesville: University Press of Florida, 1999), 86.

96   Travis Glasson, *Mastering Christianity: Missionary Anglicanism in the Atlantic World* (New York: Oxford University Press, 2011), 143, for more information on this venture see pages 141–70.

97   Dale Bisnauth, *History of Religions in the Caribbean* (Trenton: Africa World Press, Inc., 1996), 102.

98   Noel Leo Erskine, *Decolonizing Theology: A Caribbean Perspective* (Maryknoll: Orbis Books, 1981), 69.

99   Dayfoot, *West Indian Church*, 88.

100 Bisnauth, *History of Religions*, 102.

101 Patterson, *The Sociology of Slavery*, 207.

102 For information on the Baptist Missionary Society within the West Indies see: Brian Stanley, *The History of the Baptist Missionary Society, 1792-1992* (Edinburgh: T & T Clark, 1992).

103 Dayfoot, *West Indian Church*, 114.

104 Mary Turner, *Slaves and Missionaries: The Disintegration of Jamaican Slave society, 1787-1834* (Chicago: University of Illinois Press, 1982), 71.

105 The preservation of the social order became a recurring theme in the ministry of all three denominations. Even after John Wesley, the founder of Methodism, took an antislavery stance, this preservation element remained. Hunte, "Protestantism and Slavery," 103 and Goveia, *Slave Society*, 306.

106 Dayfoot, *West Indian Church*, 129, 130.

107 Turner, *Slaves and Missionaries*, 27.

108 Gordon, *Make Me Free*, 7.

109 Hunte, "Protestantism and Slavery," 101; Turner, *Slaves and Missionaries*, 84. Thus women were able to reinhabit a position they had traditionally held in African religions. See: Sylvia Frey and Betty Wood, *Come Shouting to Zion* (Chapel Hill: The University of North Carolina Press, 1998), 57, 135, 171.

110 Hunte, "Protestantism and Slavery," 101; Dayfoot, *West Indian Church*, 114; 130.

111 Patterson, *The Sociology of Slavery*, 217.

112 Turner, *Slaves and Missionaries*, 47.

113 Ibid.

114 Ibid., 39.

115 See Craton, *Testing the Chains*, 250; Gordon, *Make Me Free*, 98.

116 Johnson and Smith, *Africans in America*, 139.

117   Albert J. Raboteau, *A fire in the Bones: Reflections on African-American Religious History* (Boston: Beacon Press, 1995), 157.

118   Craton, *Testing the Chains*, 245.

119   (Guyana) Demerara in 1823, and 1831–1832 in Jamaica.

120   Gordon, *Make Me Free*, 138.

121   Erskine, *Decolonizing Theology*, 71.

122   M. Kazim Bacchus, *Education As and For Legitimacy: Developments in West Indian Education between 1846 and 1895* (Ontario: Wilfrid Laurier University Press, 1994), 15.

123   Erskine, *Decolonizing Theology*, 72.

124   Jean Besson, *Martha Brae's Two Histories: European Expansion and Caribbean Culture-building in Jamaica* (Chapel Hill: University of North Carolina Press, 2002), 129–57.

125   These church leaders were the middle-class whites in the Moravians, Methodist, and Baptist churches.

126   Erskine, *Decolonizing Theology*, 75

127   Frey and Wood, *Shouting to Zion*, 212.

128   Erskine, *Decolonizing Theology*, 78.

129   Ibid., 79.

130   This division was at times arbitrary since some people were members of both the established/mission churches and the Afro-Christian religious groups.

131   Pentecostalism arrived in the Bahamas in 1909, in Jamaica in 1914. From these two islands it expanded to the rest of the islands.

132   Hylton, *Religion in Caribbean History*, 118.

133   Vinson Synan, *The Holiness-Pentecostal Tradition: Charismatic Movements of the Twentieth Century*, 2nd ed. (Grand Rapids: Eerdmans, 1997), 7. This definition of holiness comes from the Holiness Movement, from which Pentecostalism developed.

134   Diane Austin-Broos, "Women and Jamaican Pentecostalism," in *Caribbean Portraits: Essays in Gender Ideologies and* Identities, ed. Christine Barrow (Kingston: Ian Randle, 1998), 159–60.

Chapter 2

1   Margaret Bailey, "The typical Jamaican family," October 1, 2002, http://www. jamaicans.com/culture/intro/typical_family.shtml, accessed July 11, 2008.

2   See Iain D. Campbell, *On the First Day of the Week: God, the Christian and the Sabbath* (Leominster: Day One publications, 2005), 194; Toulis, *Believing Identity*, 138.

3   Ibid., 194. See also V. S. Naipaul, "A Christmas Story," in *The Nightwatchman's Occurrence Book,* ed. V. S. Naipaul (London: Picador, 2002), 367.

4   Turner, *Slaves and Missionaries,* 84, 198–9, chapter 2, 57–71.

5   See: Daniel Lawrence, *Black Migrants, White Natives: A study of Race Relations in Nottingham* (London: Cambridge University Press, 1974), 18; Kyle D. Crowder, "Residential Segregation of West Indians in the New York/New Jersey Metropolitan Area: The Roles of Race and Ethnicity," *International Migration Review* 33, no. 1 (1999): 79, 86. Both Arnold and Aldred refute this passivity in their discussion of West Indian religious communities. See: Selwyn Arnold, *From Scepticism to Hope* (Nottingham, London: Grove Books Limited, 1992); Joe Aldred, *Respect: Understanding Caribbean British Christianity* (Peterborough: Epworth, 2005).

6   This framework was also applied to discussions on migration in other regions. See Alejandro Portes and Josh DeWind, "A Cross-Atlantic Dialogue," in *Rethinking Migration: New Theoretical and Empirical Perspectives,* ed. Alejandro Portes and Josh DeWind (New York: Berghahn Books, 2007), 6–9.

7   Elizabeth M. Thomas-Hope, *Explanation in Caribbean Migration* (London: Macmillan Press Ltd, 1992), 15.

8   Bonham C. Richardson, *Caribbean Migrants: Environment and Human Survival on St. Kitts and Nevis* (Knoxville: University of Tennessee Press, 1983), 151, 158–60, 173; Lawrence, *Black Migrants,* 18.

9   Thomas-Hope, *Caribbean Migration,* 16.

10 Alejandro Portes and József Böröcz, "Contemporary Immigration: Theoretical Perspectives on Its Determinants and Modes of Incorporation," *International Migration Review* 23, no. 3 (1989): 612; Douglass Massey, Joaquin Arango, Graeme Hugo, Ali Kouaouci, Adela Pellegrino, and J. Edward Taylor, *Worlds in Motion: Understanding International Migration at the End of the Millennium* (New York: Oxford University Press, 2005), 8–12.

11 Elizabeth Thomas-Hope, "Globalization and the Development of a Caribbean Migration Culture," in *Caribbean Migration: Globalised Identities,* ed. Mary Chamberlain (London: Routledge, 1998), 193, 196; Eugenia Georges, *The Making of a Transnational Community: Migration, Development and Cultural Change in the Dominican Republic* (New York: Columbia University Press, 1990), 150–63.

12 Richardson, *Caribbean Migrants,* 177.

13 Anthony Payne and Paul Sutton, *Charting Caribbean Development, Warwick University Caribbean Studies* (London: Macmillan, 2001), 1.

14 Ibid.

15 Portes and Böröcz "Contemporary Immigration," 609–12.

16 John U. Ogbu, *Minority Education and Caste: The American System in Cross-Cultural Perspective* (New York: Academic Press, 1978), 243.

17 Selwyn H. H. Carrington, *The Sugar Industry and the Abolition of the Slave Trade, 1775 1810* (Gainesville: University of Florida Press, 2002), 13, chapter 2.

18   Ibid., 16.

19   Ibid., 25. See also Eric Williams, *Capitalism and Slavery*, 67.

20   Ibid., 13–91.

21   Carrington, *The Sugar Industry*, 116–36.

22   William Fox, *An Address to the People of Great Britain, on the Propriety of Abstaining from West India Sugar and Rum*, 6th ed. (London: M. Gurney, 1791).

23   Thomas-Hope, "Caribbean Migration," 194.

24   Ransford W. Palmer, *Pilgrims from the Sun: West Indian Migration to America* (New York: Twayne Publishers, 1995), 2.

25   Shirley C. Gordon, *Our Cause for His Glory: Christianisation and Emancipation in Jamaica* (Kingston: The Press of the University of the West Indies, 1998), 99.

26   Mary Chamberlain, *Empire and Nation Building in the Caribbean: Barbados, 1937-66* (Manchester: Manchester University Press, 2010), 4–6.

27   Thomas-Hope, "Caribbean Migration," 189.

28   Eric Williams "American Capitalism and Caribbean Economy," in *Caribbean Freedom: Economy and Society from Emancipation to Present*, ed. Hilary Beckles and Verene Shepherd (Princeton: Markus Wiener Publishers, 1996), 342.

29   Palmer, *Pilgrims from the Sun*.

30   Dawn Marshall, "A History of West Indian Migrations: Overseas Opportunities and 'Safety-Valve' Policies," in *The Caribbean Exodus*, ed. Barry B. Levine (Westport: Praeger Publishers, 1987), 24.

31   For an in-depth discussion on the conditions in the region and specifically Barbados, see Chamberlain, *Empire and Nation Building*, 1–21.

32   Payne and Sutton, *Caribbean Development*; James Ferguson, *Far from Paradise: An Introduction to Caribbean Development* (London: Latin America Bureau, 1990).

33   Ransford W. Palmer, *Caribbean Dependence on the United States Economy* (New York: Praeger Publishers, 1979).

34   Perry Mars and Alma H. Young, ed., *Caribbean Labor and Politics: Legacies of Cheddi Jagan and Michael Manley* (Detroit: Wayne State University Press, 2004), xiii, xiv; Payne and Sutton, *Caribbean Development*, 2–15; Anthony P. Maingot "The English-Speaking Caribbean," in *The Continuing Crisis: US Policy in Central America and the Caribbean*, ed. Mark Falcoff and Robert Royal (London: Ethics and Public Policy Center, 1987), 133.

35   Ibid.

36   Norman Girvan, "Michael Manley: A Personal Perspective," in *Caribbean Labor and Politics: Legacies of Cheddi Jagan and Michael Manley*, ed. Perry Mars and Alma H. Young (Detroit: Wayne State University Press, 2004), 6.

37   Ibid.

38   Ibid., 7.

39   Manley Michael, *A Voice at the Workplace* (Washington, DC: Howard University Press, 1991), 238.

40 Catherine A. Sunshine and Keith Q. Warner, ed., *Caribbean Connections: Moving North* (Washington, DC: Network of Educators on the Americas, 1998), 7.

41 Payne and Sutton, *Caribbean Development*, 12.

42 Ibid., 13.

43 In the case of Canada see: Joe T. Darden, "The impact of Canadian Immigration Policy on the Structure of the Black Caribbean Family in Toronto," in *Inside the Mosaic*, ed. Eric Fong (London: University of Toronto Press, 2006), 146–65.

44 "The Immigration and Nationality Act of 1952 (The McCarran-Walter Act)" United States Department of State Office of the Historian. Website: http://history. state.gov/milestones/1945-1952/ImmigrationAct, accessed August 26, 2013.

45 Louise Bennett, *Jamaica Labrish* (Kingston: Sangster, 1966), 179–80.

46 "chapter 21," *Commonwealth Immigration Act 1962*. Website: http://www. britishcitizen.info/CIA1962.pdf, accessed March 12, 2008.

47 Margaret Phelan, *Immigration Law Handbook* (London: Blackstone Press Limited, 2001 [1997]), 4–67.

48 Joseph Salvo and Ronald Ortiz, *The Newest New Yorkers: An Analysis of Immigration into New York during the 1980s* (New York: New York Department of City Planning, 1992), 40.

49 Holger Henke, *The West Indian Americans* (Westport: Greenwood press, 2001), 29.

50 Ibid., 31.

51 Ibid.

52 Ellis Cose, *A Nation of Strangers: Prejudice, Politics and the Populating of America* (New York: William Marrow and Company, Inc., 1992), 190.

53 Ibid., 180, 182.

54 Doris M. Meissiner, Robert D. Hormats, Antonio Garrigues Walker, and Shijuro Ogata, *International Migration Challenges in a New Era* (New York: The Trilateral Commission, 1993), 27.

55 Cose, *Nation of Strangers*, 200.

56 Meissiner, *International Migration*, 27.

57 Thomas-Hope, "Caribbean migration," 194; Monica Boyd, "Family and Personal Networks in International Migration: Recent Developments and New Agendas," *International Migration Review* 23, no. 3 (1989): 642–3.

58 Mary Chamberlain, "Migration, the Caribbean and the Family," in *Caribbean Families in Britain and the Trans-Atlantic World*, ed. Goulbourne Harry and Chamberlain Mary (London: Macmillan Educational Ltd, 2001), 36.

59 Mary Chamberlain, *Narratives of Exile and Return*, Warwick University Caribbean Studies (London: Macmillan Caribbean, 1997), 70.

60 Interview cited in Chamberlain, *Exile and Return*, 70

61 Ibid., 75

62 First-generation male, July 11, 2007.

63 Ibid.

64   Oscar Handlin, *The Uprooted: The Epic Story of the Great Migrations that Made the American People* (New York: Grosset & Dunlap: 1981), 3.

65   Gary Gerstle, "American Freedom, American Coercion: Immigrant Journeys in the 'Promised Land,'" *Social Compass* 47, no. 1 (2000): 64.

66   Roy Simón Bryce-Laporte, "New York City and the New Caribbean Immigration: A Contextual Statement," *International Migration Review* 13, no. 2 (1979): 216.

67   Ibid., 215, 216.

68   Waters, *Black Identities*, 42.

69   Ibid.

70   See Nancy Foner, "Race and Color: Jamaican Migrants in London and New York City," *International Migration Review* 19, no. 4 (1985): 714–15.

71   Crowder, "Residential Segregation," 79.

72   Derrick Bell, *Faces at the Bottom of the Well: The Permanence of Racism* (New York: Basic Books, 1992), 3.

73   Cornel West, *Race Matters* (Boston: Beacon Press, 1993), 11–20.

74   Derrick, *Bottom of the Well*, 4.

75   Income, Poverty and Health Insurance Coverage in the United States: 2013, News release September 16, 1014: http://www.census.gov/newsroom/press-releases/2014/cb14-169.html, accessed May 15, 2015.

76   Ibid.

77   Ibid., See also: Nell Irvin Painter, *Creating Black Americans: African-American History and its Meanings, 1619 to the Present* (New York: Oxford University Press, 2007), 390–1.

78   Crowder, "Residential Segregation," 108.

79   Holger, *West Indian Americans*, 38.

80   Ibid.

81   These denominations included: Anglican/Episcopalian, Baptist, Methodist, and various Pentecostal groups.

82   Garnet A. Parris, "The African Dispora in Germany seen through the axes of Storytelling: Of Law and security and of Religious Tradition and Theology," (PhD diss., University of Birmingham, March 2008), 108–9.

83   Painter, *Creating Black Americans*, 346.

84   See Brooklyn Community District 16 profile: http://www.nyc.gov/html/dcp/pdf/lucds/bk16profile.pdf; and Brooklyn Neighborhood Report, http://issuu.com/studybrooklyn/docs/community_district_16_brooklyn_neighborhood_report, accessed May 21, 2015.

85   Elizabeth Reich Rawson, "Brownsville," in *The Encyclopedia of New York City*, ed. Kenneth Jackson, 2nd ed. (New Haven: Yale University Press, 2010), 185.

86   John B. Manbeck, *The Neighborhoods of Brooklyn* (New Haven: Yale University Press, 2004 [1998]), 40–1.

87 Rawson, "Brownsville," 185.

88 Ibid.

89 See Brooklyn Community District 18 profile: http://www.nyc.gov/html/dcp/pdf/
lucds/bk18profile.pdf, accessed May 21, 2015.

90 Manbeck, *Neighborhoods*, 123–4.

91 Ibid.

92 Dulcie Leimbach, "If You're Thinking of Living In/Flatlands; Diverse, Well-
Groomed Residential Area," *The New York Times*, February 1, 2004, accessed
March 10, 2008, http://query.nytimes.com/gst/fullpage.html?res=9D05E0DD1038
F932A35751C0A9629C8B63.

93 Ibid. Brooklyn Neighborhood Report, http://issuu.com/studybrooklyn/docs/
community-district-18-brooklyn-neighborhood-report, access May 21, 2015.

94 This brief account of the history of Latter Rain was derived from the information
documented on the church's website and from interviews with several members.

95 Following his initial contract with this denomination in his early twenties, Bishop
Davids was trained and commissioned to pastor the Mount Sinai Church in 1956.
After his tenure at Mount Sanai, he spent several years in England and in Jamaica,
prior to migrating to the United States in the 1960s.

96 These demographics are a composite of the information received from the
leadership and what I observed during fieldwork.

97 This history was compiled from information found in the Church bulletin and
from interviews with the founders of the church.

98 The Mitchell children continue to be instrumental within the church. One
daughter is the minister of music, the eldest son is the associate pastor/youth
minister, and the youngest son is the primary musician within the church.

99 In his interview, Bishop Mitchell stated that twelve people attended the Sunday
school that Sunday morning. For the official church opening, churches in the area
were invited to participate in the celebration.

100 First-generation minister, March 2007.

101 Ibid.

102 Demographics are a composite of the information received from the minister and
what I observed during fieldwork.

103 The *Empire Windrush* is the name of the ship that transported 492 passengers
from the Caribbean to Tilbury. This was the beginning of a large-scale migration
of West Indians to Britain and resulted in the ethnic diversity that would change
many facets of British society.

104 Mike Phillips and Trevor Phillips, *Windrush: The Irresistible rise of Multi-Racial
Britain* (London: HarperCollins Publishers, 1998), 4.

105 Nancy Foner, *Jamaican Farewell: Jamaican Immigrants in London* (London:
Routledge & Kegan Paul, 1979), 42.

106 Phillips and Phillips, *Windrush*, 4.

107 Edward Scobie, *Black Britannia: A History of Blacks in Britain* (Chicago: Johnson Publishing Company Inc., 1972), 196, 197.

108 For a discussion on the denigration of white working-class life in London: Michael Young, and Peter Willmott, *Family and Kinship in East London* (Berkley: University of California Press, 1992).

109 Sheila Patterson, *Dark Strangers* (London: Travistock Publications, 1963), 81, 92–103, 144.

110 Ruth Glass, *Newcomers: West Indians in London* (London: Centre for Urban Studies and George Allen & Unwin LTD, 1960), 48.

111 John Western, *Passage to England: Barbadian Londoners Speak of Home* (London: UCL Press Limited, 1992), 81. One such slum landlord was Perec "Peter" Rachman. There are also cases of other landlords, both West Indian and white, who exploited the migrants. See: Sheila Patterson, *Dark Strangers,* 181, Anita Jackson, *Catching Both Sides of the Wind: Conversations with Five Black Pastors* (London: The British Council of Churches, 1985), 89.

112 Eugene C. Black, "Sexual Roles: Victorian Progress?," in *Victorian Culture and Society*, ed. Eugene C. Black (New York: Harper & Row, Publishers, 1973), 384.

113 Patterson, *Dark Strangers*, 227.

114 Albert Hyndman, "Family Problems" and D. M. Wood, Jessie Hood, K. Aldous, and W. B. Thompson, "West Indian Welfare in Three Cities," in *The West Indian Comes to England*, ed. S. K. Ruck (London: Routledge & Kegan Paul Ltd., 1960), 123, 162.

115 Foner, *Jamaican Farewell*, 24–42; Jackson, *Catching Both Sides*, 88.

116 See pastoral profiles in the NCTG 50th anniversary booklet, *1953-2003 50 Years in His Service*.

117 The Metropolitan Railway was later renamed the Metropolitan Line.

118 See website: http://www.brent-heritage.co.uk/willesden.htm, accessed March 10, 2007.

119 See articles: "City Lawyer robbed then murdered," *BBC online news*, January 13, 2006, website: http://news.bbc.co.uk/1/hi/england/london/4609826.stm; and "Dawn raids against Crime 'Crews,'" *BBC online news*, July 16, 2003, website: http://news.bbc.co.uk/1/hi/england/london/3071091.stm, accessed March 10, 2008.

120 Arnold, *Scepticism to Hope*, 17, 18.

121 According to several respondents, church members pledged funds each week toward the cost of the building. The renovation of the building was a collective effort, with the men performing various skills (carpenters, painters, etc.) and the women cleaning up. See first-generation minister, June 2007, and first-generation female, July 10, 2007.

122 This is the governing council of the church and is comprised of twelve members.

123 This figure was cited in the senior pastor's profile in an anniversary booklet.

124 José Itzigsohn, Carlos Dore Cabral, Esther Hernandez Medina, and Obed Vasquez, 'Mapping Dominican Transnationalism: Narrow and Broad Transnational Practices,' *Ethnic and Racial Studies* 22, no. 2 (March 1999): 317; Roger Rouse, "Questions of Identity; Personhood and Collectivity in Transnational Migration to the United States," *Critique of Anthropology* 15, no. 4 (December 1995); Milton M. Gordon, *Assimilation in American Life: The Role of Race, Religion, and National Origins* (New York: Oxford University Press, 1964).

125 Linda Basch, Nina Glick Schiller, and Cristina Szanton Blanc, *Nations Unbound: Transnational Projects, Postcolonial Predicaments, and Deterritorialized Nation-States* (New York: Gordon and Breach Science Publishers, 1994), 4.

126 Ibid., 7.

127 Alejandro Portes, Luis E. Guarnizo, and Patricia Landolt, "The Study of Transnationalism: Pitfalls and Promise of an Emergent Research Field," *Ethnic and Racial Studies* 22, no. 2 (March 1999): 224–5.

128 Steven Vertovec, "Conceiving and Researching Transnationalism," *Ethnic and Racial Studies* 22, no. 2 (March 1999): 417; Itzigshon et al., "Dominican Transnationalism," 318; Portes, Guarnizo, and Landolt, "Study of Transnationalism," 223–4.

129 Basch, Glick Schiller, and Szanton Blanc, *Nations Unbound*, 52–93.

130 Portes, Guarnizo, and Landolt, "Study of Transnationalism," 220–2.

131 Alejandro Portes "Transnational Communities: Their Emergence and Significance in the Contemporary World System," in *Latin America in the World Economy*, ed, Roberto Patricio and William C. Smith (Westport: Greenwood Press, 1996), 151–68.

132 Itzigsohn et al, "Dominican transnationalism," 318.

133 Basch, Glick Schiller, and Szanton Blanc, *Nations Unbound*.

134 Ibid., 323.

135 Ibid., 318.

136 Sarah J. Mahler, "Theoretical and Empirical Contributions Towards a Research Agenda for Transnationalism," in *Transnationalism From Below*, ed. Michael P. Smith and Luis E. Guarnizo (New Brunswick: Transaction Publishers, 2002 [1998]), 64–100.

137 Itzigsohn et al., "Dominican Transnationalism," 323.

138 Ibid.

139 Afe Adogame, "Up, Up Jesus! Down, Down, Satan! African Religiosity in the former Soviet Bloc—the Embassy of the Blessed Kingdom of God for all Nations," *Exchange* 37, (2008): 323.

140 Peggy Levitt, *The Transnational Villagers* (Berkeley: University of California Press, 2001), 160.

141 Chamberlain, "Caribbean and the Family," 36; Itzigsohn et al., "Dominican Transnationalism," 325, 327; According to Rosemary Vargas-Lundius, "in 2002, remittances to the Latin America and Caribbean region amounted to approximately USD 32 billion." Rosemary Vargas-Lundius, "Remittances and Rural Development" a paper prepared for Twenty-Seventh Session of IFAD's Governing Council, Rome, February 18 to 19, 2004, accessed July 20, 2008, http://www.ifad.org/events/gc/27/roundtable/pl/discussion.pdf.

142 First-generation female, April 3, 2007. Later in the interview it was stated that her daughter stayed with her sister.

143 George Gmelch, *Double Passage: The Lives of Caribbean Migrants Abroad and Back Home* (Ann Arbor: University of Michigan Press, 1992), 51.

144 See: Karen Fog Olwig, "Narratives of the Children Left Behind: Home and Identity in Globalised Caribbean Families," *Journal of Ethnic and Migration Studies* 25, no. 2 (April 1999); Tracey Reynolds, *Caribbean Mothers: Identity and Experience in the U.K.* (London: The Tufnell Press, 2005), 36; Elaine Bauer and Paul Thompson, *Jamaican Hands Across the Atlantic* (Kingston: Ian Randle Publishers, 2006), 6–7, 192–95.

145 George Mulrain, "Caribbean," in *An Introduction to Third World Theologies*, ed. John Parratt (Cambridge: Cambridge University Press, 2004), 171.

146 Itzigsohn et al., "Dominican Transnationalism," 327.

147 Several West Indian islands have policies focused on the relocation of their expatriates.

148 Advertisements for real estate agents, properties, and buildings available for purchase can be found in the classified section of the US and UK editions of several national newspapers as well as in the online versions. See: Jamaican Gleaner: http://www.jamaica-gleaner.com/, Trinidadian Guardian: http://www.guardian.co.tt/classified/class.html, the Barbadian Nation: http://classifieds.nationnews.com/results.php?category_id=2&acTst=Grr, accessed July 22, 2008.

149 First-generation male, July 9, 2007.

150 See Reuel R. Rogers, *Afro-Caribbean Immigrants and the Politics of Incorporation: Ethnicity, Exception, or Exit* (New York: Cambridge University Press, 2006), 156–63; Gmelch, *Double Passage,* 276–7, 285; First-generation female, July 24, 2007.

151 Robert Beckford, *Dread and Pentecostal* (London: Society for Promoting Christian Knowledge, 2000), 14.

152 First-generation female, April 22, 2007.

153 First-generation female, April 3, 2007.

154 See http://www.digiceljamaica.com/home/index_v4.php, accessed July 22, 2008.

155 First-generation female, April 22, 2007.

156 Itzigsohn et al., "Dominican transnationalism," 332.

157 Second-generation female, April 11, 2007.

158 First-generation female, July 9, 2007.

159 First-generation female, April 3, 2007.

160 First-generation female, April 13, 2007.

161 Adogame, "Up, Up Jesus!" 326.

162 See NTCG Jamaican and Cayman Islands website: http://ntcgjaci.org/history.htm, accessed July 20, 2007.

163 As indicated throughout this chapter, many of these relationships favored the interest of the United States and Britain as opposed to what was most beneficial to the islands.

Chapter 3

1 Marie Gillespie, *Television, Ethnicity and Cultural Change* (London: Routledge, 1995), 19.

2 Hall, "Introduction," 4.

3 Eleanor Nesbitt, "I'm a Gujarati Lohana and a Vaishnav as Well," in *Religion, Identity and Change: Perspectives on Global Transformations*, ed. Simon Coleman and Peter Collins (Aldershot: Ashgate, 2004), 174.

4 Castells, *Power of Identity*, 7.

5 First-generation female, April 22, 2007.

6 Roy Simon Bryce-Laporte, "Black Immigrants: The Experience of Invisibility and Inequality," *Journal of Black Studies* 3, no. 1 (1972): 31. This invisibility was seen in the census statistics compiled for Flatbush (zip code 11226). This predominantly West Indian neighborhood, was listed as being 75.7 percent black/African American with no additional breakdown provided. In contrast the total Asian segment was listed along with specific numbers for particular countries. US 2010 Census Bureau fact sheet, accessed June 5, 2015, http://factfinder.census.gov/faces/tableservices/jsf/pages/productview.xhtml?src=CF.

7 Rogers, *Afro-Caribbean Immigrants*, 51. These stereotypes were not new; they had been applied to the earlier wave of West Indian migrants. Ira Reid, *The Negro Immigrant* (New York: Columbia University Press, 1939).

8 This stereotype was also very prominent among many white employers. See Waters, *Black Identities*, 118–23; Philip Kasinitz, *Caribbean New York: Black Immigrants and the Politics of Race* (Ithaca: Cornell University Press, 1992).

9 The Sylvan Learning Center offers tutoring services for students. See website: http://tutoring.sylvanlearning.com/, accessed July 29, 2008.

10 First-generation female, April 3, 2007. Italicization for emphasis.

11 First-generation male, April 22, 2007.

12 Bacchus, *West Indian Education*, 15.

13 Waters, *Black Identities;* Kasinitz, *Caribbean New York*.

14 First-generation male, March 2007.

15 Waters, *Black Identities*, 58–60.

16 First-generation female, April 3, 2007.

17 1.5-generation male, April 15, 2007.

18 Ibid.

19 Floya Anthias and Nira Yuval-Davis, *Racialized Boundaries: Race, Nation, Gender, Colour and Class and the Anti-racist Struggle* (London: Routledge, 1993), 142.

20 Roy Carr-Hill and Harbajan Chadha-Boreham, "Education," in *Britain's Black Population: A New Perspective*, ed. Ashok Bhat, Roy Carr-Hill, and Sushel Ohri (Aldershot: Gower, 1988), 14870; Gus John and Derek Humphry, *Because They're Black* (Harmondworth: Penguin Books, 1972), 119–33; Paul Gilroy, *There Ain't No Black in the Union Jack*, classic ed. (London: Routledge, 2002,), 146–98.

21 National Church Leaders Forum website: http://nationalchurchleadersforum. wordpress.com/about/.

22 Aldred, *Respect,* 76.

23 First-generation female, July 17, 2007.

24 Paul Langford, *Englishness Identified: Manners and Character 1650–1850* (Oxford: Oxford University Press, 2000).

25 Rt. Hon. David Blunkett MP, *A New England: An English identity within Britain.* Speech to the Institute for Public Policy Research, March 14, 2005, 6. See website: http://www.efdss.org/newengland.pdf, accessed July 30, 2008.

26 Ibid.

27 See Robert Beckford's discussion of this dynamic for in his father's life. Beckford, *Dread and Pentecostal*, 14–17.

28 First-generation female, July 16, 2007. Mary was a trained nurse for many years and is now retired.

29 Ibid.

30 Darcus Howe, "Turning on each Other," *The Guardian*, August 6, 2004, accessed June 16, 2015, http://www.theguardian.com/world/2004/aug/07/race. immigrationandpublicservices.

31 First-generation female, July 16, 2007. These sentiments were expressed in a letter that she wrote to her parents in Ghana.

32 Ibid.

33 First-generation female, July 19, 2007.

34 The difficulty associated with this decision was seen in June waiting two years to join her husband. First-generation female, July 19, 2007.

35 Ibid.

36 Thursday Night Service, March 29, 2007.

37 First-generation female, April 22, 2007.

38 First-generation male, April 22, 2007.

39 First-generation female, April 3, 2007.

40 Ibid.

41 Janice McLean, "Ain't I a Child of God? Gender and Christianity in Light of the Immigrant Experience," *Mission Studies* 31 (2014): 8.

42 The exception to this were the women's and youth Sunday evening services where females played a more visible role.

43 First-generation female in New York, April 3, 2007.

44 Sister Grace became licensed as a notary public to help members in some of these areas.

45 McLean, "Child of God," 9.

46 Grace Davie, *Religion In Britain since 1945: Believing without Belonging* (Oxford: Blackwell, 1994), 37.

47 Ibid., 30–4.

48 Ibid., 37.

49 First-generation female, July 9, 2007.

50 Gerrie ter Haar, *Halfway to Paradise: African Christians in Europe* (Cardiff: Cardiff Academic Press, 1998), 83.

51 First-generation male, June 2007.

52 First-generation female, July 10, 2007.

53 First-generation female, July 10, 2007. Carol has been a member of Kingsbridge for over forty years.

54 First-generation male, June 2007.

55 Janice McLean, "Make a Joyful Noise unto the Lord: Music and Song within Pentecostal West Indian Religious Communities in Diaspora," *Studies in World Christianity* 13, no. 2 (2007): 132–3.

56 First-generation female, July 16. 2007.

57 First-generation female, July 17, 2007.

58 First-generation male, July 11, 2007.

59 Anderson, *Vision of the Disinherited,* 69.

60 First-generation female, April 13, 2007.

61 Ibid.

62 Robert A. Orsi, "Introduction: Crossing the City Line," in *Gods of the City: Religion and the American Urban Landscape*, ed. Robert A. Orsi (Bloomington: Indiana University Press, 1999), 7.

63 Georg Simmel, "The Metropolis and Mental Life," in *Metropolis: Center and Symbol of Our Times*, ed. Philip Kasinitz (New York: New York University Press, 1995), 32.

64 Ibid., 33.

65 Given the licensing and ordination procedures within CoG, it does not seem likely that an undocumented person could become a licensed or ordained minister. This may be a possibility in a more independent Pentecostal church—like Latter Rain Ministries. However, I did not find this during my research.

66 First-generation male minister, March, 2007.

67 Ibid.,

68 Janice McLean-Farrell, "Uncovering an Alternative Story: Examining the Religious and Social Lives of Afro-Caribbean Youth in London and New York City," in *The Public face of African New Religious Movements in Diaspora*, ed. Afe Adogame (Burlington: Ashgate, 2014),136.

69 First-generation male minister, June 2007.

70 For data on racial wealth disparity in the United States see: Palma Joy Strand, "Inheriting Inequality: Wealth, Race, and the Laws of Succession," in *Oregon Law Review* 89 (2010): 461–77. For the United Kingdom see the report: Wealth in Great Britain, Main results from the Wealth and Assets Survey 2006/2008, http://www.ons.gov.uk/ons/rel/was/wealth-in-great-britain/main-results-from-the-wealth-and-assets-survey-2006-2008/index.html, accessed September 25, 2013.

71 See the US 2010 Census Bureau fact sheet for zip code 11212. Website: http://factfinder.census.gov/faces/tableservices/jsf/pages/productview.xhtml?src=CF, accessed June 5, 2015.

72 Second-generation female, July 9, 2007, McLean, "Appropriating Faith."

73 First-generation female, July 16, 2007.

74 McLean, "Make a Joyful Noise," 130.

75 Ibid., 135.

76 Within the Jamaican context the Rally was not limited to Pentecostal churches but is found in several denominations. During my childhood, the Rally was an established program within the Anglican Church calendar.

Chapter 4

1 In this chapter, "immigrant youth" was used to refer to the members of the 1.5, second, and third generations. Given the age range among these generations, it was necessary to find a term that communicated this diversity.

2 Toulis, *Believing Identity*, 170; R Cohen, *Frontiers of Identity: The British and the Others* (London: Longman, 1994), 199–200.

3 Simon Coleman and Peter Collins, "Introduction," in *Religion Identity and Change: Perspectives on Global Transformations*, ed. Simon Coleman and Peter Collins (Aldershot: Ashgate, 2004), 5.

4   Erik Erikson, *Identity: Youth and Crisis* (London: Faber & Faber Ltd., 1968), 155.

5   G. S. Hall, *Adolescence, its Psychology, and its Relation to Physiology, Anthropology, Sociology, Sex, Crime, Religion and Education*, vol. 2 (New York: D. Appleton & Co, 1904).

6   Geoffrey L. Ream and Ritch C. Savin-Williams, "Religious Development in Adolescence," in *Blackwell Handbook of Adolescence*, ed. Gerald R. Adams and Michael D. Berzonsky (Oxford: Blackwell Publishing, 2006 [2003]), 53.

7   Sherri-Ann Butterfield, "We're Just Black: The Racial and Ethnic Identities of Second-generation West Indians in New York," in *Becoming New Yorkers: Ethnographies of the New Second-generation*, ed. Philip Kasinitz, John Mollenkopf and Mary C. Waters (New York: Russell Sage Foundation, 2004), 293–5.

8   Robert E. Park and Ernest W. Burgess, *Introduction to the Science of Sociology* (Chicago: University of Chicago Press, 1921), 735.

9   Richard Alba and Victor Nee, "Rethinking Assimilation Theory for a New Era of Immigration," *International Migration Review* 31, no. 4 (1997): 826–74.

10 Gordon, *Assimilation in American Life*, 84–114.

11 Ibid., 71, 77.

12 Ibid.

13 Ibid., 77, 78, 80–1.

14 Mary C. Waters, *Ethnic Options, Choosing Identities in America* (Berkeley: University of California Press, 1990), 90–4.

15 Alba and Nee, "Rethinking Assimilation," 845.

16 Ruben Rumbaut, "The Crucible within: Ethnic Identity, Self-Esteem, and Segmented Assimilation among Children of Immigrants," *International Migration Review* 28, no. 4 (1994): 753; Min Zhou, "Segmented Assimilation: Issues, Controversies, and Recent Research on the New Second-generation," *International Migration Review* 31, no. 4 (1997): 975–1008.

17 According to the US Census in 1990, the majority of the immigrants to the United States are nonwhite—primarily from Asia and Latin America including the Caribbean. See US Bureau of the Census Report Table 3: *Region and Country or Area of Birth of the Foreign-Born Population: 1960 to 1990*. Internet Release date: March 9, 1999 at website: http://www.census.gov/population/www/ documentation/twps0029/tab03.html, accessed April 29, 2008.

18 Rumbaut, "Crucible within," 751.

19 Ibid., 753.

20 Margaret Byron and Stéphanie Candon, *Migration in Comparative Perspective: Caribbean Communities in Britain and France* (New York: Routledge, 2008), 129; Boyd, "Family and Personal Networks," 642–3.

21 Byron and Candon, *Comparative Perspective*, 153.

22   Ibid. 185; Milton Vickerman, "Jamaica," in *The New Americans: A Guide to Immigration Since 1965*, ed. Mary C. Waters, and Reed Ueda, with Helen Marrow (Cambridge, MA: Harvard University Press, 2007), 488–9.

23   Bennett Harrison, *Lean and Mean: The Changing Landscape of Corporate Power in the Age of Flexibility* (New York: Basic Books, 1994).

24   Katherine S. Newman, *No Shame in My Game: The Working Poor in the Inner City* (New York: Vintage Books and Russell Sage Foundations, 1999), xii.

25   See the median salaries for these professions at: http://money.usnews.com/careers/best-jobs/plumber/salary, accessed June 10, 2015.

26   Byron and Candon, *Comparative Perspective*, 86.

27   Ibid., 90.

28   David Gillborn and Heidi Mirza, *Educational inequality: Mapping Race, Class and Gender* (London: Office for standards in Education, 2000); Tessa Blackstone, "Towards a Learning Society: Can Ethnic Minorities Participate Fully?," in *Race Relations in Britain*, ed. Tessa Blackstone, Bhikhu Parech, and Peter Sanders (London: Routledge, 1998), 96–110; John Rex and Sally Tomlinson, *Colonial Immigrants in a British City: A class analysis* (London: Routledge & Kegan Paul, 1979), 216–21.

29   Richard Berthoud, *Young Caribbean Men and the Labour Market: A Comparison with Other Ethnic Groups* (New York: Joseph Rowntree Foundation, 1999), 23; Gillborn and Mirza, *Educational inequality*, 23–4.

30   Ibid., 56.

31   Martin Carnoy, *Faded Dreams: The Politics and Economics of Race in America* (New York: Cambridge University Press, 1994), 129.

32   Zhou, "Segmented Assimilation," 988. Many of these schools were segregated and had a very high African American and Puerto Rican student population.

33   Carnoy, *Faded Dreams*, 131–2.

34   Public Education Finances, 2013, Educational Finance Branch, issued June 2015, https://www.census.gov/content/dam/Census/library/publications/2015/econ/g13-aspef.pdf, accessed September 7, 2015.

35   See Ibid., 136.

36   Zhou, "Segmented Assimilation," 987.

37   Ogbu, *Minority Education*, 199–200.

38   Ken Pryce, *Endless Pressure: A Study of West Indian Life styles in Bristol* (Middlesex: Penguin Books, 1979), 120.

39   Ibid. Rex and Tomlinson, *Colonial Immigrants*, 208; Brian Richardson, Diane Abbott, and Bernard Coard, *Tell it Like it is: How our Schools Fail Black Children* (London: Bookmarks, 2005).

40   Richard Majors, "Introduction: Understanding the Current Educational Status of Black Children," in *Educating Our Black Children: New Directions and Radical Approaches*, ed. Richard Majors (London: RoutldedgeFalmer, 2001), 2.

41   Ibid., 5.

42 McLean-Farrell, "Alternative Story," 136.

43 Robert Beckford, *God and the Gangs* (London: Darton, Longman & Todd, 2004), 32.

44 Philomena Essed, *Understanding Everyday Racism: An Interdisciplinary Theory* (London: Sage Productions, 1991), 50

45 Ibid., 169.

46 Ibid., 52.

47 Mekada Graham, *Black Issues in Social Work and Social Care* (Bristol: Policy Press, 2007), 56.

48 The pervasiveness of racism in the lives of blacks is bolstered by location, that is, by living and working in close proximity to whites.

49 McLean-Farrell, "Alternative Story," 139.

50 According to Gilroy, racial issues in Britain did not emerge from the perceived corruption of the romanticized homogeneous cohesive social-democratic regime by the "other." In reality, he suggests "that these chronic difficulties which periodically produce acute bouts of racial and national anxiety arise from melancholic responses to the loss of imperial pre-eminence and the painful demand to adjust the life of the national collective to a severely reduced sense of itself as a global power." See Paul Gilroy, *There Ain't No Black in the Union Jack*, xxxvii. While I agree that Britain's reduced sense of itself as a global power did contribute to the racism that minorities experienced, I would also argue that the racial characterization of black and nonwhite phenotypes were prominent even when Britain was the primary global power, and formed the basis for the slavery system in the West Indies, and the policies that were instituted throughout the Commonwealth.

51 Ibid., xxiv.

52 Howard Schuman, Charlotte Steeh, Lawrence Bobo and Maria Krysan, *Racial Attitudes in America: Trends and Interpretations* (Cambridge, MA: Harvard University Press, 1997 [1985]).

53 Alba and Nee, "Assimilation Theory," 846.

54 Ibid.

55 Second-generation male, April 15, 2007.

56 Second-generation female, April 15, 2007. The incident referenced by the respondent was regarding a nationally syndicated radio program called *Imus in the Morning*, where the host referred to the African American members of Rutgers University collegiate women's basketball team as "nappy head hos." The outrage generated by this comment eventually resulted in CBS terminating his employment and a resurgence of discussion concerning race in the telecommunication industries. Imus's program was later picked up by Citadel Broadcasting and is now distributed nationally through ABC Radio networks. See: http://www.cbsnews.com/stories/2007/04/12/national/main2675273.shtml, accessed on May 7, 2008.

57 The perception and actual experience of prejudice was more prominent among second-generation males than among females. This was consistent with the phenomenon of gendered racism.

58 1.5-generation male, April 15, 2007.

59 Rumbaut, "Crucible within," 770.

60 Second-generation male, April 19, 2007.

61 Ibid.

62 Second-generation male, April 15, 2007.

63 Waters, *Black Identities*, 290.

64 Waters, *Black Identities*, 293.

65 Vickerman, "Jamaica," 488.

66 Waters, *Black Identities*, 290–7.

67 Waters, *Black Identities*, 296.

68 Ibid., 307.

69 Ibid., 298–301.

70 Waters, *Black Identities*, 202.

71 One 1.5-generation respondent received a weekly stipend from his church "mother" to cover the cost of lunch. Oftentimes when he needed money, his biological mother encouraged him to call his church "mother" for assistance.

72 Such relationships are also present with other immigrant groups. See Karen Chai, "Competing for the Second-generation: English-Language Ministry at a Korean Protestant Church," in *Gatherings in Diaspora: Religious Communities and the New Immigrants*, ed. R. Stephen Warner and Judith Wittner (Philadelphia: Temple University Press, 1998), 298–9.

73 McLean, "Child of God," 10

74 McLean-Farrell, "Alternative Story," 140.

75 Painter, *Creating Black Americans*, 384. Also see the portrayal of masculinity in the following movies about urban life in America—Jim Sheridan, *Get Rich or Die Tryin* (Hollywood: Paramount films, 2005); and Ridley Scott, *American Gangster* (Hollywood: Universal Studios, 2007).

76 McLean-Farrell, "Alternative Story," 131.

77 Janice McLean, "The Place of the Second-Generation in West Indian Pentecostalism in the Diaspora—New York City and London," in *African Traditions in the Study of Religion, Diaspora and Gendered Societies*, ed. Afe Adogame, Ezra Chitando, and Bolaji Bateye (Burlington: Ashgate, 2013), 124.

78 Second-generation male, April 19, 2007; Waters, *Black Identities*, 296–300.

79 Pryce, *Endless Pressure*, 176–218.

80 C. Eric Lincoln and Lawrence H. Mamiya, *The Black Church in the African American Experience* (Durham: Duke University Press, 1990), 227–8.

81 Second-generation female, April 22, 2007.

82 Second-generation female, April 15, 2007.

83 Second-generation male, April 15, 2007.

84 Kirk Franklin is a prominent urban contemporary gospel artist, who incorporates hip-hop and Rhythm and Blues (R&B) into his gospel songs.

85 Second-generation male, April 15, 2007.

86 Interview with second-generation male, April 15, 2007.

87 Christian Smith with Melinda Lundquist Denton, *Soul Searching: The Religious and Spiritual Lives of American Teenagers* (New York: Oxford University Press, 2005).

88 Ernest Cashmore and Barry Troyna, eds, *Black Youth in Crisis* (London: George Allen & Unwin, 1982). These social realities were further compounded by marked poverty within the Afro-Caribbean community. According to data from a Poverty and Social Exclusion (PSE) survey, "ethnicity is a key factor predisposing children and their families to poverty". See Eva Lloyd, "Children, Poverty and Social Exclusion," in *Poverty and Social Exclusion in Britain: The Millennium Survey*, ed., Christina Pantazis, David Gordon, and Ruth Levitas (Bristol: The Policy Press, 2006), 328–9.

89 McLean-Farrell, "Alternative Story," 131–2.

90 Second-generation female, July 16, 2007.

91 Third-generation female, July 9, 2007.

92 Peter Weinreich "Ethnicity and Adolescent Identity Conflicts: A Comparative Study," in *Minority Families in Britain: Support and Stress*, ed. Verity Saifullah Khan (London: Macmillan Press, 1979), 103.

93 McLean-Farrell, "Alternative Story," 132.

94 Second-generation male, July 12, 2007.

95 1.5-generation male, July 11, 2007. This respondent was born in Jamaica and came to the United Kingdom as a child. Later in the interview he stated that he knew very little about Jamaica except what he has heard from other people. For him, Jamaica was a halfway step between Africa and the United Kingdom.

96 Claire Alexander, *The Art of Being Black: The Creation of Black British Youth Identities* (New York: Oxford University Press, 1996), 30–70.

97 Alexander, *The Art of Being Black*, 3, 4; Scobie, *Black Britannia*; and James Walvin, *Black and White: The Negro and English Society 1555–1945* (London: Allen Lane The Penguin Press, 1973).

98 Ibid; See Parris, "African Dispora in Germany," 137–47.

99 Although some third-generation West Indians were included in this study, the majority were between ages nine and thirteen. As such, their identity may have been tied to that of their parents. Erikson, *Identity*.

100 Arnold, *Scepticism to Hope*, 41.

101 Ibid., 26.

102 1.5-generation male, July 11, 2007.

103 Second-generation male, July 8, 2007.

104 First-generation minister, June 2007.

105 Second-generation female, July 9, 2007.

106 Ibid.

107 Ibid. The appointment of women to the pastoral council requires a majority vote at the CoG General Assembly. Although the issue has been voted on on several occasions, it has never won a majority.

108 Second-generation female, July 17, 2007.

109 Second-generation female, April 22, 2007.

110 McLean, "Second-Generation Youth," 124–5. This evangelist was one of the youth group leaders and functioned as the "father" figure for the group.

111 This youth leader was the vice president of the youth group. During fieldwork, the president became ill. As a result the vice president's duties became more significant and as the male leader, he also functioned as the "father" figure for the group.

112 Group interview, April 11, 2007, McLean, "Appropriating Faith,"

113 1.5-generation male, April 15, 2007.

114 McLean-Farrell, "Alternative Story," 134.

115 McLean, "Second-Generation Youth," 125.

116 Ibid., 125–6.

117 This is a space free of the potential of exposure to drugs, violence, or gang affiliation.

118 According to one respondent, the Saturday school was started in Kingsbridge Church in 1997 "as a means of supporting Black children in the community schools." This program has since expanded to include children from other nationalities. See interview with second-generation male, July 11, 2007.

119 This conversation with a mother occurred during a Friday youth club meeting that was held in the church hall, London, July 2007.

120 Waters, *Black Identities*, 296–300.

121 Group interview, April 11, 2007.

122 In many of these congregations the senior minister and founder has primary authority over every aspect of the church. Thus, to seek to change any element without their approval could be seen as trying to usurp or undermine their authority.

123 Acquiring specific figures on the number of youth who left was difficult given the complex dynamics surrounding this type of "exodus" and the diversity of perspectives and experiences about this subject among the leadership, the laity, and those who left. Added to this were certain complications related to ascertaining the root cause for the exodus, while also navigating what would

be the ongoing interaction between the church and those who had left. The myriad issues, feelings, traditions, etc., that accompanied the interrogation of the "departure" made this subject one that many leaders, laity, and youth did not readily choose to discuss.

124 McLean, "Second-Generation Youth," 127.

125 This could be gang related and criminal activities, as well as the organization of protests marches in response to perceived police injustice.

126 McLean, "Second-Generation Youth," 128.

127 This dynamic was noted in several of the Friday youth meetings that I attended. During these meetings, young people would lead praise and worship and prayer. The majority of the choruses sung were of West Indian origin. This was followed by a forty-five minute talk or Bible study led by one of the adult leaders—this focused on admonishing the young people to live in accordance with the scriptures and not to "sell out" to the world. After this an offering was collected, and the meeting closed in prayer.

128 Although contemporary choruses are incorporated into the service they are limited to the praise and worship section. This hymnal, published in the late-nineteenth-early-twentieth century has become a staple in Jamaica within several Pentecostal churches. While visiting a church in Jamaica where Bishop Davids had previously served as a minister, it was observed that this hymnal was used during services.

129 The first generation (now older than 60) are experiencing decline due to death or return migration to their island homes.

130 First-generation minister, June 2007.

131 Although many first-generation members would have desired for the religious and cultural traditions to remain West Indian, they are aware of the need to change. A prominent theme among several first-generation respondents was their children's "exodus."

132 These are Bibles that have been bought or donated to the church for use during the Sunday and midweek worship services. These Bibles are normally stamped with the church's address, and kept in the sanctuary.

133 Second-generation minister, July 24, 2007.

Chapter 5

1 Andrew Walls, "Mission and Migration: the Diaspora Factor in Christian History," *Journal of African Christian Thought* 5, no. 2 (2002): 3–12.

2 For some migrants, underlying their decision is a sense of being compelled by the Holy Spirit to go and fulfill the divine mandate or calling. Ruth Tucker, *From*

Jerusalem to Irian Jaya: A Biographical History of Christian Missions (Grand Rapids: Zondervan, 2004 [1983]).

3 Andrew F. Walls, *The Cross-Cultural Process in Christian History* (New York: Orbis Books, 2002), 85; Lamin Sanneh, *Whose Religion is Christianity?* (Grand Rapids: Eerdmans, 2003); Philip Jenkins, *The Next Christendom: The Coming of Global Christianity* (New York: Oxford University Press, 2002). This shift was a product of migration and mission. The growth in adherents to Christianity observed in the Southern continents highlighted that the existence of "a great family of churches in all parts of Asia and Africa and the islands of the sea [was] the fruit of the missionary effort of the past two hundred years." See: Lesslie Newbigin, A *Word in Season: Perspectives on Christian World Missions* (Edinburgh: Saint Andrew Press, 1994), 10.

4 See: Manuel Castells, Mireia Fernandez Ardevol, Jack Linchuan Qiu, Araba Sey et al., *Mobile Communication and Society: A Global Perspective* (Cambridge: Massachusetts Institute of Technology Press, 2007); Robert Flanagan, *Globalization and labor Conditions: Working Conditions and Worker Rights in a Global Economy* (New York: Oxford University Press, 2006); Samir Dasgupta and Ray Kiely, eds, *Globalization and After* (London: Sage Publications, 2006).

5 According to Cecil Robeck, this debate is primarily political since "denominational, cultural, racial and ethnic agendas, as well as the call to conform to certain standard of political correctness, are only a few of the agendas that have been brought to bear on the discussion of Pentecostal origins." See: Cecil M. Robeck Jr., "Pentecostalism and Mission: From Azusa Street to the Ends of the Earth," *Missiology: An International Review* 35, no. 1 (2007): 76.

6 David Allen, *The Unfailing Stream: A Charismatic Church History in Outline* (Tonbridge: Sovereign World, 1994), 80–92.

7 Gordon Strachan, *The Pentecostal Theology of Edward Irving* (London: Darton, Longman & Todd, 1973), 19; James R. Goff, *Fields white unto Harvest: Charles F. Parham and the Missionary Origins of Pentecostalism* (London: University of Arkansas Press, 1988).

8 Walter J. Hollenweger, *The Pentecostals: The Charismatic Movement in the Churches* (Minneapolis: Augsburg Publishing House, 1972); Edwin Villafañe, *Liberating Spirit* (Grand Rapids: Eerdmans, 1993); Anderson, *Vision of the Disinherited*; Iain MacRobert, *The Black Roots and White Racism of Early Pentecostalism in the USA* (Basingstoke: Macmillan Press, 1988).

9 Carl Brumback, *Suddenly . . . From Heaven: A History of The Assemblies of God* (Springfield: Gospel Publishing House, 1961), 48

10 Ibid.

11 Anderson, *Vision of the Disinherited*, 45; Allan Anderson, *An Introduction to Pentecostalism: Global Charismatic Christianity* (New York: Cambridge University Press, 2004), 302.

12 See Walter Hollenweger cited in Cecil M. Robeck Jr., "Pentecostalism and Mission: From Azusa Street to the Ends of the Earth," *Missiology: An International Review* 35, no. 1 (2007): 76.

13 Edith Blumhofer "Azusa Street Revival," *The Christian Century* 123, no. 5 (2006): 22. For Dale Irvin, this caution was expressed as not making "Azusa Street—or any other local event in Pentecostal history—the determining factor for Pentecostal histories elsewhere in the world." Dale Irvin "Pentecostal Historiography and Global Christianity: Rethinking the Questions of Origin," *Pneuma: The Journal of the Society for Pentecostal Studies* 27, no. 1 (2005): 44.

14 Such a criticism was especially valid since some forms of Pentecostalism originated in different locations. See: Ogbu Kalu, *African Pentecostalism: An Introduction* (New York: Oxford University Press, 2008).

15 Robert Beckford, *Dread and Pentecostal*, 171; Allan Anderson, *Spreading Fires: The Missionary Nature of Early Pentecostalism* (London: SCM Press, 2007).

16 Pomerville, *The Third Force*; Gary B. McGee, "Pentecostal and Charismatic Missions," in *Toward the 21st Century in Christian Mission*, ed. James M. Philips and Robert T. Coote (Grand Rapids: Eerdmans, 1998 [1993]), 46.

17 For additional information on Azusa Street see Anderson, *Introduction to Pentecostalism*.

18 This doctrine was formulated by Charles F. Parham at the Bethel Bible School in Topeka, Kansas.

19 McGee, "Pentecostal and Charismatic Missions," 46.

20 Millard J. Erickson, *Christian Theology*, 2nd ed. (Grand Rapids: Baker Books, 2002), 889.

21 Ibid., 880.

22 Scriptures like Mark 1:15 and Matthew 7:21 highlight these two dimensions of the kingdom of God—a reign that began with Christ's coming, and also one which has a future dimension. The Second Advent is interpreted in several ways: pre-millennial, post-millennial, and A-millennial. See the following: William C. Placher, ed., *Essentials of Christian Theology* (Louisville: Westminster John Knox Press, 2003); Alister E. McGrath, *Christian Theology: An Introduction* (Oxford: Blackwell Publishers, 2001); and Hans Schwarz, *Eschatology* (Grand Rapids: Eerdmans, 2000).

23 Goff, *White unto harvest*, 72; Anderson, *Vision of the Disinherited*, 90–2.

24 Harvey Cox, *Fire from Heaven: The Rise of Pentecostal Spirituality and the Reshaping of Religion in the Twenty-First Century* (Reading, PA: Addison-Wesley Publishing Company, 1995), 87.

25 Steven Jack Land, *Pentecostal Spirituality: A Passion for the Kingdom*, Journal of Pentecostal Theology. Supplement Series; 1 (Sheffield: Sheffield Academic Press, 1993), 111.

26 Ibid.

27 Goff, *White unto Harvest*, 51–5.

28 David W. Faupel, *The Everlasting Gospel: The Significance of Eschatology in the Development of Pentecostal Thought, Journal of Pentecostal Theology. Supplement Series; 10* (Sheffield: Sheffield Academic Press, 1996), 219–20.

29 Within six months of beginning of the revival, thirty-eight foreign and home missionaries were commissioned. See: Anderson, *Vision of the Disinherited*, 72.

30 Anderson, *Introduction to Pentecostalism*, 40, 57–9; Cox, *Fire from Heaven*, 56–9; Synan, *Holiness-Pentecostal Tradition*, 103–6.

31 Anderson, *Vision of the Disinherited*, 71.

32 E. Franklin Frazier, *The Negro Church in America* (New York: Schocken Books, 1964); Melville J. Herskovits, *The Myth of the Negro Past* (New York: Harper & Bothers, 1941); Gayraud S. Wilmore *Black Religion and Black Radicalism: An Interpretation of the Religious History of African Americans*, 3rd ed. (Maryknoll: Orbis Books, 1998); Albert Raboteau, *Slave Religion: the "invisible institution" in the Antebellum South* (New York: Oxford University Press, 1978).

33 Wilmore, *Black Religion*, 18; Raboteau *Slave Religion*, 4–5; James Cone, *The Spirituals and the Blues: An Interpretation* (New York: Orbis Books, 1992), 29–30.

34 Cheryl Bridges Johns, *Pentecostal Formation: A Pedagogy among the Oppressed* (Sheffield: Sheffield Academic Press, 1993), 87.

35 Ibid., 89.

36 The idealism of this belief was later revealed as certain gender roles, leadership hierarchies, racial distinctions, etc., persisted.

37 Faupel, *Everlasting Gospel*, 210.

38 Ibid.

39 Ibid., 211.

40 Anderson, *Vision of the Disinherited*, 69.

41 "Missionary" is used to call attention to the evangelistic fervor that propelled the Barrs to return to the Bahamas. In this manner they continued a process began at Azusa Street in which after receiving spirit baptism, foreigners felt compelled by the Holy Spirit to take that experience to their homelands. Anderson, *Spreading Fires*, 197.

42 Diane Austin-Broos, *Jamaica Genesis: Religion and the Politics of Moral Orders* (Chicago: The University of Chicago Press, 1997), 96–114.

43 George Olson started the Holiness CoG in Jamaica. He came in response to a letter sent by Isaac Delevante to the Holiness CoG in Anderson Indiana, describing the devastating earthquake that had occurred in January 1907 and also appealing for missionaries. One distinct belief within the Holiness CoG was "sanctification" through the in-filling of the Holy Spirit. This in-filling, manifested in the "capacity to abstain from sin," was received quietly, or "as an 'intellectual' experience." See Austin-Broos, *Jamaica Genesis*, 97–8.

44 Barry Chevannes, "Introducing the Native Religions of Jamaica," in *Rastafari and Other African-Caribbean Worldviews*, ed. Barry Chevannes (New Brunswick: Rutgers University Press, 1998 [1995]), 9.

45 Gordon, *Make Me Free*, 129.

46 Nathaniel Samuel Murrell, *Afro-Caribbean Religions: An Introduction to Their Historical, Cultural, and Sacred Traditions* (Philadelphia: Temple University Press, 2010), 251.

47 Ennis B. Edmonds and Michelle A. Gonzalez, *Caribbean Religious History: An Introduction* (New York: New York University Press, 2010), 126.

48 Ibid., 126; Erskine, *Decolonizing Theology*, 31; Hylton, *Caribbean History*, 172–3; Chevannes, "Native Religions," 6–7.

49 Ibid.

50 Chevannes, "Native Religions," 5. This is a spirit associated with either the Holy Spirit or a benevolent spirit within the African-derived pantheon.

51 Jean Besson, "Religion as Resistance in Jamaican Peasant Life," in *Rastafari: Roots and Ideology*, ed. Barry Chevannes (New York: Syracuse University Press,1994), 61; Leonard Barrett, *The Sun and the Drum: African Roots in Jamaican Folk Tradition* (Kingston: Sangster's Book Stores, 1976), 57.

52 George Eaton Simpson, "Jamaican Revivalist Cults," *Social and Economic Studies* 5, no. 4 (1956): 352.

53 Erskine, *Decolonizing Theology*, 105.

54 Austin-Broos, *Jamaica Genesis*, 63.

55 Ibid., 99, 105.

56 Extract from a Revivalist sermon cited in Ibid., 100.

57 Kortwright Davis, *Emancipation Still Comin': Explorations in Caribbean Emancipatory Theology* (Maryknoll: Orbis Books, 1990).

58 George Mulrain, "Caribbean," in *An Introduction to Third World Theologies*, ed. John Parratt (Cambridge: Cambridge University Press, 2004), 165.

59 Ibid., 164.

60 This belief existed simultaneously with the West African concept of multiple souls. See: Simpson, "Jamaican Revivalist Cults," 346.

61 Noel Leo Erskine, "How do We Know What to Believe: Revelation and Authority," in *Essentials of Christian Theology*, ed. William C. Placher (Louisville: Westminster John Knox Press, 2003), 35.

62 Ibid., 36.

63 Ibid., 37. This perspective could be applied to people within the entire Caribbean region. See section entitled "Self-Affirmation" in Mulrain, "Caribbean," 172–3.

64 Erskine, "How do We Know," 37.

65 Diane Austin-Broos, "Jamaican Pentecostalism: Transnational Relations and the Nation-State," in *Between Babel and Pentecost: Transnational Pentecostalism*

in Africa and Latin America, ed. André Corten and Ruth Marshall-Fratani (Bloomington: Indiana University Press, 2001), 145.

66 Austin-Broos, "Jamaican Pentecostalism," 144.

67 Austin-Broos, "Jamaican Pentecostalism," 146.

68 Turner, *Slaves and Missionaries*, 76–7; Janice McLean, "Enslaving liberators? An examination of Evangelical Missionaries in Pre and Post-emancipation Jamaica" (paper presented at the Yale-Edinburgh Conference, Edinburgh, July 3–5, 2008).

69 Horace O. Russell, *The Missionary Outreach of the West Indian Church: Jamaica Baptist Missions to Africa in the Nineteenth Century* (New York: Peter Lang, 2000); Bakary Gibba, "The West Indian Mission to West Africa: The Rio Pongas Mission 1850-1963" (PhD diss. University of Toronto, 2011).

70 Mulrain, "Caribbean," 171.

71 Church website, accessed on May 12, 2007.

72 Church website, accessed on June 5, 2007.

73 This practice of an "altar call" is not restricted to Pentecostalism. Precursors can be found in the evangelical movement from the time of the American Evangelist Charles Finney and also in Revivalism. Simpson, "Jamaican Revivalist Cults," 354

74 Within certain contexts, this invitation could involve some manipulation—where the "unsaved" is told that their failure to respond positively to this invitation could result in them not having another opportunity to do so before they die. And to die without salvation meant going to hell.

75 During this prayer individuals confess that they are sinners, repent of the sins they have committed, acknowledge that Jesus died on the cross to atone for their sins, accept that atonement, and ask Jesus to come into their lives.

76 This constitutes the beginning of a series of the new converts or discipleship classes which conclude with the water baptism by immersion of the individual.

77 Janice McLean, "'By My Spirit says the Lord: Mission Perspectives among Pentecostal West Indians Religious Communities in New York City and London," in *Mission and Migration*, ed. Stephen Spencer (Hope Valley: Cliff College Publishing, 2008), 87.

78 First-generation female, April 3, 2007.

79 First-generation male, July 11, 2007.

80 Ibid.

81 Second-generation female, July 19, 2007.

82 Group interview, April 11, 2007.

83 Second-generation male, April 15, 2007.

84 Second-generation male, July 8, 2007.

85 Second-generation female, July 9, 2007.

86 Group interview, second-generation male, April 11, 2007.

87 Group interview, 1.5-generation male, April 11, 2007.

88 This report documented the quantity of printed literature that was distributed and the number of conversions within the church over a certain time period.

89 First-generation male minister, June 2007.

90 McLean, "By my Spirit," 88. In her interview, this respondent spoke about experiencing discrimination from several coworkers and how these experiences made her workplace a difficult place to work.

91 McLean, "By my Spirit," 89.

92 First-generation female, April 3, 2007. During fieldwork I was not able to ascertain why this technology was not being used.

93 First-generation male, April 22, 2007.

94 First-generation male minister, March 2007.

95 Emmanuel Egbunu, "To Teach, Baptise, and Nurture New Believers (i)," in *Mission in the 21st Century*, ed. Andrew Walls and Cathy Ross (London: Darton, Longman and Todd, 2008), 25–6; Andrew Lord, *Spirit, Kingdom and Mission: A Charismatic Missiology* (Cambridge: Grove Books Limited, 2002), 3; Anderson, *Introduction to Pentecostalism*, 261.

96 Villafañe, The *Liberating Spirit*, 202.

97 Donald E. Miller and Tetsunao Yamamori, *Global Pentecostalism: The New Face of Christian Social Engagement* (Berkeley: University of California Press, 2007); For an overview of Latin American Pentecostals involvement in social action and politics, see: Anderson, *Introduction to Pentecostalism*, 72–3; David Martin, *Tongues of Fire: The Explosion of Protestantism in Latin America* (Oxford: Basil Blackwell Ltd, 1990), 66.

98 See Robert Beckford's discussion of embracing certain aspects of Rastafarianism within a particular expression of Pentecostalism he is advocating for within the British context. Beckford engages with these issues as a second-generation West Indian male who is involved in the NTCG denomination. Beckford, *Dread and Pentecostal*.

99 According to Ande Titre, "The aim of God's mission is the transformation of life, not only of individuals but also of the whole society, even the created order." See Ande Titre, "To Teach, Baptise, and Nurture New Believers (ii)," in *Mission in the 21st Century*, ed. Andrew Walls and Cathy Ross (London: Darton, Longman and Todd, 2008), 37.

100 According to one respondent at Kingsbridge, there is a lack of understanding within many local NTCG churches about this dynamic. For many members, denominational leadership was associated with the national NTCG, without the realization that the NTCG was also a part of the CoG denomination. Although Beulah reported directly to the CoG headquarters in Tennessee—the fact that the majority of senior leadership within the denomination was white was lost on most of the black members of the church. This was because the leadership

at local and regional levels was predominantly black. In both Kingsbridge and Beulah, exposure and awareness of the white American organizational leadership of Church came with one's attendance at the general assembly that was held once every four years. See interview with second-generation female, July 9, 2007.

101 Arnold, *Scepticism to Hope*, Doreen Morrison, "Reaching for the Promised Land: The role of Culture, issues of Leadership and Social stratification with British Caribbean Christianity" (PhD diss. University of Birmingham, 2012).

102 Walter Hollenweger, *The Future of Mission and the Mission of the Future*, Occasional paper no. 2 (Birmingham: Selly Oak Colleges, 1990), 5.

103 Ter Haar, *Strangers and Sojourners*, 167–71.

104 Gracie Davie, *Europe: The Exceptional Case: Parameters of Faith in the Modern World* (London: Darton, Longman and Todd Ltd, 2002), 110.

105 Lesslie Newbigin, *Foolishness to the Greeks: The Gospel and Western Culture* (Grand Rapids: Eerdmans, 1986), 147; See also: Andrew Walls, "Afterword: Christian Mission in a Five-hundred-year Context," in *Mission in the 21st Century*, ed. Andrew Walls and Cathy Ross (London: Darton, Longman and Todd, 2008), 204.

106 Ibid., 204.

Conclusion

1 Helen Rose Ebaugh and Janet Saltzman Chafetz, eds, *Religion and the New Immigrants: Continuities and Adaptations in Immmigrant Congregations* (Walnut Creek: Altamira Press, 2000); Foley, and Hoge, *New Immigrants*; Olupona and Gemignani, eds, *African Immigrant Religions*. Two exceptions are: Warner and Wittner, *Gatherings in Diaspora*, in which one chapter is dedicated to Rastafari and Haitian Voodoo, and Delroy A. Reid-Salmon, *Home Away From Home: The Caribbean Diasporan Church in the Black Atlantic Tradition* (London: Equinox, 2008).

2 Within the majority of the studies on West Indian migrants in the United States, the role of the faith communities is given only a cursory glance. Waters, *Black Identities*; Constance R. Sutton, and Elsa M. Chaney, eds, *Caribbean Life in New York City: Sociocultural dimensions* (New York: Center for Migration Studies of New York, Inc., 1994), Milton Vickerman, *Crosscurrents: West Indian Immigrants and Race* (New York: Oxford University Press, 1999).

3 Aldred, *Respect*; Malcolm J. C. Calley, *God's People: West Indian Pentecostal Sects in England* (London: Oxford University Press, 1965); Jackson, *Catching Both Sides*; Toulis, *Believing Identity*.

4 Some exceptions are: Arnold, *Scepticism to Hope*, Morrison, "Promised Land."

5 These dualistic elements are not distinctive to only Christian communities but are also evident within other religious communities. See Adam Unterman discussion of the Reform, Conservative and Orthodox traditions within Judaism and Alford T. Welch's presentation on Islamic movements. Adam Unterman "Judaism," in *The New Penguin Handbook of Living Religions*, ed. John R. Hinnells (Oxford: Blackwell Publishers Ltd, 1997), 37–44; Alford T. Welch "Islam," in *Living Religions*, ed. Hinnells, 208–22.

6 Immigrant youth were one of the main agents behind the incorporation of social engagement within the conception and practice of mission.

7 According to the Youth and United Nations website, 85 percent of the world's youth live in the non-Western world. This includes 62.4 percent in Asia, 14.1 percent in Africa, and 9.3 percent in Latin America and the Caribbean. See website: http://www.un.org/esa/socdev/unyin/qanda.htm, accessed October 29, 2008.

8 See: John Cotterell, *Social Networks in Youth and Adolescence* (London: Routledge, 2007); Kip Pegley, *Coming to You Wherever You Are: MuchMusic, MTV and Youth Identities* (Middletown: Wesleyan University Press, 2008). The importance of youth within the society is also highlighted within various governmental reports. See: UK government Green Papers, *Youth Matters* (July 2005) and *Youth Matters Next Step* (March 2006). Websites: http://www.everychildmatters.gov.uk/_files/Youth%20Matters.pdf, http://www.everychildmatters.gov.uk/_files/38 04D7C4B4D206C8325EA1371B3C5F81.pdf, accessed November 22, 2008. Also see the National Survey on Drug Use and Health reports on teens that focus on various subjects like underage drinking, mental health, drug use etc. Website: http://ncadistore.samhsa.gov/catalog/results.aspx?h=drugs&topic=10, accessed November 22, 2008.

9 One book that highlights some of the ways in which these issues are being addressed especially within the non-Western context is: Miller and Yamamori, *Global Pentecostalism*, 68–98.

10 Fundraising was conducted locally or with assistance from the "parent" church in the home country. See: Scott Farwell's article, "Nigerian Church brings noise, passion to Texan town," *The Dallas Morning News*, June 21, 2008, accessed November 22, 2008, http://www.dallasnews.com/sharedcontent/dws/dn/yahoolatestnews/stories/062108dnmetnigerians.435c001.html?npc. In this article Farwell documents how over the past eight years the Redeemed Church of God (RCCG) has purchased 700 acres of land and several homes and built an elementary school size church and a parking lot. See also: Afe Adogame, "Towards a 'Christian Disneyland'? Negotiating Space and Identity in the New African Religious Diaspora" (paper presented at the Gwendolen M. Carter Conference, University of Florida, Gainesville, February 15 to 16, 2008).

11 Lamin Sanneh, "Conclusion: The Current Transformation of Christianity," in *The Changing Face of Christianity*, ed. Lamin Sanneh and Joel A. Carpenter (New York: Oxford University Press, 2005), 214.

Postscript

1 Mark Sherry, "Insider/Outsider Status," in *The Sage Encyclopedia of Qualitative Methods*, ed. Lisa M Given, Vol 2 (Thousand Oaks: Sage Publications, 2008), 433; Brian Edwards, "Deep Insider Research," *Qualitative Research Journal* 2, no. 1 (2002): 71–84; Thomas Headland, Kenneth L. Pike, and Marvin Harris eds, *Emics and etics: The insider/outsider debate* (Thousand Oaks: Sage Publications, 1990).

2 Adbi M. Kusow, "Beyond Indigenous Authenticity: Reflections on the Insider/ Outsider Debate in Immigration Research," *Symbolic Interaction* 26, no. 4 (Fall 2003): 591–9; Rubén G. Rumbaut, "Immigration Research in the United States: Social Origins and Future Orientations," *American Behavioral Scientist* 42, no. 9 (1999): 1285–301; Kirin Narayan, "How Native Is a 'Native' Anthropologist?" *American Anthropologist, New Series* 95, no. 3 (September 1993): 671–86.

3 Ann Gleig, "Researching New Religious Movements from the Inside Out and the Outside In: Methodological Reflections from Collaborative and Participatory Perspectives," *Nova Religio: The Journal of Alternative and Emergent Religions* 16, no. 1 (August 2012): 89.

4 Robert Alexander Innes, "'Wait a Second. Who Are You Anyways?' The Insider/ Outsider Debate and American Indian Studies," *American Indian Quarterly* 33, no. 4 (Fall 2009): 440.

5 These ties include having relatives who reside, work and/or have citizenship in these countries.

6 Kusow, "Indigenous Authenticity," 592.

7 Kusow, "Indigenous Authenticity," 598; Rumbaut, "Immigrant Research," 1285–301.

Bibliography

Primary sources

Interviews

New York

First-generation male. March 2007. Digital recording. Senior minister.
Second-generation male. April 1, 2007. Digital recording.
First-generation female. April 3, 2007. Digital recording.
Group interview. April 11, 2007. Digital recording.
First-generation female. April 13, 2007. Digital recording.
1.5-generation male. April 15, 2007. Digital recording.
Second-generation female. April 15, 2007. Digital recording.
Second-generation male. April 15, 2007. Digital recording.
Second-generation male. April 15, 2007. Digital recording.
Second-generation female. April 15, 2007. Digital recording.
Second-generation male. April 19, 2007. Digital recording.
Second-generation female. April 22, 2007. Digital recording.
First-generation male. April 22, 2007. Digital recording.
First-generation female. April 22, 2007. Digital recording.
Second-generation female. April 22, 2007. Digital recording.

London

First-generation male. June 2007. Digital recording. Senior minister.
Group interview. July 2007. Digital recording.
Second-generation male. July 8, 2007. Digital recording.
First-generation female. July 9, 2007. Digital recording.
Second-generation female. July 9, 2007. Digital Recording.
Third-generation female. July 9, 2007. Digital recording.
First-generation male. July 9, 2007. Digital recording.
First-generation female. July 10, 2007. Digital recording.
First-generation female. July 10, 2007. Digital recording.
1.5-generation male. July 11, 2007. Digital recording.
First-generation male. July 11, 2007. Digital recording.
Second-generation male. July 12, 2007. Digital recording.
Second-generation female. July 13, 2007. Digital recording.

Second-generation female. July 16, 2007. Digital recording.

First-generation female. July 16, 2007. Digital recording.

First-generation female. July 16, 2007. Digital recording.

Second-generation female. July 17, 2007. Digital recording.

First-generation female. July 17, 2007. Digital recording.

Second-generation female. July 19, 2007. Digital recording.

First-generation female. July 19, 2007. Digital recording

First-generation male. July 19, 2007. Digital recording.

Second-generation female. July 22, 2007. Digital recording.

First-generation female. July 24, 2007. Digital recording.

Second-generation male. July 24, 2007. Digital recording. Associate minister.

Published sources

Church publications

New York

"Bishop's Profile," April 2007.

"The Call of God to Ministry: A brief history of Bishop's fifty years in ministry," May 2006.

"The Christian manner of dress," a gospel tract distributed at Latter Rain Ministries on March 29, 2007.

Bulletin for Sunday, January 28, 2007.

Bulletin for Sunday, February 18, 2007.

Bulletin for Men's Sunday, March 11, 2007. This was also an appreciation service for a minister and his family who was leaving to plant a church.

Bulletin for Sunday, March 18, 2007.

Bulletin for Sunday March 25, 2007.

Bulletin for Sunday, April 1, 2007.

Bulletin for Sunday, April 8, 2007.

Bulletin for Sunday, April 15, 2007.

Bulletin for Sunday, April 22, 2007.

London

Welcome booklet.

The New Testament Church of God 50th anniversary booklet, *1953-2003 50 Years in His Service*

Bulletin for Sunday, June 3, 2007. This bulletin reminded members that the Rally would take place on Saturday June 9, 2007.

Bulletin for Sunday, June 17, 2007.

Bulletin for Sunday June 24, 2007.

Bulletin for Sunday, July 1, 2007.

Bulletin for Sunday July 8, 2007.

Bulletin for Sunday July 22, 2007.

Secondary sources

Published sources

Journal and Newspaper articles

Alba, Richard and Victor Nee. "Rethinking Assimilation Theory for a New Era of Immigration." *International Migration Review* 31, no. 4 (1997): 826–74.

Adogame, Afe. "Up, Up Jesus! Down, Down, Satan! African Religiosity in the former Soviet Bloc—the Embassy of the Blessed Kingdom of God for all Nations." *Exchange* 37 (2008): 310–36.

Blumhofer, Edith. "Azusa Street Revival." *The Christian Century* 123, no. 5 (2006): 20–2.

Boyd, Monica, "Family and Personal Networks in International Migration: Recent Developments and New Agendas." *International Migration Review* 23, no. 3 (1989): 638–70.

Bryce-Laporte, Roy Simon. "Black Immigrants: The Experience of Invisibility and Inequality." *Journal of Black Studies* 3, no. 1 (1972): 29–56.

Bryce-Laporte, Roy Simon. "New York City and the New Caribbean Immigration: A Contextual statement." *International Migration Review* 13, no. 2 (1979): 214–34.

"City Lawyer robbed then murdered." *BBC Online News*, January13, 2006. Accessed March 10, 2008, http://news.bbc.co.uk/1/hi/england/london/4609826.stm.

Crowder, Kyle D. "Residential Segregation of West Indians in the New York/New Jersey Metropolitan Area: The Roles of Race and Ethnicity." *International Migration Review* 33, no. 1 (1999): 79–113.

Dadzie, Stella. "Searching for the Invisible Woman; Slavery and Resistance in Jamaica." *Race and Class* 32, no. 2 (1990): 21–38.

"Dawn raids against Crime 'Crews.'" *BBC Online News*, July 16, 2003. Accessed March 10, 2008, http://news.bbc.co.uk/1/hi/england/london/3071091.stm.

Edwards, Brian. "Deep Insider Research." *Qualitative Research Journal* 2, no. 1 (2002): 71–84.

Farwell, Scott. "Nigerian Church brings noise, passion to Texan town," *The Dallas Morning News*, June 21, 2008. Accessed November 22, 2008, http://www.dallasnews.com/sharedcontent/dws/dn/yahoolatestnews/stories/062108dnmetnigerians.4 35c001.html?npc.

Foner, Nancy. "Race and Color: Jamaican Migrants in London and New York City." *International Migration Review* 19, no. 4 (1985): 708–27.

Geene, Jack P. "Society and Economy in the British Caribbean during the Seventeenth and Eighteenth Century." *The American Historical Review* 79, no. 5 (1974): 1499–517.

Gerstle, Gary. "American Freedom, American Coercion: Immigrant Journeys in the 'Promised Land,'" *Social Compass* 47, no. 1 (2000): 63–76.

Gleig, Ann. "Researching New Religious Movements from the Inside Out and the Outside In: Methodological Reflections from Collaborative and Participatory Perspectives." *Nova Religio: The Journal of Alternative and Emergent Religions* 16, no. 1 (2012): 88–103.

Howe, Darcus. "Turning on each Other." *The Guardian*, August 6, 2004. Accessed June 16, 2015, http://www.theguardian.com/world/2004/aug/07/race. immigrationandpublicservices.

Innes, Robert Alexander. "'Wait a Second. Who Are You Anyways?' The Insider/ Outsider Debate and American Indian Studies." *American Indian Quarterly* 33, no. 4 (2009): 440–61.

Irvin, Dale. "Pentecostal Historiography and Global Christianity: Rethinking the Questions of Origin." *Pneuma: The Journal of the Society for Pentecostal Studies* 27, no. 1 (2005): 35–50.

Itzigsohn, José, Carlos Dore Cabral, Esther Hernandez Medina, and Obed Vasquez. "Mapping Dominican Transnationalism: Narrow and Broad Transnational Practices." *Ethnic and Racial Studies* 22, no. 2 (1999): 316–39.

Kusow, Adbi M. "Beyond Indigenous Authenticity: Reflections on the Insider/Outsider Debate in Immigration Research." *Symbolic Interaction* 26, no. 4 (2003): 591–9.

Leimbach, Dulcie. "If You're Thinking of Living In Flatlands; Diverse, Well-Groomed Residential Area." *The New York Times*, February 1, 2004. Accessed March 10, 2008, http://query.nytimes.com/gst/fullpage.html?res=9D05E0DD1038F932A35751C0A9 629C8B63.

Marrin, Minette. "Should we limit immigrants to Europeans?" *The Sunday Times*, June 17, 2007. Accessed October 9, 2008, http://www.timesonline.co.uk/tol/comment/ columnists/minette_marrin/article1942934.ece.

McLean, Janice. "Ain't I a Child of God? Gender and Christianity in Light of the Immigrant Experience." *Mission Studies* 31 (2014): 364–76.

McLean, Janice. "Make a Joyful Noise unto the Lord: Music and Song within Pentecostal West Indian Religious Communities in Diaspora." *Studies in World Christianity* 13, no. 2 (2007): 127–41.

Narayan, Kirin. "How Native Is a 'Native' Anthropologist?" *American Anthropologist New Series* 95, no. 3 (1993): 671–86.

Navarrette, Ruben Jr. "Commentary: Immigrants melting into the pot as usual." *CNN Politics.Com*, May 27, 2008. Accessed October 9, 2008, http://edition.cnn.com/2008/ POLITICS/05/27/navarette.may.27/index.html.

Olwig, Karen Fog. "Narratives of the Children Left Behind: Hone and Identity in Globalised Caribbean Families." *Journal of Ethnic and Migration Studies* 25, no. 2 (1999): 319–29.

Portes, Alejandro, Luis E. Guarnizo, and Patricia Landolt. "The Study of Transnationalism: Pitfalls and Promise of an Emergent Research Field." *Ethnic and Racial Studies* 22, no. 2 (1999): 217–37.

Portes, Alejandro, Luis E. Guarnizo, Patricia Landolt, and József Böröcz. "Contemporary Immigration: Theoretical Perspectives on Its Determinants and Modes of Incorporation." *International Migration Review* 23, no. 3 (1989): 606–30.

Robeck Jr., Cecil M. "Pentecostalism and Mission: From Azusa Street to the Ends of the Earth." *Missiology: An International Review* 35, no. 1 (2007): 75–92.

Rouse, Roger. "Questions of Identity; Personhood and Collectivity in Transnational Migration to the United States." *Critique of Anthropology* 15, no. 4 (1995): 351–80.

Rumbaut, Rubén G. "The Crucible within: Ethnic Identity, Self-Esteem, and Segmented Assimilation among Children of Immigrants." *International Migration Review* 28, no. 4 (1994): 748–94.

Rumbaut, Rubén G. "Immigration Research in the United States: Social Origins and Future Orientations." *American Behavioral Scientist* 42, no. 9 (1999): 1285–301.

Sheridan, R. B. "The Wealth of Jamaica in the Eighteenth Century." *The Economic History Review* 18, no. 2 (1965): 292–311.

Simpson, George Eaton. "Jamaican Revivalist Cults." *Social and Economic Studies* 5, no. 4 (1956): 320–442.

Strand, Palma Joy. "Inheriting Inequality: Wealth, Race, and the Laws of Succession." *Oregon Law Review* 89 (2010): 453–504.

Vertovec, Steven. "Conceiving and Researching Transnationalism," *Ethnic and Racial Studies* 22, no. 2 (1999): 447–62.

Walls, Andrew. "Mission and Migration: The Diaspora Factor in Christian History." *Journal of African Christian Thought* 5, no. 2 (2002): 3–12.

Waters, Mary C. "Ethnic and Racial Identities of Second-Generation Black Immigrants in New York City." *International Migration Review* 28, no. 4 (1994): 795–820.

Zhou, Min. "Segmented Assimilation: Issues, Controversies, and Recent Research on the New Second Generation." *International Migration Review* 31, no. 4 (1997): 975–1008.

"500 years of Indigenous Resistance." *Oh-Toh-Kin*, Vol. 1 No. 1 (Winter/Spring 1992). Accessed March 2004, http://www.dickshovel.com/500.html.

Books

Adogame, Afe and Cordula Weissköppel. eds. *Religion in the Context of African Migration*. Bayreuth: Pia Thielmann & Eckhard Breitinger, 2005.

Aimable, Twagilimana. *The Debris of Ham*. New York: University Press of America, 2003.

Aldred, Joe. *Respect: Understanding Caribbean British Christianity*. Werrington: Epworth, 2005.

Alexander, Claire. *The Art of Being Black: The Creation of Black British Youth Identities*. New York: Oxford University Press, 1996.

Allen, David. *The Unfailing Stream: A Charismatic Church History in Outline*. Tonbridge: Sovereign World, 1994.

Anderson, Allan. *An Introduction to Pentecostalism: Global Charismatic Christianity*. Cambridge: Cambridge University Press, 2004.

Anderson, Allan. *Spreading Fires: The Missionary Nature of Early Pentecostalism.* London: SCM Press, 2007.

Anderson, Ray S., ed. *Theological Foundations for Ministry.* Grand Rapids: Eerdmans, 1979.

Anderson, Robert Mapes. *Vision of the Disinherited the Making of American Pentecostalism.* New York: Oxford University Press, 1979.

Anthias, Floya and Nira Yuval-Davis. *Racialized Boundaries: Race, Nation, Gender, Colour and Class and the Anti-racist Struggle.* London: Routledge, 1993.

Arnold, Selwyn. *From Scepticism to Hope.* Nottingham: Grove Books, 1992.

Arthur, John A. *The African Diaspora in the United States and Europe: The Ghanaian Experience.* Aldershot: Ashgate Publishing, 2008.

Austin-Broos, Diane. *Jamaica Genesis: Religion and the Politics of Moral Orders.* Chicago: The University of Chicago Press, 1997.

Austin-Broos, Diane. "Jamaican Pentecostalism: Transnational Relations and the Nation-State." In *Between Babel and Pentecost: Transnational Pentecostalism in Africa and Latin America*, edited by André Corten and Ruth Marshall-Fratani, 142–62. Bloomington: Indiana University Press, 2001.

Austin-Broos, Diane. "Women and Jamaican Pentecostalism." In *Caribbean Portraits: Essays in Gender Ideologies and Identities*, edited by Christine Barrow, 156–73. Kingston: Ian Randle, 1998.

Bacchus, M. Kazim. *Education As and For Legitimacy: Developments in West Indian Education between 1846 and 1895.* Waterloo, ON: Wilfrid Laurier University Press, 1994.

Barrett, Leonard. *The Sun and the Drum: African roots in Jamaican folk tradition.* Kingston: Sangster's Book Stores, 1976.

Basch, Linda, Nina Glick Schiller, and Cristina Szanton Blanc. *Nations Unbound: Transnational Projects, Postcolonial Predicaments, and Deterritorialized Nation-States.* New York: Gordon and Breach Science Publishers, 1994.

Bauer, Elaine and Paul Thompson. *Jamaican Hands across the Atlantic.* Kingston: Ian Randle Publishers, 2006.

Bean, Richard. *The British Trans-Atlantic Slave Trade, 1650—1775.* Ann Arbor, MI: University Microfilms, 1971.

Beckford, Robert. *Dread and Pentecostal.* London: Society for Promoting Christian Knowledge, 2000.

Beckford, Robert. *God and the Gangs.* London: Darton, Longman & Todd, 2004.

Bell, Derrick. *Faces at the Bottom of the Well: The Permanence of Racism.* New York: Basic Books, 1992.

Bennett, Louise. *Jamaica Labrish.* Kingston: Sangster, 1966.

Berry, James. *When I Dance.* London: Penguin Books, 1990 [1988].

Berthoud, Richard. *Young Caribbean Men and the Labour Market: A Comparison with Other Ethnic Groups.* New York: Joseph Rowntree Foundation, 1999.

Besson, Jean. *Martha Brae's Two Histories: European Expansion and Caribbean Culture-building in Jamaica.* Chapel Hill: University of North Carolina Press, 2002.

Besson, Jean. "Religion as Resistance in Jamaican Peasant Life." In *Rastafari and Other African-Caribbean Worldviews*, edited by Barry Chevannes, 43–75. New Brunswick: Rutgers University Press, 1998 [1995].

Bevans, Stephen B., and Roger Schroeder. *Constants in Context: A Theology of Mission for Today, American Society of Missiology Series; no. 30.* Maryknoll: Orbis Books, 2004.

Bisnauth, Dale. *History of Religions in the Caribbean.* Trenton: Africa World Press, Inc., 1996.

Black, Eugene C. "Sexual Roles: Victorian Progress?" In *Victorian Culture and Society*, edited by Eugene C. Black, 384–93. New York: Harper & Row, Publishers, 1973.

Blackstone, Tessa. "Towards a Learning Society: Can Ethnic Minorities Participate Fully?" In *Race Relations in Britain*, edited by Tessa Blackstone, Bhikhu Parech, and Peter Sanders, 96–110. London: Routledge, 1998.

Bosch, David. *Transforming Mission: Paradigm Shifts in Theology of Mission.* Maryknoll: Orbis Books, 1998.

Brumback, Carl. *Suddenly . . . From Heaven: A History of The Assemblies of God.* Springfield: Gospel Publishing House, 1961.

Burton, Richard D. E. *Afro-Creole: Power, Opposition, and Play in the Caribbean.* Ithaca: Cornell University Press, 1997.

Butterfield, Sherri-Ann. "We're Just Black: The Racial and Ethnic Identities of Second-generation West Indians in New York." In *Becoming New Yorkers: Ethnographies of the New Second-generation*, edited by Philip Kasinitz, John Mollenkopf and Mary Waters, 288–313. New York: Russell Sage Foundation, 2004.

Byran, Patrick "The White Minority in Jamaica at the end of the Nineteenth Century." In *The White Minority in the Caribbean*, edited by Howard Johnson and Karl Watson, 116–32. Kingston: Ian Randle Publishers, 1998.

Byron, Margaret and Stéphanie Candon. *Migration in Comparative Perspective: Caribbean Communities in Britain and France.* New York: Routledge, 2008.

Calley, Malcolm J. C. *God's People: West Indian Pentecostal Sects in England.* London: Oxford University Press, 1965.

Campbell, Iain D. *On the First Day of the Week: God, the Christian and the Sabbath.* Leominster: Day One publications, 2005.

Carnoy, Martin. *Faded Dreams: The Politics and Economics of Race in America.* New York: Cambridge University Press, 1994.

Carr-Hill, Roy and Harbajan Chadha-Boreham. "Education." In *Britain's Black Population: A New Perspective*, edited by Ashok Bhat, Roy Carr-Hill, and Sushel Ohri, 147–76. Aldershot: Gower, 1988.

Carrington, Selwyn H. H. *The Sugar Industry and the Abolition of the Slave Trade, 1775 1810.* Gainesville: University of Florida Press, 2002.

Cashmore, Ernest and Barry Troyna. eds., *Black Youth in Crisis.* London: George Allen & Unwin, 1982.

Castells, Manuel, Mireia Fernàndez-Ardèvol, Jack Linchuan Qui, and Araba Sey. *The Information Age: Economy, Society, Culture.* vol. 2 The Power of Identity. Oxford: Blackwell Publishing, 2004 [1997].

Castells, Manuel, Mireia Fernàndez-Ardèvol, Jack Linchuan Qui, and Araba Sey. *Mobile Communication and Society: A Global Perspective*. Cambridge, MA: MIT Press, 2007.

Chai, Karen. "Competing for the Second Generation: English-Language Ministry at a Korean Protestant Church." In *Gatherings in Diaspora: Religious Communities and the New Immigration*, edited by R. Stephen Warner and Judith Wittner, 295–331. Philadelphia: Temple University Press, 1998.

Chamberlain, Mary. *Empire and Nation Building in the Caribbean: Barbados, 1937-66*. Manchester: Manchester University Press, 2010.

Chamberlain, Mary. "Migration, the Caribbean and the Family." In *Caribbean Families in Britain and the Trans-Atlantic World*, edited by Harry Goulbourne and Mary Chamberlain, 32–47. London: Macmillan, 2001.

Chamberlain, Mary. *Narratives of Exile and Return*. Warwick University Caribbean Studies. London: Macmillan Caribbean, 1997.

Chevannes, Barry. "Introducing the Native Religions of Jamaica." In *Rastafari and Other African-Caribbean Worldviews*, edited by Barry Chevannes, 1–19. New Brunswick: Rutgers University Press, 1998 [1995].

Cohen, R. *Frontiers of Identity: The British and the Others*. London: Longman, 1994.

Coleman, Simon and Peter Collins. *Religion Identity and Change: Perspectives on Global Transformations*. Aldershot: Ashgate, 2004.

Cone, James. *The Spirituals and the Blues: An Interpretation*. New York: Orbis Books, 1992.

Cose, Ellis. *A Nation of Strangers: Prejudice, Politics and the Populating of America*. New York: William Marrow and Company, Inc., 1992.

Cotterell, John. *Social Networks in Youth and Adolescence*. London: Routledge, 2007.

Cox, Harvey. *Fire from Heaven: The Rise of Pentecostal Spirituality and the Reshaping of Religion in the Twenty-First Century*. Reading: Addison-Wesley Publishing Company, 1995.

Craton, Michael. *Testing the Chains: Resistance to Slavery in the British West Indies*. Ithaca: Cornell University Press, 1982.

Darden, Joe T. "The impact of Canadian Immigration Policy on the Structure of the Black Caribbean Family in Toronto." In *Inside the Mosaic*, edited by Eric Fong, 146–68. London: University of Toronto Press, 2006.

Dasgupta, Samir and Ray Kiely. eds. *Globalization and After*. London: Sage Publications, 2006.

Davenport, Frances Gardiner. ed. *European Treaties Bearing on the History of the United States and its Dependencies to 1648*. Washington, DC: Carnegie Institution of Washington, 1917.

Davie, Grace. *Europe: The Exceptional Case: Parameters of Faith in the Modern World*. London: Darton, Longman and Todd Ltd, 2002.

Davie, Grace. *Religion in Britain since 1945: Believing without Belonging*. Oxford: Blackwell, 1994.

Dayfoot, Arthur Charles. *The Shaping of the West Indian Church, 1942—1962*. Gainesville: University Press of Florida, 1999.

Deerr, Noël. *History of Sugar*. London: Chapman and Hall Ltd., 1949.

Denevan, William M. "Introduction." In *The Native Population of the Americas in 1492*, edited by William M. Denevan, 1-12. Madison: The University of Wisconsin Press, 1976.

Ebaugh, Helen Rose and Janet Saltzman Chafetz. eds. *Religion and the New Immigrants: Continuities and Adaptations in Immigrant Congregations*. Walnut Creek: Altamira Press, 2000.

Edmonds, Ennis B., and Michelle A. Gonzalez, *Caribbean Religious History: An Introduction*. New York: New York University Press, 2010.

Egbunu, Emmanuel. "To Teach, Baptise, and Nurture New Believers (i)." In *Mission in the 21st Century*, edited by Andrew Walls and Cathy Ross, 25–36. London: Darton, Longman and Todd, 2008.

Erickson, Millard J. *Christian Theology*. 2nd ed. Grand Rapids: Baker Books, 2002 [1983, 1984, 1985, 1998].

Erikson, Erik. *Identity: Youth and Crisis*. London: Faber & Faber Ltd., 1968.

Erskine, Noel Leo. *Decolonizing Theology: A Caribbean Perspective*. Maryknoll: Orbis Books, 1981.

Erskine, Noel Leo. "How do We Know What to Believe: Revelation and Authority." In *Essentials of Christian Theology*, edited by William C. Placher, 33–49. Louisville: Westminster John Knox Press, 2003.

Essed, Philomena. *Understanding Everyday Racism: An Interdisciplinary Theory*. Newbury Park: Sage Productions, 1991.

Faupel, David W. *The Everlasting Gospel: The Significance of Eschatology in the Development of Pentecostal Thought*. Journal of Pentecostal Theology. Supplement Series: 10. Sheffield: Sheffield Academic Press, 1996.

Ferguson, James. *Far from Paradise: An Introduction to Caribbean Development*. London: Latin America Bureau, 1990.

Flanagan, Robert. *Globalization and Labor Conditions: Working Conditions and Worker Rights in a Global Economy*. New York: Oxford University Press, 2006.

Foley, Michael W., and Dean R. Hoge. *Religion and the New Immigrants: How Faith Communities Form Our Newest Citizens*. New York: Oxford University Press, 2007.

Foner, Nancy. *Jamaican Farewell: Jamaican migrants in London*. London: Routledge & Kegan Paul, 1979 [Berkeley: University of California Press, 1978].

Fox, William. *An Address to the People of Great Britain, on the Propriety of Abstaining from West India Sugar and Rum*. 6th ed. London: M. Gurney, 1791.

Frazier, E. Franklin. *The Negro Church in America*. New York: Schocken Books, 1964.

Frey, Sylvia and Betty Wood. *Come Shouting to Zion*. Chapel Hill: The University of North Carolina Press, 1998.

Georges, Eugenia. *The Making of a Transnational Community: Migration, Development and Cultural Change in the Dominican Republic*. New York: Columbia University Press, 1990.

Gillborn, David and Heidi Mirza, *Educational Inequality: Mapping Race, Class and Gender.* London: Office for standards in Education, 2000.

Gillespie, Marie. *Television, Ethnicity and Cultural Change.* London: Routledge, 1995.

Gilroy, Paul. *There Ain't No Black in the Union Jack.* London: Routledge, 2002.

Girvan, Norman. "Michael Manley: A Personal Perspective." In *Caribbean Labor and Politics: Legacies of Cheddi Jagan and Michael Manley*, edited by Perry Mars and Alma H. Young, 3–9. Detroit: Wayne State University Press, 2004.

Glass, Ruth *Newcomers: West Indians in London.* London: Centre for Urban Studies and George Allen & Unwin LTD, 1960.

Glasson, Travis. *Mastering Christianity: Missionary Anglicanism in the Atlantic World.* New York: Oxford University Press, 2011.

Gmelch, George. *Double Passage: The Lives of Caribbean Migrants Abroad and Back Home.* Ann Arbor: University of Michigan Press, 1992.

Gnanakan, Ken. "To proclaim the Good News of the Kingdom (i)." In *Mission in the 21st Century*, edited by Andrew Walls and Cathy Ross, 3–10. London: Darton, Longman and Todd, 2008.

Goff, James R. *Fields white unto Harvest: Charles F. Parham and the Missionary Origins of Pentecostalism.* London: University of Arkansas Press, 1988.

González, Justo L. Foreword to *A Violent Evangelism: The Political and Religious Conquest of the Americas*, by Luis N. Rivera, ix–xi. Louisville: Westminster/John Knox Press, 1992.

Gonzalez, Ondina E., and Justo L. Gonzalez, *Christianity in Latin America: A History.* New York: Cambridge University Press, 2008.

Gordon, Milton M. *Assimilation in American Life: The Role of Race, Religion, and National Origins.* New York: Oxford University Press, 1964.

Gordon, Shirley C. *God Almighty Make Me Free: Christianity in Preemancipation Jamaica.* Bloomington: Indiana University Press, 1996.

Gordon, Shirley C. *Our Cause for His Glory: Christianisation and Emancipation in Jamaica.* Kingston: The Press University of the West Indies, 1998.

Goveia, Elsa V. *Slave Society in the British Leeward Islands.* Forge Village: Murray Printing Company, 1969 [1965].

Graham, Mekada. *Black Issues in Social Work and Social Care.* Bristol: Policy Press, 2007.

Hall, G. S. *Adolescence, its Psychology, and its Relation to Physiology, Anthropology, Sociology, Sex, Crime, Religion and Education.* vol. 2. New York: D. Appleton & Co, 1904.

Hall, Stuart. "Introduction: Who needs 'Identity'?" In *Questions of Cultural Identity*, edited by Stuart Hall and Paul Du Gay, 1–17. London: Sage Publications, 1996.

Handlin, Oscar. *The Uprooted: The Epic Story of the Great Migrations that Made the American People.* New York: Grosset & Dunlap, 1981.

Hanke, Lewis. *Aristotle and the American Indians.* Chicago: Henry Regnery Company, 1959).

Headland, Thomas, Kenneth L. Pike, and Marvin Harris. eds. *Emics and etics: The insider/outsider debate.* Thousand Oaks: Sage Publications, 1990.

Henke, Holger. *The West Indian Americans.* Westport: Greenwood press, 2001.

Herskovits, Melville J. *The Myth of the Negro Past.* New York: Harper & Bothers, 1941.

Hollenweger, Walter J. *The Future of Mission and the Mission of the Future.* Occasional paper no. 2. Birmingham: Selly Oak Colleges, 1990.

Hollenweger, Walter J. *The Pentecostals: The Charismatic Movement in the Churches.* Minneapolis: Augsburg Publishing House, 1972.

Hunte, Keith. "Protestantism and Slavery in the British Caribbean." In *Christianity in the Caribbean: Essays on Church History,* edited by Armando Lampe, 86–125. Kingston: University of West Indies Press, 2001.

Hylton, Patrick. *The Role of Religion in Caribbean History.* Kearney: Morris Publishing, 2002.

Hyndman, Albert. "Family Problems." In *The West Indian Comes to England,* edited by S. K. Ruck, 119–36. London: Routledge & Kegan Paul Ltd., 1960.

Jackson, Anita. *Catching Both Sides of the Wind: Conversations with Five Black Pastors.* London: The British Council of Churches, 1985.

Jenkins, Philip. *The Next Christendom: The Coming of Global Christianity.* New York: Oxford University Press, 2002.

John, Gus and Humphry Derek. *Because They're Black.* Harmondworth: Penguin Books, 1972.

Johns, Cheryl Bridges. *Pentecostal Formation: A Pedagogy Among the Oppressed.* Sheffield: Sheffield Academic Press, 1993.

Johnson, Charles and Patricia Smith. *Africans in America.* New York: Harcourt Brace & Company, 1998.

Kalu, Ogbu. *African Pentecostalism: An Introduction.* New York: Oxford University Press, 2008.

Kasinitz, Philip. *Caribbean New York: Black Immigrants and the Politics of Race.* Ithaca: Cornell University Press, 1992.

Kidd, Colin. *The Forging of Races: Race and Scripture in the Protestant Atlantic World, 1600—2000.* Cambridge: Cambridge University Press, 2006.

Land, Steven Jack. *Pentecostal Spirituality: A Passion for the Kingdom.* Journal of Pentecostal Theology. Supplement Series: 1. Sheffield: Sheffield Academic Press, 1993.

Langford, Paul. *Englishness Identified: Manners and Character 1650—1850.* Oxford: Oxford University Press, 2000.

Las Casas, Bartolomé De. *A Short Account of the Destruction of the Indies.* New York: Penguin Books, 1992.

Lawler, Steph. *Identity: Sociological Perspectives.* Cambridge: Polity Press, 2008.

Lawrence, Daniel. *Black Migrants: White Natives: A Study of Race Relations in Nottingham.* London: Cambridge University Press, 1974.

Levitt, Peggy. *The Transnational Villagers.* Berkeley: University of California Press, 2001.

Lincoln, C. Eric. *Race, Religion and the Continuing American Dilemma*. rev. ed. New York: Hill & Wang, 1999 [1984].

Lincoln, C. Eric and Lawrence H. Mamiya. *The Black Church in the African American Experience*. Durham: Duke University Press, 1990.

Lloyd, Eva. "Children, Poverty and Social Exclusion." In *Poverty and Social Exclusion in Britain: The Millennium Survey*, edited by Christina Pantazis, David Gordon, and Ruth Levitas, 315–46. Bristol: The Policy Press, 2006.

Lord, Andrew. *Spirit, Kingdom and Mission: A Charismatic Missiology*. Cambridge: Grove Books Limited, 2002.

MacRobert, Iain. *The Black Roots and White Racism of Early Pentecostalism in the USA*. Basingstoke: Macmillan Press, 1988.

Mahler, Sarah J. "Theoretical and Empirical Contributions Towards a Research Agenda for Transnationalism." In *Transnationalism From Below*, edited by Michael P. Smith and Luis E. Guarnizo, 64–79. New Brunswick: Transaction Publishers, 2002 [1998].

Maingot, Anthony P. "The English-Speaking Caribbean." In *The Continuing Crisis: U.S. Policy in Central America and the Caribbean*, edited by Mark Falcoff and Robert Royal, 129–46. London: Ethics and Public Policy Center, 1987.

Majors, Richard. "Introduction: Understanding the Current Educational Status of Black Children." In *Educating Our Black Children: New Directions and Radical pbhnkm Approaches*, edited by Richard Majors, 1–10. London: RoutldedgeFalmer, 2001.

Manbeck, John B. *The Neighborhoods of Brooklyn*. New Haven: Yale University Press, 2004 [1998].

Manley, Micheal. *A Voice at the Workplace*. Washington, DC: Howard University Press, 1991.

Mars, Perry and Alma H. Young. eds. *Caribbean Labor and Politics: Legacies of Cheddi Jagan and Michael Manley*. Detroit: Wayne State University Press, 2004.

Marshall, Dawn. "A History of West Indian Migrations: Overseas Opportunities and 'Safety-Valve Policies." In *The Caribbean Exodus*, edited by Barry B. Levine, 15–31. New York: Praeger Publishers, 1987.

Martin, David. *Tongues of Fire: The Explosion of Protestantism in Latin America*. Oxford: Basil Blackwell Ltd, 1990.

Massey, Douglass, Joaquin Arango, Graeme Hugo, Ali Kouaouci, Adela Pellegrino, and J. Edward Taylor. *Worlds in Motion: Understanding International Migration at the End of the Millennium*. New York: Oxford University Press, 2005.

McGee, Gary B. "Pentecostal and Charismatic Missions." In *Toward the 21st Century in Christian Mission*, edited by James M. Philips and Robert T. Coote, 41–56. Grand Rapids: Eerdmans, 1998 [1993].

McGrath, Alister E. *Christian Theology: An Introduction*. Oxford: Blackwell Publishers, 2001.

McLean-Farrell, Janice. "Uncovering an Alternative Story: Examining the Religious and Social Lives of Afro-Caribbean Youth in London and New York City." In *The Public*

Face of African New Religious Movements in Diaspora, edited by Afe Adogame, 25–145. Burlington: Ashgate, 2014.

McLean, Janice. "Appropriating Faith within the City: An Examination of Urban Youth Ministry in Immigrant Churches." In *Reaching the City: Reflections on Urban Mission for the Twenty-first Century*, edited by Gary Fujino, Timothy R. Sisk, and Tereso C. Casiño, 219–32. Pasadena: William Carey Library, 2012.

McLean, Janice. "Mission Perspectives Among Pentecostal West Indians Religious Communities in New York City and London: 'By My Spirit' says the Lord." In *Mission and Migration*, edited by Stephen Spencer, 79–91. Hope Valley: Cliff College Publishing, 2008.

McLean, Janice. "The Place of the Second-Generation in West Indian Pentecostalism in the Diaspora—New York City and London." In *African Traditions in the Study of Religion, Diaspora and Gendered Societies*, edited by Afe Adogame, Ezra Chitando, and Bolaji Bateye, 115–31. Burlington: Ashgate, 2013.

Meissiner, Doris M., Robert D. Hormats, Antonio Garrigues Walker, and Shijuro Ogata. *International Migration Challenges in a New Era*. New York: The Trilateral Commission, 1993.

Miller, Donald E., and Tetsunao Yamamori. *Global Pentecostalism: The New Face of Christian Social Engagement*. London: University of California Press, 2007.

Morison, Samuel Eliot and Maurico Obregón. *Admiral of the Ocean: A Life of Christopher Columbus*. Boston: Little, Brown and Company, 1942.

Morison, Samuel Eliot and Maurico Obregón. *The Caribbean as Columbus saw it*. Boston: Little, Brown and Company, 1964.

Mulrain, George. "Caribbean." In *An Introduction to Third World Theologies*, edited by John Parratt, 163–81. Cambridge: Cambridge University Press, 2004.

Murrell, Nathaniel Samuel. *Afro-Caribbean Religions: An Introduction to Their Historical, Cultural, and Sacred Traditions*. Philadelphia: Temple University Press, 2010.

Naipaul, V. S. *The Nightwatchman's Occurrence Book*. London: Picador, 2002.

Nesbitt, Eleanor. "I'm a Gujarati Lohana and a Vaishnav as Well." In *Religion, Identity and Change: Perspectives on Global Transformations*, edited by Simon Coleman and Peter Collins, 174–90. Aldershot: Ashgate, 2004.

Newbigin, Lesslie. *Foolishness to the Greeks: The Gospel and Western Culture*. Grand Rapids: Eerdmans, 1986.

Newbigin, Lesslie. *A Word in Season: Perspectives on Christian World Missions*. Edinburgh: Saint Andrew Press, 1994.

Newman, Katherine S. *No Shame in My Game: The Working Poor in the Inner City*. New York: Vintage Books and Russell Sage Foundations, 1999.

Novo, De Orbe. *The Eight Decades of Peter Martyr D'Anghera*. trans. Francis Augustus MacNutt. vol. 1. New York: Burt Franklin, 1970 [1912].

Ogbu, John U. *Minority Education and Caste: The American System in Cross-Cultural Perspective*. New York: Academic Press, 1978.

Olupona, Jacob K., and Regina Gemignani. eds. *African Immigrant Religions in America*. New York: New York University Press, 2007.

Orsi, Robert A. "Introduction: Crossing the City Line." In *Gods of the City: Religion and the American Urban Landscape*, edited by Robert A. Orsi, 1–78. Bloomington: Indiana University Press, 1999.

Pagden, Anthony. *The Fall of Natural Man: The American Indian and the Origins of Comparative Ethnology*. New York: Cambridge University Press, 1982.

Painter, Nell Irvin. *Creating Black Americans: African-American History and its Meanings, 1619 to the Present*. New York: Oxford University Press, 2007.

Palmer, Geoff. *The Enlightenment Abolished*. Penicuik: Henry Publishing, 2007.

Palmer, Ransford W. *Caribbean Dependence on the United States Economy*. New York: Praeger Publishers, 1979.

Palmer, Ransford W. *Pilgrims from the Sun: West Indian Migration to America*. New York: Twayne Publishers, 1995.

Park, Robert E., and Ernest W. Burgess. *Introduction to the Science of Sociology*. Chicago: University of Chicago Press, 1921.

Patterson, Orlando. *The Sociology of Slavery*. London: Macgibbon & Kee Ltd, 1967.

Patterson, Sheila. *Dark Strangers*. London: Travistock Publications, 1963.

Payne, Anthony and Paul Sutton. *Charting Caribbean Development*. Warwick University Caribbean Studies. London: Macmillan, 2001.

Pegley, Kip. *Coming to You Wherever You Are: MuchMusic, MTV and Youth Identities*. Middletown: Wesleyan University Press, 2008.

Phelan, Margaret. *Immigration Law Handbook*. London: Blackstone Press Limited, 2001 [1997].

Phillips, Mike and Trevor Phillips. *Windrush: The Irresistible Rise of Multi-Racial Britain*. London: HarperCollins Publishers, 1998.

Placher, William C. ed. *Essentials of Christian Theology*. Louisville: Westminster John Knox Press, 2003.

Pomerville, Paul A. *The Third Force in Missions*. Peabody: Hendrickson Publishers, 1985.

Portes, Alejandro and Josh DeWind. "A Cross-Atlantic Dialogue." In *Rethinking Migration: New Theoretical and Empirical Perspectives*, edited by Alejandro Portes and Josh DeWind, 3–28. New York: Berghahn Books, 2007.

Portes, Alejandro. "Transnational Communities: Their Emergence and Significance in the Contemporary World System." In *Latin America in the World Economy*, edited by Roberto Patricio Korzeniewicz and William C. Smith, 151–68. Westport: Greenwood Press, 1996.

Price, Richard. *Maroon Societies Rebel Slave Communities in the Americas*. Baltimore: The John Hopkins University Press, 1979.

Pryce, Ken. *Endless Pressure: A Study of West Indian Life Styles in Bristol*. Middlesex: Penguin Books, 1979.

Purseglove, J. W. *Tropical Crops: Monocotyledons*. London: Longman Group Ltd., 1974.

Raboteau, Albert J. *A Fire in the Bones: Reflections on African-American Religious History*. Boston: Beacon Press, 1995.

Raboteau, Albert J. *Slave Religion: The "invisible institution" in the Qntebellum South.* New York: Oxford University Press, 1978.

Rawson, Elizabeth Reich. "Brownsville." In *The Encyclopedia of New York City,* edited Kenneth Jackson, 2nd ed, 184–5. New Haven: Yale University Press, 2010.

Ream, Geoffrey L., and Ritch C. Savin-Williams. "Religious Development in Adolescence." In *Blackwell Handbook of Adolescence,* edited by Gerald R. Adams and Michael D. Berzonsky, 51–9. Oxford: Blackwell Publishing, 2006 [2003].

Reid, Ira. *The Negro Immigrant.* New York: Columbia University Press, 1939.

Reid-Salmon, Delroy A. *Home Away from Home: The Caribbean Diasporan Church in the Black Atlantic Tradition.* London: Equinox, 2008.

Rex, John and Sally Tomlinson, *Colonial Immigrants in a British City: A Class Analysis.* London: Routledge & Kegan Paul, 1979.

Reynolds, Tracey. *Caribbean Mothers: Identity and Experience in the U.K.* London: The Tufnell Press, 2005.

Richardson, Bonham C. *Caribbean Migrants: Environment and Human Survival on St. Kitts and Nevis.* Knoxville: University of Tennessee Press, 1983.

Richardson, Brian, Diane Abbott, and Bernard Coard. *Tell it Like it is: How our Schools Fail Black Children.* London: Bookmarks, 2005.

Rivera, Luis N. *A Violent Evangelism: The Political and Religious Conquest of the Americas.* Louisville: Westminster/John Knox Press, 1992.

Rogers, Reuel R. *Afro-Caribbean Immigrants and the Politics of Incorporation: Ethnicity, Exception, or Exit.* New York: Cambridge University Press, 2006.

Roozen, David A., William McKinney, and Jackson W. Carroll. *Varieties of Religious Presence: Mission in Public Life.* Cleveland: The Pilgrim Press, 1984.

Rumbaut, Ruben G., and Kenji Ima. *The Adaptation of Southeast Asian Refugee Youth: A Comparative Study.* Washington, DC: U.S. Office of Refugee Resettlement, 1998.

Salvo, Joseph and Ronald Ortiz. *The Newest New Yorkers: An Analysis of Immigration into New York during the 1980s.* New York: New York Department of City Planning, 1992.

Sanneh, Lamin. "Conclusion: The Current Transformation of Christianity." In *The Changing Face of Christianity,* edited by Lamin Sanneh and Joel A. Carpenter, 213–24. New York: Oxford University Press, 2005.

Sanneh, Lamin. *Whose Religion is Christianity?* Grand Rapids: Eerdmans, 2003.

Schuman, Howard, Charlotte Steeh, Lawrence Bobo, and Maria Krysan. *Racial Attitudes in America: Trends and Interpretations.* Cambridge, MA: Harvard University Press, 1997 [1985].

Schwarz, Hans. *Eschatology.* Grand Rapids: Eerdmans, 2000.

Scobie, Edward. *Black Britannia: A History of Blacks in Britain.* Chicago: Johnson Publishing Company Inc., 1972.

Scott, Ridley. *American Gangster.* Hollywood: Universal Studios, 2007.

Shedden, Roscow. *Ups and Downs in a West Indian Diocese.* London: A. R. Mowbray & Co. Ltd., 1927.

Sheridan, Jim. *Get Rich or Die Tryin.* Hollywood: Paramount films, 2005.

Sherlock, Philip and Hazel Bennett. *The Story of the Jamaican People.* Kingston: Ian Randle Publishers Limited, 1998.

Sherry, Mark. "Insider/Outsider Status." In *The Sage Encyclopedia of Qualitative Methods,* edited by Lisa M Given, Vol. 2, 433. Thousand Oaks: Sage Publications, 2008.

Simmel, Georg. "The Metropolis and Mental Life." In *Metropolis: Center and Symbol of Our Times,* edited by Philip Kasinitz, 30–45. New York: New York University Press, 1995.

Smith, Christian, with Melinda Lundquist Denton. *Soul Searching: The Religious and Spiritual Lives of American Teenagers.* New York: Oxford University Press, 2005.

Smith, Sidonie. *Where I'm Bound: Patterns of Slavery and Freedom in Black American Autobiography.* Westport: Greenwood Press, 1974.

Sokolow, Jayme A. *The Great Encounter: Native Peoples and European Settlers in the Americas, 1492-1800.* London: M. E. Sharpe, 2003.

Stanley, Brian. *The History of the Baptist Missionary Society, 1792-1992.* Edinburgh: T & T Clark, 1992.

Stevenson, David. "Cromwell, Scotland and Ireland." In *Oliver Cromwell and the English Revolution,* edited by John Morrill, 149–80. London: Longman, 1990.

Strachan, Gordon. *The Pentecostal Theology of Edward Irving.* London: Darton, Longman & Todd, 1973.

Sunshine, Catherine A., and Keith Q. Warner. eds. *Caribbean Connections: Moving North.* Washington, DC: Network of Educators on the Americas, 1998.

Sutton, Constance R., and Elsa M. Chaney. eds. *Caribbean Life in New York City: Sociocultural Dimensions.* New York: Center for Migration Studies of New York, Inc., 1994 [1987].

Synan, Vinson. *The Holiness-Pentecostal Tradition: Charismatic Movements of the Twentieth Century.* 2nd ed. Grand Rapids: Eerdmans, 1997.

Ter Haar, Gerrie. "African Christians in the Netherlands." In *Strangers and Sojourners: Religious Communities in the Diaspora,* edited by Gerrie ter Haar, 153–72. Leuven: Peeters, 1998.

Ter Haar, Gerrie. *Halfway to Paradise: African Christians in Europe.* Cardiff: Cardiff Academic Press, 1998.

Thomas-Hope, Elizabeth M. *Explanation in Caribbean Migration.* London: Macmillan Press Ltd, 1992.

Thomas-Hope, Elizabeth M. "Globalization and the Development of a Caribbean Migration Culture." In *Caribbean Migration: Globalised Identities,* edited by Mary Chamberlain, 194–09. London: Routledge, 1998.

Thomas, Hugh. *The Slave Trade, The history of the Atlantic Slave Trade: 1440—1870.* London: Papermac, 1998 [1997].

Titre, Ande. "To Teach, Baptise, and Nurture New Believers (ii)." In *Mission in the 21st Century,* edited by Andrew Walls and Cathy Ross, 37–45. London: Darton, Longman and Todd, 2008.

Toulis, Nicole Rodriguez. *Believing Identity: Pentecostalism and the Mediation of Jamaican Ethnicity and Gender in England.* Oxford: Berg, 1997.

Tucker, Ruth. *From Jerusalem to Irian Jaya: A Biographical History of Christian Missions.* Grand Rapids: Zondervan, 2004 [1983].

Turner, Mary. *Slaves and Missionaries: The Disintegration of Jamaican Slave Society, 1787-1834.* Chicago: University of Illinois Press, 1982.

Unterman, Adam, "Judaism," In *The New Penguin Handbook of Living Religions,* edited by John R. Hinnells, 11–54. Oxford: Blackwell Publishers Ltd, 1997.

Vickerman, Milton. *Crosscurrents: West Indian Immigrants and Race.* New York: Oxford University Press, 1999.

Vickerman, Milton. "Jamaica." In *The New Americans: A Guide to Immigration Since 1965,* edited by Mary C. Waters, and Ueda Reed, with Marrow Helen, 479–90. Cambridge, MA: Harvard University Press, 2007.

Villafañe, Edwin. *Liberating Spirit.* Grand Rapids: Eerdmans, 1993.

Walls, Andrew F. "Afterword: Christian Mission in a Five-hundred-year Context." In *Mission in the 21st Century,* edited by Andrew Walls, and Cathy Ross, 193–204. London: Darton, Longman and Todd, 2008.

Walls, Andrew F. *The Cross-Cultural Process in Christian History.* New York: Orbis Books, 2002.

Walvin, James. *Black and White: The Negro and English Society 1555—1945.* London: Allen Lane the Penguin Press, 1973.

Walvin, James. *Making the Black Atlantic: Britain and the African Diaspora.* London: Cassell, 2000.

Warner, R. Stephen and Judith G. Wittner. eds. *Gatherings in Diaspora: Religious Communities and the New Immigration.* Philadelphia: Temple University Press, 1998.

Waters, Mary C. *Black Identities: West Indian Immigrant Dreams and American Realities.* Cambridge, MA: Harvard University Press, 1999.

Waters, Mary C. *Ethnic Options, Choosing Identities in America.* Berkley: University of California Press, 1990.

Watts, David. *The West Indies: Patterns of Development, Culture and Environmental Change Since 1492.* New York: Cambridge University Press, 1990 [1987].

Weinreich, Peter. "Ethnicity and Adolescent Identity Conflicts: A Comparative Study." In *Minority Families in Britain: Support and Stress,* edited by Verity Saifullah Khan, 88–107. London: Macmillan Press, 1979.

Welch, Alford T. "Islam." In *The New Penguin Handbook of Living Religions,* edited by John R. Hinnells, 162–35. Oxford: Blackwell Publishers Ltd, 1997.

West Cornel, *Prophesy Deliverance/An Afro-American Revolutionary Christianity.* Philadelphia: Westminster Press, 1982.

West Cornel. *Race Matters.* Boston: Beacon Press, 1993.

Western John, *Passage to England: Barbadian Londoners Speak of Home.* London: UCL Press Limited, 1992.

Williams, Eric. "American Capitalism and Caribbean Economy." In *Caribbean Freedom: Economy and Society from Emancipation to Present*, edited by Hilary Beckles and Verene Shepherd. Kingston: Ian Randle Publishers Limited, 1993.

Williams, Eric. *Capitalism and Slavery*. London: Andre Deutsch Limited, 1964.

Williams, Eric. "Capitalism and Slavery." In *Caribbean Slave Society and Economy*, edited by Hilary Beckers and Verene Shepherd, 120–9. Kingston: Ian Randle Publishers Limited, 1991.

Williams, Eric. *From Columbus to Castro: The History of the Caribbean 1492—1969*. London: Andre Deutsch Ltd., 1970.

Wilmore, Gayraud S. *Black Religion and Black Radicalism: An Interpretation of the Religious History of African Americans*, 3rd ed. Maryknoll: Orbis Books, 1998.

Wood, D. M., Jessie Hood, K. Aldous and W. B. Thompson. "West Indian Welfare in Three Cities." In *The West Indian Comes to England*, edited by S. K. Ruck, 155–67. London: Routledge & Kegan Paul Ltd., 1960.

Yeboah, Samuel. *The Ideology of Racism*. London: Hanslib Publishing Limited, 1988.

Young, Michael and Peter Willmott. *Family and Kinship in East London*. Berkley: University of California Press, 1992.

Unpublished sources

Adogame, Afe. "Towards a 'Christian Disneyland'? Negotiating Space and Identity in the New African Religious Diaspora." Paper presented at the Gwendolen M. Carter Conference, University of Florida, Gainesville, February 15 to 16, 2008.

McLean, Janice. "Enslaving liberators? An examination of evangelical missionaries in pre and post-emancipation Jamaica." Paper presented at the Yale-Edinburgh Conference, University of Edinburgh, Edinburgh, July 3 to 5, 2008.

Morrison, Doreen. "Reaching for the Promised Land: The role of Culture, issues of Leadership and Social stratification with British Caribbean Christianity." PhD diss. University of Birmingham, 2012.

Parris, Garnet A. "The African Dispora in Germany seen through the axes of Storytelling: Of Law and security and of Religious Tradition and Theology." PhD diss., University of Birmingham, 2008.

Websites

Bailey, Margaret. "The typical Jamaican family." Published October 1, 2002. Accessed July 11, 2008, http://www.jamaicans.com/culture/intro/typical_family.shtml.

Barbadian Nation. Accessed July 22, 2008, http://classifieds.nationnews.com/results.php?category_id=2&acTst=Grr.

Blunkett, David. *A New England: An English identity within Britain.* Speech to the Institute for Public Policy Research, March 14, 2005. Accessed July 30, 2008, http://www.efdss.org/newengland.pdf.

"Brent county." Accessed March 10, 2007, http://www.brent-heritage.co.uk/willesden. htm.

"Brooklyn Community District 16 profile." Accessed May 21, 2015, http://www.nyc.gov/ html/dcp/pdf/lucds/bk16profile.pdf.

"Brooklyn Community District 16 Neighborhood Report." Accessed May 21, 2015, http://issuu.com/studybrooklyn/docs/community_district_16_brooklyn_ neighborhood_report.

"Brooklyn Community District 18 profile." Accessed May 21, 2015, http://www.nyc.gov/ html/dcp/pdf/lucds/bk18profile.pdf.

"Brooklyn Community District 18 Neighborhood Report." Access May 21, 2015, http://issuu.com/studybrooklyn/docs/community-district-18-brooklyn-neighborhood-report.

"Chapter 21." *Commonwealth Immigration Act 1962.* Accessed March 12, 2008, http://www.britishcitizen.info/CIA1962.pdf.

Davidson, Marcia. "Anancy Introduction." *Jamaican Culture.* Accessed September 19, 2013, http://www.jamaicans.com/culture/anansi/anancy_intro.shtml.

Digicel Telecommunications. Accessed July 22, 2008, http://www.digiceljamaica.com/ home/index_v4.php.

"Don Imus." Accessed on May 7, 2008, http://www.cbsnews.com/stories/2007/04/12/ national/main2675273.shtml.

"Eastern District of New York Press Release." Released May 25, 2005. Accessed March 4, 2009, http://www.usdoj.gov/usao/nye/pr/2005/2005may25.html.

Essix, Donna. *Brief History of Jamaica.* Accessed February 2005, http://www.jamaicans. com/info/brief.htm.

"Income, Poverty and Health Insurance Coverage in the United States: 2013." News release, September 16, 1014. Accessed May 15, 2015, http://www.census.gov/ newsroom/press-releases/2014/cb14-169.html.

Jamaican Gleaner. Accessed July 22, 2008, http://www.jamaica-gleaner.com/.

Median salaries. Accessed June 10, 2015, http://money.usnews.com/careers/best-jobs/ plumber/salary.

"National Church Leaders Forum." Accessed October 2008, http://nationalchurch leadersforum.wordpress.com/about/.

"National Survey on Drug Use and Health Reports." Accessed November 22, 2008, http://ncadistore.samhsa.gov/catalog/results.aspx?h=drugs&topic=10.

New Testament Church of God—Jamaican and Cayman Islands. Accessed July 20, 2007, http://ntcgjaci.org/history.htm.

Public Education Finances 2013. Educational Finance Branch, issued June 2015. Accessed September 7, 2015, https://www.census.gov/content/dam/Census/library/ publications/2015/econ/g13-aspef.pdf.

Sharpe Peter, *Sugar Cane: Past and Present*. Accessed October 10, 2007, http://www.siu.edu/~ebl/leaflets/sugar.htm.

Sylvan Learning Center. Accessed July 29, 2008, http://tutoring.sylvanlearning.com/.

"The Immigration and Nationality Act of 1952 (The McCarran-Walter Act)." *United States Department of State Office of the Historian*. Accessed August 26, 2013, http://history.state.gov/milestones/1945-1952/ImmigrationAct.

Trinidadian Guardian, Accessed July 22, 2008, http://www.guardian.co.tt/classified/class.html.

"Youth Matters." *UK government Green Papers*, July 2005. Accessed November 22, 2008, http://www.everychildmatters.gov.uk/_files/Youth%20Matters.pdf.

"Youth Matters Next Step" *UK government Green Papers*, March 2006. Accessed November 22, 2008, http://www.everychildmatters.gov.uk/_files/3804D7C4B4D206C8325EA1371B3C5F81.pdf.

US Census Bureau. Accessed March 16, 2005, http://www.census.gov/Press-Release/www/2002/cb02-124.html.

US Census Bureau fact sheet for zip code 11226. Accessed June 5, 2015, http://factfinder.census.gov/faces/tableservices/jsf/pages/productview.xhtml?src=CF.

US 2010 Census Bureau fact sheet for zip code 11212. Accessed June 5, 2015, http://factfinder.census.gov/faces/tableservices/jsf/pages/productview.xhtml?src=CF.

US Bureau of the Census 1990 Report Table 3: *Region and Country or Area of Birth of the Foreign-Born Population: 1960 to 1990*. Internet Release date March 9, 1999. Accessed April 29, 2008, http://www.census.gov/population/www/documentation/twps0029/tab03.html.

Vargas-Lundius, Rosemary. "Remittances and Rural Development." Paper prepared for Twenty-Seventh Session of IFAD's Governing Council, Rome, February 18 to 19, 2004. Accessed July 20, 2008, http://www.ifad.org/events/gc/27/roundtable/pl/discussion.pdf.

"Wealth in Great Britain, Main results from the Wealth and Assets Survey 2006/2008." Accessed September 25, 2013, http://www.ons.gov.uk/ons/rel/was/wealth-in-great-britain/main-results-from-the-wealth-and-assets-survey-2006-2008/index.html.

Index